Mid-Century Conductors
More Viennese Singers

Discographies
compiled by John Hunt

Dedicated to the
Clifford Elkin Collection

ISBN 0 951 0268 5 2

1992

Acknowledgement

This publication has been made possible by generous support from the following:

Y. Asada	R. Ames
D. Carroll	J. Baker
E. Chibas	J. Bartley
J. Derry	R. Benson
E. Kaskey	J. Brookner
E. Lumpe	D. Creighton
T. Omoto	E. Dervos
J. Parsons	R. Donaldson
G. Söderwall	M. Hickley
K. Soma	H. Kimura
Y. Suzuki	N. MacDougall
A. Tingström	B. Morrison
	T. Potter
	D. Priddon
	G. Reeves
	D. Selwyn
	C. Shepherd
	N. Sumpter
	T. Spoors
	A. Warren

Contents

7   Karl Böhm

85   Victor de Sabata

115   Hans Knappertsbusch

163   Tullio Serafin

195   Clemens Krauss

249   Anton Dermota

297   Leonie Rysanek

329   Eberhard Wächter

363   Maria Reining

381   Erich Kunz

409   Rita Streich: additions

Mid-Century Conductors
Published by John Hunt.
Designed by Richard Chluparty
© 1992 John Hunt
reprinted 2009
ISBN 978-0-951026-85-4

Sole distributors:
Travis & Emery.
17 Cecil Court,
London, WC2N 4EZ,
United Kingdom.
(+44) 20 7 459 2129.
sales@travis-and-emery.com

Foreword

After publication of the volume of discographies which included the Italians Toscanini, Giulini and Cantelli I was asked from many sides why Victor De Sabata and Tullio Serafin had not been included. They certainly occupy equally illustrious positions in the history of Italian conducting, so with the help of Angelo Scottini I have now redressed the balance.

As far as the three prominent Austro-German conductors in this book are concerned, I hope that my work will help to bring awareness to modern collectors of the repertoire covered by Hans Knappertsbusch and Clemens Krauss in particular, some of which has never reappeared since the days of 78s.

As before, my aim is to give the general history of each recording, quoting first issue numbers, some important reissues and the most recent or currently available versions. There is no claim to have included all issues in all countries of any recording. However, I have tried to cover all commercially made records, including some never published, and the ever-growing number of unofficial publications. In the cases of Krauss and Knappertsbusch I have also added a list of further private, and so far unissued, recordings which may in future provide the basis for new publications.

As many of these artists recorded for Decca in the early days of LP, I have attempted to capture the "flavour" of the period by including the potted biographies which appeared in the "Decca Book of Opera". This was a scholarly publication giving the plots of all the main operas in the repertoire of the day. Although the book emanated from a specific record company and obviously served an advertising function, it remained remarkably free of the publicity "hype" which would surround such a project nowadays.

Those collectors whose main interest is the Viennese singers featured in this volume will find that there is a bonus. Contained within the discography of the conductor Clemens Krauss is that of his wife, the soprano Viorica Ursuleac. She performed and recorded together with her husband to such an extent that I know of only one extant recording, a "Tristan und Isolde" from Argentina in 1948 where Ursuleac takes the part of Brangäne under the baton of Erich Kleiber, in which she is not partnered by her husband.

Also appertaining to Krauss, I should draw attention to the existence of a series of little-known records which he in made in 1949-1950 for the Czech firm Supraphon, just prior to his signing the exclusive contract with Decca which resulted in that fine harvest of LPs. The Supraphon records appear to have had a very restricted circulation and some were even withdrawn for contractual reasons.

As far as abbreviations are concerned, I have kept these to the barest minimum, using only ones known to most collectors. I have taken the liberty of using VPO (Vienna Philharmonic Orchestra) to cover that orchestra even when they recorded in their other guise of Vienna State Opera Orchestra, and have used the description Berlin RO (Berlin Radio Orchestra) to cover the various ensembles which existed at various times under names such as RIAS, RSO and so on. The abbreviation "np" occasionally occurs to denote a record which was allocated catalogue number but subsequently not issued in that particular format.

Finally I must thank the friends, colleagues and enthusiasts who have assisted me with information and suggestions for these discographies. They are, in alphabetical order,
Y. Asada, S. Clark, C. Elkin,
M. Erhard, J. Gratz, A. Jefferson,
A. Kaine, R. Krüsemann, E. Lumpe,
Y. Nakanishi, T. Omoto, J. Raymon,
H. Reysen, A. Scottini, T. Suzuki,
J. Schundelmaier, J. Vieten,
M. Walker and G. Walter.

John Hunt

Karl Böhm
Discography

Compiled by John Hunt

KARL BÖHM

THE FORMER Generalmusikdirektor of the Vienna State Opera is a native of Graz. His first appointment was in his native city from 1917 to 1920. He spent the next seven years in Munich. From 1927 to 1931, he was Generalmusikdirektor at Darmstadt; then in 1931 he succeeded Karl Muck as chief conductor at Hamburg, where he remained until 1934, when he went to the Dresden State Opera in succession to Fritz Busch. He remained at Dresden until 1941. It was during his period there that he paid his first visit to London, conducting the Dresden Company at Covent Garden in November 1936. During his directorship of the Dresden Opera he conducted a number of important premières, including *Die schweigsame Frau* and *Daphne* by Richard Strauss, *Romeo und Julia* and *Die Zauberinsel* by Sutermeister, and the new realization of Monteverdi's *Orfeo* by Carl Orff.

In 1941 Böhm went to Vienna, and has conducted at the State Opera there ever since. He has appeared with great success at the San Carlo, Naples, where his performances of *Wozzeck* in 1949 caused a sensation. He was in charge of the German performances at the Teatro Colon, Buenos Aires, from 1950 to 1953, and is a regular visitor to the Salzburg Festival, where he conducted the world première of Einem's *Der Prozess* in 1953.

SALZBURGER FESTSPIELE 1962

IPHIGENIE IN AULIS

OPER IN DREI AKTEN
VON LE BLANC DU ROULLET

Deutsche Bühnenfassung
nach Glucks letzter Partitureinrichtung von 1775
von
Paul Friedrich und Günther Rennert

Musik von Christoph Willibald Gluck

DIRIGENT
KARL BÖHM

INSZENIERUNG
GÜNTHER RENNERT

BÜHNENBILD UND KOSTÜME
CASPAR NEHER

CHOREOGRAPHIE
ERICH WALTER

ORCHESTER
DIE WIENER PHILHARMONIKER
CHOR DER WIENER STAATSOPER
EIN KAMMERCHOR DER SALZBURGER FESTSPIELE

Bach

Air (Orchestral Suite No 3)

Vienna   VPO   78: Electrola DB 7651
1942

Beethoven

Symphony No 1

Vienna September 1971	VPO	LP: DG 2530 958 LP: DG 2721 154/2740 115/2720 045 LP: DG 2543 163 CD: 429 1522

Symphony No 2

Vienna Date uncertain	VPO	LP: Discocorp IGI 384
Salzburg August 1968	BPO	CD: Bella Musica BMF 967 CD: Curcio-Hunt CONB 05
Vienna May 1971	VPO	LP: DG 2530 448 LP: DG 2721 154/2740 115/2720 045 LP: DG 2543 164

Symphony No 3 "Eroica"

Berlin December 1961	BPO	LP: DG LPM 18 814/SLPM 138 814 LP: DG 2535 101
Vienna September 1971	VPO	LP: DG 2530 437 LP: DG 2721 154/2740 115/2720 045 LP: DG 2543 165 LP: DG 413 2211 CD: DG 427 1942

Symphony No 4

Berlin April 1952	BPO	LP: Movimento Musica 08.001
Budapest November 1969	VPO	CD: Curcio-Hunt CONB 04
Vienna September 1971	VPO	LP: DG 2530 451 LP: DG 2721 154/2740 115/2720 045 LP: DG 2543 166 CD: DG 429 1522
Tokyo March 1975	VPO	LP: DG (Japan) 92MG-0752-5

Symphony No 5

Berlin March 1953	BPO	78: DG LVM 72346-8 LP: DG LPM 18 097 2nd movement only LP: DG LPEM 19 078
Vienna April 1970	VPO	LP: DG 2530 062 LP: DG 2721 154/2740 115/2720 045 LP: DG 2543 167/2543 506 CD: DG 413 1442

Symphony No 6 "Pastoral"

Vienna May 1971	VPO	LP: DG 2530 142 LP: DG 2721 154/2740 115/2720 045 LP: DG 2543 168 LP: DG 413 9771/419 6441 CD: DG 413 1442/413 7212

Symphony No 7

Berlin April 1958	BPO	LP: DG LPM 18 514/SLPM 138 018 LP: DG 2535 147
Vienna September 1971	VPO	LP: DG 2530 421 LP: DG 2721 154/2740 115/2720 045 LP: DG 2543 169 CD: DG 429 5092
Tokyo March 1975	VPO	LP: DG (Japan) 92MG-0650-3

Symphony No 8

Vienna May 1953	VPO	LP: Decca LXT 2824/LXT 5361 LP: Decca LW 5259 LP: Decca ACL 86 LP: Decca ECM 558/ECS 558
Vienna May 1971	VPO	LP: DG 2707 073/2721 080 LP: DG 2721 154/2740 115/2720 045 LP: DG 2543 163

Symphony No 9 "Choral"

Dresden 1941	Dresden Staatskapelle Dresden Opera Chorus Teschemacher, Höngen, Ralf, J.Herrmann	78: Electrola DB 5652-5650 LP: Electrola 1C 137 53508-13M
Frankfurt September 1954	Hessischer Rundfunk Chorus & Orchestra Stich-Randall, Höffgen, Friedrich, Frick	LP: Longanesi periodici GCL 03 LP: Foyer FO 1033
Vienna June 1957	VSO Vienna Opera Chorus Stich-Randall, Rössl-Majdan, Dermota, Schöffler	LP: Philips 698 000 CL/494 022 EE LP: Philips GL 5810 LP: Philips 6833 080 Last movement only LP: Philips 6833 188
Bayreuth July 1963	Bayreuth Festival Chorus & Orchestra Janowitz, Bumbry, Thomas, London	LP: Melodram MEL 650 CD: Classical Collection CD3-CLC 4015 Classical Collection omits third movement
Vienna April 1970	VPO Vienna Opera Chorus Jones, Troyanos, Thomas, Ridderbusch	LP: DG 2707 073/2721 080 LP: DG 2721 154/2740 115/2720 045 LP: DG 413 2211 CD: DG 427 1962
Vienna November 1980	VPO Vienna Opera Concert Choir Norman, Fassbänder, Domingo, Berry	LP: DG 2741 009 CD: DG 413 7212/427 8022

Choral Fantasy

Vienna June 1957	VSO Vienna Opera Chorus Stich-Randall, Hellwig, Dermota, Rössl-Majdan, Majkut, Schöffler	LP: Philips 663 000 ER LP: Philips 6833 188 Only recorded version to include vocal soloists in addition to chorus

Piano Concerto No 1

Vienna	VPO	LP: Decca LXT 2627
May 1951	Gulda	LP: Decca ACL 84

Piano Concerto No 3

Dresden	Dresden	78: Electrola DB 5506-5510
1939	Staatskapelle	LP: Electrola 1C 137 53500-4M
	Kolessa	
Vienna	VPO	LP: Decca LXT 2553
September 1950	Backhaus	LP: Decca ECM 524/ECS 524
Turin	RAI Turin Orchestra	LP: Fonit Cetra LAR 46
May 1952	Del Pueyo	
Vienna	VPO	LP: DG 2531 057
November 1977	Pollini	LP: DG 2740 284
		LP: DG 2543 170
		LP: DG 419 8091
		CD: DG 413 4462/419 7932

Piano Concerto No 4

Dresden	Dresden	78: Columbia (Germany) LWX 288-191
1939	Staatskapelle	78: Columbia LX 847-850/LX 8462-8465 auto
	Gieseking	LP: Electrola 1C 137 53500-4M
Vienna	VPO	LP: DG 2530 791
June 1976	Pollini	LP: DG 2740 284
		LP: DG 2543 171
		LP: DG 419 8091
		CD: DG 413 4452/419 7932
		CD: DG 435 0912/435 0982

Piano Concerto No 5 "Emperor"

Dresden	Dresden	78: Electrola DB 5511-5515
1939	Staatskapelle	LP: Electrola 1C 137 53500-4M
	Fischer	
Vienna	VPO	LP: DG 2531 194
May 1978	Pollini	LP: DG 2740 284
		LP: DG 2543 172
		LP: DG 419 8091
		CD: DG 413 4472/419 7932
		CD: DG 435 0912/435 0982

Violin Concerto

Dresden 1939	Dresden Staatskapelle Strub	78: Electrola DB 5516-5520 LP: Electrola 1C 137 53500-4M
Place and date uncertain	Orchestra Ferras	LP: Longanesi periodici GCL 39

Missa Solemnis

Berlin 1955	BPO St Hedwig's Choir Stader, Radev, Dermota, Greindl	LP: DG LPM 18224-5/LPM 18232-3 auto LP: DG 89679-80 LP: Discocorp IGI 384 Discocorp incorrectly labelled as a wartime performance
Vienna October 1974	VPO Vienna Opera Concert Choir M.Price, C.Ludwig, Ochman, Talvela	LP: DG 2707 080 LP: DG 413 1911 Sanctus LP: DG 2545 055

Coriolan, Overture

Berlin December 1958	BPO	LP: DG LPM 18 514/SLPM 138 018 LP: DG 2535 147
Vienna September 1971	VPO	LP: DG 2720 045/2740 115 LP: DG 2535 135 LP: DG 2543 164 LP: DG 419 9771 CD: DG 429 5092

Egmont, Overture

Dresden 1935	Dresden Staatskapelle	78: Electrola EH 919 78: HMV C 2780 LP: Electrola 1C 137 53500-4M
Vienna September 1971	VPO	LP: DG 2720 045/2740 115 LP: DG 2535 135 LP: DG 2543 166 LP: DG 419 6441 CD: DG 413 1442/429 5092

Fidelio

Vienna May 1944	VPO Vienna Opera Chorus Konetzni, Seefried, Klein, Ralf, Alsen, Schöffler, Neralcic	LP: Acanta DE 23116-7 Excerpts LP: Vox OPL 370/SOPL 5370
Vienna November 1955	VPO Vienna Opera Chorus Mödl, Seefried Dermota, Kmennt, Weber, Schöffler, Kamann	LP: Melodram MEL 008 CD: Frequenz CMM 2 CD: Movimento Musica 051.024 Excerpts CD: Melodram CDM 26522
New York March 1960	Metropolitan Opera Chorus & Orchestra Nilsson, Hurley, Vickers, Anthony, Tozzi, Uhde, Czerwenka	LP: Melodram MEL 045 Ha! Welch ein Augenblick LP: Melodram MEL 094
San Francisco November 1968	San Francisco Opera Chorus & Orchestra Rysanek, Blegen, Vickers, Dickie, Tozzi, Berry, Macurdy	LP: Melodram CDM 27086
Dresden March 1969	Dresden Staatskapelle Dresden Opera Chorus Leipzig Radio Choir Jones, Mathis, King, Schreier, Adam, Crass, Talvela	LP: DG 2709 031 LP: DG 2720 113/2721 136 Excerpts LP: DG 2537 002 Overture LP: DG 2530 958 LP: DG 2535 135 CD: DG 413 1452 CD: DG 427 1942 Leonore No 3 Overture LP: DG 2530 958 LP: DG 2535 135 CD: DG 413 1452 CD: DG 427 1942

Fidelio: Excerpt (Gott, welch Dunkel hier)

Vienna September 1951	VPO Patzak	78: Decca X 489/K 23076 LP: Decca LXT 2672 LP: Decca BR 3062 LP: Decca ECS 812 LP: Decca 414 1781

Leonore No 3, Overture

Dresden 1938	Dresden Staatskapelle	78: Electrola DB 4558-9 LP: Electrola 1C 137 53500-4M
Tokyo March 1975	VPO	LP: DG (Japan) 92-MG 0650-3 LP: DG (Japan) 92-MG 0752-5 <u>These are 2 separate versions taken from live performances during a VPO tour 1975</u>

Prometheus, Overture

Berlin 1952	Berlin RO	LP: Melodram MEL 218
Vienna September 1971	VPO	LP: DG 2720 045/2740 115 LP: DG 2530 448 LP: DG 2535 135 LP: DG 2543 164 CD: DG 429 5092

Berg

Lulu

Berlin February 1968	Deutsche Oper Orchestra Lear, Johnson, Grobe, Driscoll, Dicks, Feldhoff, Fischer-Dieskau, Greindl	LP: DG SLPM 139 273-5 LP: DG 2709 029 LP: DG 413 7971/413 8071 CD: DG 435 7052

Wozzeck

Berlin April 1965	Deutsche Oper Chorus & Orchestra Lear, Melchert, Wunderlich, Fischer-Dieskau, Stolze, Kohn	LP: DG SLPM 138 991-2 LP: DG 2707 023 LP: DG 413 7971/413 8041 CD: DG 435 7052

Wozzeck: Excerpt (Death of Marie)

New York March 1959	Metropolitan Opera Orchestra Steber, Uhde	LP: Melodram MEL 094

Berger

Rondino giocoso

Dresden 1940	Dresden Staatskapelle	78: Columbia (Germany) LWX 335 LP: Electrola 1C 137 53508-13M

Berlioz

La Damnation de Faust, Hungarian March

Dresden 1939	Dresden Staatskapelle	78: Electrola DB 5559 78: Electrola 1C 137 53505-7M

Bizet

Carmen: Excerpts

Dresden 1942	Dresden Staatskapelle Dresden Opera Chorus Höngen, Trötschel, Ralf, J.Herrmann Sung in German	LP: BASF 10.213625 C'est toi! C'est moi! LP: BASF 72.221792

Brahms

Symphony No 1

Vienna 1942	VPO	78: Electrola DB 7715-9 This version may not have been published; an Electrola studio recording by Furtwängler is also supposed to have been made in 1942 or 1944 in Vienna
Berlin Date uncertain	BPO	LP: Longanesi periodici GCL 55 LP: Foyer FO 1033
Berlin October 1959	BPO	LP: DG LPM 18 613/SLPM 138 113 LP: DG 2535 102 CD: DG 413 4242
Tokyo March 1975	VPO	LP: DG (Japan) 92-MG 0650-3 LP: DG (Japan) 92-MG 0752-3 CD: DG (Japan) F35G-20016 The 2 LP versions are of 2 different performances from the 1975 VPO tour
Vienna May 1975	VPO	LP: DG 2530 959 LP: DG 2711 017/2740 154 LP: DG 2543 173

Symphony No 2

Vienna 1942	VPO	78: Electrola DB 7693-8 This version may not have been published
Berlin December 1956	BPO	LP: DG LPM 18 360 LP: DG 89 595
Vienna May 1975	VPO	LP: DG 2530 960 LP: DG 2711 017/2740 154 LP: DG 2543 174

Symphony No 3

Vienna June 1953	VPO	LP: Decca LXT 2843 LP: Decca ACL 14 LP: Vox STPL 513
Vienna June 1975	VPO	LP: DG 2530 992 LP: DG 2711 017/2740 154 LP: DG 2543 175

Symphony No 4

Dresden 1939	Dresden Staatskapelle	78: Electrola DB 4684-9/8776-8781 auto LP: Electrola 1C 137 53508-13M
Vienna May 1975	VPO	LP: DG 2530 894 LP: DG 2711 017/2740 154 LP: DG 2543 176 CD: DG 413 4242

Piano Concerto No 1

Vienna June 1953	VPO Backhaus	LP: Decca LXT 2866/LXT 5364 LP: Decca (France) 592.135
Vienna December 1979	VPO Pollini	LP: DG 2531 294 LP: DG 2707 127/2740 276 LP: DG 2543 177 CD: DG 419 4702

Piano Concerto No 2

Dresden 1939	Dresden Staatskapelle Backhaus	78: Electrola DB 5500-5505 LP: Electrola 1C 053 01362M LP: Toshiba GR 2078 LP: Pathé 2C 051 01362 LP: Electrola 1C 137 53505-7M
Vienna April 1967	VPO Backhaus	LP: Decca SXL 6322 CD: Decca 414 1422

Violin Concerto

Dresden 1940	Dresden Staatskapelle Schneiderhan	78: Columbia (Germany) LWX 331-335 LP: Electrola 1C 137 53505-7M

Tragic Overture

Vienna	VPO	LP: DG 2530 894
February 1977		LP: DG 2536 396

Haydn Variations (St Antoni Chorale)

Vienna	VPO	LP: DG 2530 960
February 1977		LP: DG 2536 396

Alto Rhapsody

Vienna	VPO	LP: DG 2530 992
June 1976	Singverein	LP: DG 2536 396
	C.Ludwig	LP: DG 2543 175

Hungarian Dances Nos 5 and 6

Dresden	Dresden	78: Electrola DA 4443
1938	Staatskapelle	LP: Electrola 1C 137 53505-7M

Bruckner

Symphony No 3

Vienna September 1970	VPO	LP: Decca SXL 6505 CD: Decca future release

Symphony No 4 "Romantic"

Dresden 1936	Dresden Staatskapelle	78: Electrola DB 4450-4457 LP: Electrola 1C 053 28924M LP: Electrola 1C 137 53508-13M
Vienna November 1973	VPO	LP: Decca 6BB 171-2 LP: Decca JB 120 CD: Decca 411 5812 CD: Decca 433 3402/433 3302

Symphony No 5

Dresden 1936	Dresden Staatskapelle	78: Electrola DB 4486-4494 LP: Electrola 1C 137 535 08-13M LP: Discocorp IGI 452

Symphony No 7

Vienna 1948	VPO	LP: Vox VSPS 5 LP: Discocorp IGI 365 LP: Intercord 155.801
Vienna September 1976	VPO	LP: DG 2709 068/2740 179 LP: DG 2727 015 LP: DG 413 9781 CD: DG 419 8582

Symphony No 8

Vienna February 1976	VPO	LP: DG 2709 068/2740 179 LP: DG 2727 011

Dvorak

Symphony No 9 "From the New World"

Berlin December 1951	BPO	LP: Movimento Musica 01.024
Vienna May 1978	VPO	LP: DG 2531 098 LP: DG 2543 178

Gluck

Iphigenie in Aulis

Salzburg July 1962	VPO Vienna Opera Chorus C.Ludwig, Borkh, King, Berry, Edelmann	LP: Penzance Records PR 25 Excerpt LP: Melodram MEL 098

Gounod

Faust: Excerpt (Soldiers' Chorus)

Dresden 1939	Dresden Staatskapelle Dresden Opera Chorus Sung in German	78: Electrola DA 4457 LP: Electrola 1C 137 53514-9M

Handel

Giulio Cesare: Excerpts

Berlin April 1960	Berlin RO Seefried, Fischer-Dieskau	LP: DG LPM 18 637/SLPM 138 637 Tu la mia stella sei LP: DG LPEM 19 477/SLPEM 136 477 LP: DG 410 8471 Più amabile beltà LP: DG 410 8471

Haydn

Symphony No 88

Vienna September 1972	VPO	LP: DG 2530 343 LP: DG 2535 445/2543 179 CD: DG 429 5232

Symphony No 89

Vienna September 1972	VPO	LP: DG 2530 343 LP: DG 2543 179 CD: DG 429 5232

Symphony No 90

Vienna May 1973	VPO	LP: DG 2530 398 LP: DG 2535 445/2543 180

Symphony No 91

Vienna September 1973 and April 1974	VPO	LP: DG 2530 524 LP: DG 2543 180

Symphony No 92 "Oxford"

Vienna April 1974	VPO	LP: DG 2530 524 LP: DG 2531 190 LP: DG 2543 181 CD: DG 429 5232

Sinfonia concertante for wind

Vienna May 1973	VPO Küchl, Scheiwein, Mayrhofer, Zeman	LP: DG 2530 398 LP: DG 2543 181

Die Jahreszeiten

Vienna April and June 1967	VSO Singverein Janowitz, Schreier, Talvela	LP: DG 2709 026 CD: DG 423 9222 Excerpts LP: DG 2535 480

London Symphony Orchestra
Principal Conductor André Previn   Leader John Brown

Karl Böhm
conductor

Mozart
Symphony K201

Strauss
Don Juan

Interval

Schubert
Symphony No. 9

Greater London Council
Royal Festival Hall
Director John Denison CBE

Sunday 29th June at 7.30 pm

Programme Book 25p.

DIE WIENER PHILHARMONIKER AUF DECCA-LANGSPIELPLATTEN

BEETHOVEN
Symphonie Nr. IX d-moll, op. 125
Hilde Güden - Sieglinde Wagner - Anton Dermota - Ludwig Weber
Singverein der Gesellschaft der Musikfreunde, Wien
Dirigent: ERICH KLEIBER
LXT 2725/26

SCHUBERT
Symphonie Nr. V B-dur
Symphonie Nr. VIII h-moll „Unvollendete"
Dirigent: KARL BÖHM LXT 2998

BRAHMS
Klavierkonzert Nr. 2 B-dur, op. 83
Wilhelm Backhaus, Klavier
Dirigent: CARL SCHURICHT
LXT 2723

BRUCKNER
Symphonie Nr. III d-moll
Dirigent: HANS KNAPPERTSBUSCH
LXT 2967

DVORAK
Cellokonzert h-moll, op. 104
Pierre Fournier, Violoncello
Dirigent: RAFAEL KUBELIK
LXT 2999

R. STRAUSS
Don Juan, op. 20
Till Eulenspiegels lustige Streiche, op. 28
Dirigent: CLEMENS KRAUSS LXT 2549

MOZART
Die Zauberflöte, Oper in 2 Akten
Kurt Böhme (Sarastro) - Leopold Simoneau (Tamino) - Paul Schöffler (Sprecher) - Wilma Lipp (Königin der Nacht) - Hilde Güden (Pamina) Walter Berry (Papageno) - Emmy Loose (Papagena) - August Jaresch (Monostatos) u. a.
Chor der Wiener Staatsoper
Dirigent: KARL BÖHM
LXT 5085-87 (3 Platten)

R. STRAUSS
Der Rosenkavalier, Komöd. f. Musik in 3 Akt.
Maria Reining (Feldmarschallin) - Ludwig Weber (Ochs) - Sena Jurinak (Oktavian) - Alfred Poell (Faninal) - Hilde Güden (Sophie) - Judith Hellwig (Jungfer Marianne Leitmetzerin) - Peter Klein (Valsacchi) - Hilde Rössl-Majdan (Annina) Anton Dermota (Sänger) u. a.
Chor der Wiener Staatsoper
Leitung: ERICH KLEIBER
LXT 2954-57 (4 Platten)

SCHALLPLATTEN

Preis jeder 30 cm Langspielplatte DM 24.–

Humperdinck

Hänsel und Gretel, Overture

| Dresden | Dresden | 78: Electrola DB 4648 |
| 1939 | Staatskapelle | LP: Electrola 1C 137 53514-9M |

Leoncavallo

I Pagliacci, Intermezzo

Dresden	Dresden	78: Electrola DB 4556
1938	Staatskapelle	45: HMV 7R 158
		LP: Electrola 1C 137 53514-9M

Lortzing

Undine, Ballet Music

| Dresden | Dresden | 78: Electrola EH 916 |
| 1935 | Staatskapelle | LP: Electrola 1C 137 53505-7M |

Zar und Zimmermann, Clog Dance

| Dresden | Dresden | 78: Electrola EH 916 |
| 1935 | Staatskapelle | LP: Electrola 1C 137 53505-7M |

Mahler

Kindertotenlieder

Salzburg August 1962	BPO Fischer-Dieskau	LP: Melodram MEL 712
Berlin April 1963	BPO Fischer-Dieskau	LP: DG LPM 18 879/SLPM 138 879 LP: DG 2531 375 LP: DG 2726 066 LP: DG 2543 182 LP: DG 413 6311 CD: DG 415 1912

Rückert-Lieder: Ich atmet' einen linden Duft; Blicke mir nicht in die Lieder; Ich bin der Welt abhanden gekommen; Um Mitternacht

Berlin April 1963	BPO Fischer-Dieskau	LP: DG LPM 18 879#SLPM 138 879 LP: DG 2531 375 LP: DG 2726 065 LP: DG 2543 182 LP: DG 413 5281 CD: DG 415 1912

Marx

Orchesterlieder: Selige Nacht; Venezianisches Wiegenlied; Marienlied; Waldseligkeit; Erinnerung; Hat dich die Liebe berührt

Berlin April 1951	Berlin RO Linhard-Böhm	LP: Melodram MEL 218

Mascagni

Cavalleria Rusticana, Intermezzo

Dresden 1938	Dresden Staatskapelle	78: Electrola DB 4556 45: HMV 7R 158 LP: Electrola 1C 137 53514-9M

Cavalleria Rusticana: Excerpt (Easter Hymn)

Dresden 1939	Dresden Staatskapelle Dresden Opera Chorus Goltz Sung in German	78: Electrola DB 5558 LP: Electrola 1C 137 53514-9M

Mozart

Symphony No 1 K16; Symphony No 4 K19; Symphony No 5 K22; Symphony in F K76 (42a); Symphony No 6 K43; Symphony No 7 K45; Symphony in B flat K45b

Berlin	BPO	LP: DG 2720 044
February-November		LP: DG 2740 109
1968		CD: DG 427 2412

Symphony No 8 K48; Symphony No 9 K73; Symphony No 10 K74; Symphony No 11 K84 (73q); Symphony in D K95 (73n); Symphony in D K97 (73m); Symphony in F K75; Symphony No 12 K110 (75b); Symphony in C K96 (111b); Symphony No 13 K112; Symphony No 14 K114; Symphony No 15 K124

Berlin	BPO	LP: DG 2720 044
October-November		LP: DG 2740 109
1968		CD: DG 427 2412

Symphony No 16 K128; Symphony No 17 K129; Symphony No 18 K130; Symphony No 19 K132; Symphony No 20 K133

Berlin	BPO	LP: DG 2720 044
February-November		LP: DG 2740 109
1968		CD: DG 427 2412

Symphony No 21 K134; Symphony No 22 K162; Symphony No 23 K181 (162b); Symphony No 24 K 182 (173dA)

Berlin	BPO	LP: DG 2720 044
February-March		LP: DG 139 405
1968		LP: DG 2740 109
		CD: DG 427 2412

Symphony No 25 K183 (173dB)

Vienna	VPO	78: HMV C 4086-4088/7843-7845 auto
November and		
December 1947		

Berlin	BPO	LP: DG 2720 044
February-March		LP: DG 2535 479
1968		LP: DG 2740 110
		LP: DG 2543 183
		CD: DG 427 2412

Symphony No 26 K184 (161a)

Vienna December 1947	VPO	HMV unpublished
Amsterdam September 1955	Concertgebouw Orchestra	LP: Philips A 00318 L LP: Philips G 05314 R LP: Philips 6833 214
Berlin February-March 1968	BPO	LP: DG 2720 044 LP: DG 139 159 LP: DG 135 125 LP: DG 2740 110 LP: DG 2530 120 LP: DG 2535 425/2542 127/2543 183 CD: DG 427 2412

Symphony No 27 K199 (161b)

Berlin February-March 1968	BPO	LP: DG 2720 044 LP: DG 2740 110 LP: DG 2530 120 LP: DG 2543 183 CD: DG 427 2412

Symphony No 28 K200 (189k)

Berlin February-March 1968	BPO	LP: DG 2720 044 LP: DG 139 406 LP: DG 2740 110 LP: DG 2543 184 CD: DG 427 2412

Symphony No 29 K201 (186a)

Berlin February-March 1968	BPO	LP: DG 2720 044 LP: DG 139 406 LP: DG 2740 110 LP: DG 2543 184 CD: DG 427 2412
Vienna June 1980	VPO	LP: DG 2531 335 LP: DG 2740 268 CD: DG 413 7342 CD: DG 429 8002/429 8032

Symphony No 30 K202 (186b)

Berlin February-March 1968	BPO	LP: DG 2720 044 LP: DG 2740 110 CD: DG 427 2412

Symphony No 31 K297 (300a) "Paris"

Berlin February-March 1968	BPO	LP: DG 2720 044 LP: DG 139 159 LP: DG 2535 425 LP: DG 2740 110 LP: DG 2542 127/2543 185 CD: DG 413 1512 CD: DG 427 2102/427 2412

Symphony No 32 K318

Amsterdam September 1955	Concertgebouw Orchestra	LP: Philips A 00318 L LP: Philips 6833 214
Berlin October 1959	BPO	LP: DG LPM 18 612/SLPM 138 112 LP: DG 2720 044 LP: DG 2535 229/2535 385 LP: DG 2740 110 LP: DG 2542 119/2543 186 LP: DG 419 0171 CD: DG 413 1512 CD: DG 427 2412

Symphony No 33 K319

Berlin February 1968	BPO	LP: DG 2720 044 LP: DG 2740 110 CD: DG 427 2412

Symphony No 34 K338, with Minuet K409

Vienna November 1954	VPO	LP: Decca LXT 5111 LP: Decca LW 5299 LP: Decca LXT 6277-80/SXL 6277-80
Berlin February 1966	BPO	LP: DG 2720 044 LP: DG 139 159 LP: DG 2740 110 LP: DG 2543 185 CD: DG 427 1412

Symphony No 35 K385 "Haffner"

Vienna 1942	VPO	78: Electrola DB 7649-7651
Berlin February 1954	BPO	LP: Longanesi periodici GCL 07 LP: Foyer FO 1033 <u>Incorrectly labelled Berlin RO 1951</u>
Berlin October 1959	BPO	LP: DG LPM 18 612/SLPM 138 112 LP: DG 2720 044 LP: DG 2535 385 LP: DG 2740 110 LP: DG 2542 119/2543 186 LP: DG 413 1512/419 0171 CD: DG 427 1412/429 5212
Vienna June 1980	VPO	LP: DG 2531 335 LP: DG 2740 268 CD: DG 413 7342 CD: DG 427 2412 CD: DG 429 8002/429 8032

Symphony No 36 K425 "Linz"

Vienna September 1950	VPO	LP: Decca LXT 2558/LXT 2562 LP: Decca ACL 147
Berlin February 1966	BPO	LP: DG 2720 044 LP: DG 139 160 LP: DG 2535 385 LP: DG 2740 110 LP: DG 2542 119/2543 186 CD: DG 427 2412 CD: DG 429 5212

Symphony No 38 K504 "Prague"

Vienna November 1954	VPO	LP: Decca LXT 5111 LP: Decca LW 5316 LP: Decca LXT 6277-6280/SXL 6277-6280
Berlin October 1959	BPO	LP: DG LPM 18 612/SLPM 138 112 LP: DG 2720 044 LP: DG 2535 425 LP: DG 2740 110 LP: DG 2542 127/2543 187 LP: DG 2726 504 LP: DG 413 5311/423 0041 CD: DG 427 2412 CD: DG 429 5212
Vienna March 1979	VPO	LP: DG 2531 206 LP: DG 2740 268 CD: DG 413 7352

Symphony No 39 K543

Amsterdam September 1955	Concertgebouw Orchestra	LP: Philips A 00319 L LP: Philips 6833 214
Berlin February 1966	BPO	LP: DG 2720 044 LP: DG 139 160 LP: DG 2740 110 LP: DG 2726 504 LP: DG 2543 187/2543 527 LP: DG 413 5311/423 0041 CD: DG 427 2412
Vienna March 1979	VPO	LP: DG 2531 206 LP: DG 2740 258 CD: DG 413 7352

Symphony No 40 K550

Amsterdam September 1955	Concertgebouw Orchestra	LP: Philips A 00319 L LP: Philips G 05314 R LP: Philips 6527 035/6540 077
Berlin December 1961 and March 1962	BPO	LP: DG LPM 18 815/SLPM 138 815 LP: DG 2720 044 LP: DG 2535 479 LP: DG 2740 110 LP: DG 2726 504 LP: DG 2543 188/2543 527 LP: DG 413 1512/413 5311/419 6461 CD: DG 427 2102/427 2412
Salzburg August 1962	BPO	LP: Melodram MEL 712 <u>1st movement only</u> CD: Classical Collection CD 3CLC-4015 <u>Classical Collection incorrectly dated February 1968</u>
Vienna April 1976	VPO	LP: DG 2530 780 LP: DG 2740 268 CD: DG 413 5472

Symphony No 41 K551 "Jupiter"

Vienna March 1949	VPO	78: HMV C 3884-3998/7759-7762 auto 78: HMV DB 11532-11535 LP: Victor LBC 1018 LP: Vox (Japan) H 5062 CD: EMI CHS 764 2942/CDH 764 2952 <u>Vox incorrectly dated 1952</u>
Amsterdam September 1955	Concertgebouw Orchestra	LP: Philips A 00318 L LP: Philips G 03014 L LP: Philips 6527 035/6540 077
Berlin December 1961 and March 1962	BPO	LP: DG LPM 18 815/SLPM 138 815 LP: DG 2720 044 LP: DG 2740 110 LP: DG 2726 504 LP: DG 2543 188 LP: DG 413 1512/413 5311/419 0171/419 64 CD: DG 427 2102/427 2412
Tokyo March 1975	VPO	LP: DG (Japan) 92MG-0650-3
Vienna April 1976	VPO	LP: DG 2530 780 LP: DG 2531 190 LP: DG 2740 268 CD: DG 413 5472

Divertimento No 11 K251: First movement

Vienna 1947	VPO	78: HMV C 4088

Serenade No 6 K239 "Serenata notturna"

Vienna December 1947	VPO	HMV unpublished <u>First three movements only</u>
Berlin September 1957	BPO	LP: DG LPE 17 101 45: DG EPL 30 422
Berlin May 1970	BPO	LP: DG 2530 082 LP: DG 2535 492 LP: DG 2543 191 CD: DG 427 2082

Serenade No 7 K250 "Haffner"

Berlin May 1970 and May 1972	BPO	LP: DG 2530 290 LP: DG 2543 190 LP: DG 419 8661 CD: DG 419 8662 CD: DG 429 8002/429 8062

Serenade No 7 K250 "Haffner": Rondo, Minuet and Trio

Vienna	VPO	Rondo
December 1947		78: HMV C 3990
		Minuet and Trio
		HMV unpublished

Serenade No 9 K320 "Posthorn"

Berlin	BPO	LP: DG 2530 082
May 1970		LP: DG 2531 191
		LP: DG 2543 191
		LP: DG 415 8431
		LP: DG 423 0071
		CD: DG 415 8432
		CD: DG 427 8002/427 8072

Serenade No 10 for 13 winds K361

Berlin	BPO	LP: DG 2530 136
May 1970		LP: DG 2543 192

Serenade No 13 K525 "Eine kleine Nachtmusik"

Dresden	Dresden	78: Electrola DB 4548-9
1938	Staatskapelle	LP: Electrola 1C 137 53500-4M
Berlin	BPO	78: HMV DB 11514-5
Date uncertain		May not have been published
Berlin	BPO	LP: Movimento Musica 01.035
February 1954		LP: Melodram MEL 218
		Melodram incorrectly labelled
		Berlin RO 1953
Berlin	BPO	LP: DG LPE 17 101
December 1956		
Vienna	VPO	LP: DG 2530 731/2531 191
October 1974		LP: DG 2535 492
		LP: DG 2536 173/2536 381
		LP: DG 2543 193/2546 303
		LP: DG 2721 205/2721 231
		LP: DG 415 8431
		CD: DG 413 1522
		CD: DG 415 8432
		CD: DG 427 2082

Masonic Funeral Music K477

Vienna	VPO	LP: DG 2531 335
March 1979		LP: DG 2740 268
		LP: DG 413 1512
		CD: DG 413 7342
		CD: DG 429 8002/429 8032

Bassoon Concerto K191

Vienna	VPO	LP: DG 2530 411
May 1973	Zeman	LP: DG 2740 231
		LP: DG 2543 196
		LP: DG 413 0211
		CD: DG 429 8002/429 8162

Clarinet Concerto K622

Vienna	VPO	LP: DG 2530 411
September 1972	Prinz	LP: DG 2740 231
		LP: DG 2543 196
		LP: DG 413 0211
		CD: DG 413 5522
		CD: DG 429 8002/429 8162

Flute Concerto No 1 K313

Vienna	VPO	LP: DG 2530 527
May 1973	Tripp	LP: DG 2740 231
		LP: DG 2543 194
		LP: DG 2726 522
		LP: DG 413 0211/419 8651
		CD: DG 413 7372

Flute and Harp Concerto K299

Vienna	VPO	LP: DG 2530 715
May 1975	Schulz,	LP: DG 2740 231
	Zabaleta	LP: DG 2543 193
		CD: DG 413 5522
		CD: DG 429 8002/429 8152

Horn Concerto No 1 K412

Vienna	VPO	LP: DG 2531 274
December 1979	Högner	LP: DG 2740 231
		LP: DG 2543 195
		LP: DG 413 0211
		CD: DG 413 7922

Horn Concerto No 2 K417

Vienna	VPO	LP: DG 2531 274
March 1979	Högner	LP: DG 2740 231
		LP: DG 2543 195
		CD: DG 413 7922

Horn Concerto No 3 K447

Dresden 1940	Dresden Staatskapelle Zimolog	78: Electrola DB 5628-9 LP: Electrola 1C 137 53500-4M
Vienna November 1978	VPO Högner	LP: DG 2531 274 LP: DG 2740 231 LP: DG 2543 195 CD: DG 413 7922

Horn Concerto No 4 K495

Vienna December 1979	VPO Högner	LP: DG 2531 274 LP: DG 2740 231 LP: DG 2543 195 CD: DG 413 7922

Oboe Concerto K285d (314)

Vienna April and May 1974	VPO Turetschek	LP: DG 2530 527 LP: DG 2740 231 LP: DG 2726 522 LP: DG 2543 194 LP: DG 413 0211/419 8651 CD: DG 413 7372 CD: DG 429 8002/429 8162

Piano Concerto No 19 K459

Vienna April 1976	VPO Pollini	LP: DG 2530 716 LP: DG 2543 197 CD: DG 413 7932 CD: DG 429 8002/429 8122 Laserdisc: DG 072 1021

Piano Concerto No 21 K467

Berlin December 1951	BPO Askenase	LP: Movimento Musica 01.035

Piano Concerto No 23 K488

Vienna April 1976	VPO Pollini	LP: DG 2530 716 LP: DG 2543 197 CD: DG 413 7932 CD: DG 429 8002/429 8122 Laserdisc: DG 072 1021

Piano Concerto No 27 K595

Vienna May and June 1955	VPO Backhaus	LP: Decca LXT 5123 LP: Decca ECS 749 Also issued by Decca on 10" LP
Salzburg August 1960	VPO Backhaus	LP: Longanesi periodici GCL 14 LP: Seven Seas K22C-168
Vienna September and November 1973	VPO Gilels	LP: DG 2530 456 LP: DG 2543 198 LP: DG 419 0591 CD: DG 419 0592 CD: DG 429 8002/429 8102

Concerto for 2 pianos K365

Vienna September and November 1973	VPO Elena and Emil Gilels	LP: DG 2530 456 LP: DG 2543 198 LP: DG 419 0591 CD: DG 419 0592

Violin Concerto No 4 K218

Berlin 1951	Berlin RO Menuhin	LP: Longanesi periodici GCL 42 CD: Foyer CDS 16006

Violin Concerto No 5 K219

Dresden 1938	Dresden Staatskapelle Dahmen	78: Electrola DB 4578-4581 LP: Electrola 1C 137 53500-4M

Sinfonia concertante for violin and viola K364

Berlin December 1964	BPO Brandis, Cappone	LP: DG 139 156 LP: DG 2535 492/2538 262 LP: DG 2543 189 CD: DG 427 2982 CD: DG 429 8002/429 8132

Sinfonia concertante for winds K297b

Berlin February 1966	BPO Steins, Leister, Seifert, Piesk	LP: DG 139 156 LP: DG 2535 492 LP: DG 2543 189 CD: DG 413 1522
Vienna May 1975	VPO Lehmayer, Schmidl, Högner, Faltl	LP: DG 2530 715 LP: DG 2740 231 CD: DG 429 8002/429 8132

Requiem K626

Vienna November 1956	VSO Vienna Opera Chorus Stich-Randall, Malaniuk, Kmennt, Böhme	LP: Philips G 03088 L LP: Philips GL 5709 CD: Classical Collection CD 3CLC-4015 CD: Philips 420 7722
Vienna April 1971	VPO Vienna Opera Chorus Mathis, Hamari, Ochman, Ridderbusch	LP: DG 2530 143 LP: DG 2543 199 CD: DG 413 5532 Dies irae LP: DG 2535 654/2563 632

La Clemenza di Tito K621

Dresden January and March 1979	Dresden Staatskapelle Leipzig Radio Choir Berganza, Mathis, Varady, Schiml, Schreier, Adam	LP: DG 2709 092 LP: DG 2740 208/2740 222 CD: DG 429 8782/435 3962 Excerpts LP: DG 2537 054

Così fan tutte K588

Geneva January 1949	Suisse Romande Chorus & Orchestra Danco, Simionato, Morel, De Lucia, Cortis, Stabile	LP: Rodolphe RP 12456-8
Vienna May 1955	VPO Vienna Opera Chorus Della Casa, Loose, C.Ludwig, Dermota, Kunz, Schöffler	LP: Decca LXT 5107-9 LP: Decca GOM 543-5/GOS 543-5 Excerpts LP: Decca LXT 5277/LXT 5511/SXL 2058 45: Decca CEP 572 LP: Decca BR 3085 LP: Decca ADD 208/SDD 208/SDD 288
Salzburg July 1960	VPO Vienna Opera Chorus Schwarzkopf, C.Ludwig, Sciutti, Kmennt, Prey, Dönch	LP: Melodram MEL 708 LP: Movimento Musica 03.026 Excerpts LP: Melodram MEL 082/MEL 088 CD: Melodram MEL 16501
Salzburg August 1962	VPO Vienna Opera Chorus Schwarzkopf, C.Ludwig, Sciutti, Kmennt, Prey, Dönch	CD: Hunt CDMP 455
London September 1962	Philharmonia Chorus & Orchestra Schwarzkopf, C.Ludwig, Steffek, Kraus, Taddei, Berry	LP: EMI AN 103-6/SAN 103-6 LP: EMI SLS 5028 CD: EMI CMS 769 3302 Excerpts LP: EMI ALP 2265/ASD 2265 LP: EMI SXLP 30457 LP: Electrola 1C 187 29225-6M
Salzburg August 1974	VPO Vienna Opera Chorus Janowitz, Fassbänder, Grist, Schreier, Panerai, Prey	LP: DG 2709 059 LP: DG 2740 118 LP: DG 2740 206/2740 222 CD: DG 429 8742/435 3942 Excerpts LP: DG 2537 037 CD: DG 427 7122 CD: DG 429 8002/429 8242 Overture LP: DG 2535 229/2535 383

Così fan tutte K588: Excerpts

Salzburg August 1958	VPO Vienna Opera Chorus Schwarzkopf, C.Ludwig, Sciutti, Alva, Panerai, Schmidt	LP: Gioielli della lirica GML 52

SALZBURGER FESTSPIELE 1961

COSÌ FAN TUTTE

KOMISCHE OPER IN ZWEI AKTEN VON LORENZO DA PONTE

MUSIK VON
WOLFGANG AMADEUS MOZART

DIRIGENT
KARL BÖHM

INSZENIERUNG
GÜNTHER RENNERT

BÜHNENBILD UND KOSTÜME
LENI BAUER-ECSY

ORCHESTER
DIE WIENER PHILHARMONIKER
CHOR DER WIENER STAATSOPER

COSÌ FAN TUTTE
(In italienischer Sprache)
Komische Oper in zwei Akten von Lorenzo da Ponte
MUSIK VON WOLFGANG AMADEUS MOZART

Fiordiligi	Schwestern	Elisabeth Schwarzkopf
Dorabella		Christa Ludwig
Guglielmo, Offizier, Fiordiligis Bräutigam . .		Hermann Prey
Ferrando, Offizier, Dorabellas Bräutigam . .		Waldemar Kmentt
Despina, Kammermädchen der Damen . . .		Graziella Sciutti
Don Alfonso, ein Philosoph		Carl Dönch

Nach dem ersten Akt eine größere Pause

Technische Einrichtung und Beleuchtung: Hermann Andre

Der offizielle Almanach „Salzburg — Festspiele 1961" ist auch für Sie der unentbehrliche Ratgeber
The official almanac "Salzburg Festivals 1961" is an indispensable guide for all Festival visitors
L'almanach officiel «Salzbourg Festival 1961» est indispensable à tous ceux qui s'intéressent au Festival

Don Giovanni K527

New York December 1957	Metropolitan Opera Chorus & Orchestra Steber, Della Casa, Peters, Peerce, Siepi	LP: Melodram MEL 439 Excerpts CD: Legato BIM 712
New York January 1967	Metropolitan Opera Chorus & Orchestra Sutherland, Hurley, Lorengar, Gedda, Siepi	CD: Nuova Era 6708 Excerpt CD: Di Stefano GDS 21017
Prague February and March 1967	Prague National Chorus & Orchestra Arroyo, Nilsson, Grist, Schreier, Fischer-Dieskau	LP: DG 2711 006 LP: DG 2740 119 LP: DG 2740 108 LP: DG 2740 205/2740 222 CD: DG 429 8702/435 3942 Excerpts LP: DG 2537 014 Overture LP: DG 2535 229
Salzburg July and August 1977	VPO Vienna Opera Chorus Tomowa-Sintov, Zylis-Gara, Mathis, Schreier, Berry, Milnes	LP: DG 2709 085 LP: DG 2740 194 LP: DG 413 2821 Excerpts LP: DG 2537 050 CD: DG 429 8002/429 8232 CD: DG 431 1812

Don Giovanni K527: Excerpts

Vienna November 1955	VPO Jurinac, Seefried, Della Casa, Kunz, Dermota, London Sung in German	LP: Amadeo 412 8211 LP: DG 415 4491 Excerpts CD: Di Stefano GDS 1206/GDS 2204 CD: Melodram CDM 26522/CDM 26526
New York February 1959	Metropolitan Opera Orchestra Della Casa, London, Flagello	CD: Melodram CDM 26526

Don Giovanni K527: Excerpts (Dalla sua pace; Il mio tesoro)

Vienna September 1950	VPO Dermota	LP: Decca LXT 2685 LP: Telefunken 642.233 LP: Everest 3202

Don Giovanni K527: Excerpt (Madamina)

Vienna September 1950	VPO Schöffler	78: Decca K 23305 LP: Decca LXT 2554/LXT 2685 LP: Decca 414 4531

Die Entführung aus dem Serail K384

Dresden September 1973	Dresden Staatskapelle Leipzig Radio Choir Auger, Grist, Schreier, Moll, Neukirch	LP: DG 2709 051 LP: DG 2740 102 LP: DG 2740 203/2740 222 CD: DG 423 4592 CD: DG 429 8682/435 3952 Excerpts LP: DG 2537 035 LP: DG 413 1812 Overture LP: DG 2535 229/2535 627 LP: DG 2563 649/2721 205
Munich 1979	Bavarian State Chorus & Orchestra Gruberova, Grist, Araiza, Orth, Talvela	VHS Video: DG 072 4083 Laserdisc: DG 072 4081

Die Entführung aus dem Serail K384, Overture

Dresden 1939	Dresden Staatskapelle	78: Electrola DB 4692 LP: Electrola 1C 137 53514-9M

Idomeneo K366

Salzburg August 1956	VPO Vienna Opera Chorus Hillebrecht, Goltz, Schock, Kmennt	LP: Movimento Musica 03.017
Dresden September and November 1977	Dresden Staatskapelle Leipzig Radio Choir Mathis, Varady, Schreier, Ochman	LP: DG 2711 023 LP: DG 2740 195 LP: DG 2740 202/2740 222 CD: DG 429 8642/435 3962 <u>Excerpts</u> LP: DG 2537 051

Der Schauspieldirektor K486

Dresden September 1973	Dresden Staatskapelle Auger, Grist, Schreier, Moll	LP: DG 2740 102 LP: DG 2709 051 LP: DG 2740 203/2740 222 CD: DG 419 5662 CD: DG 429 8772/435 3952 <u>Overture</u> LP: DG 2535 229

Der Schauspieldirektor K486, Overture

Vienna 1949	VPO	78: HMV C 3887

Le Nozze di Figaro K492

Stuttgart October 1938	Stuttgart Radio Chorus & Orchestra Teschemacher, Cebotari, Kolniak, Ahlersmayer, Böhme, Schöffler Sung in German	LP: Acanta DE 23.133-4 CD: Preiser 90035 Excerpt LP: BASF 72.221792
Vienna 1955	VSO Vienna Opera Chorus Jurinac, Streich, C.Ludwig, Berry, Schöffler	LP: Philips A 00357-9 L LP: Philips GL 5777-9 LP: Philips SFL 14012-4 LP: Philips 6706 006 Excerpts LP: Philips GL 5666 LP: Philips G 03069 L 45: Philips ABE 10129
Salzburg July 1957	VPO Vienna Opera Chorus Schwarzkopf, Kunz, Seefried, C.Ludwig, Fischer-Dieskau	LP: Melodram MEL 709 CD: Di Stefano GDS 31019 Excerpts LP: Melodram MEL 047 CD: Virtuoso 269.7152 CD: Verona 27092-4
Berlin March 1968	Deutsche Oper Chorus & Orchestra Janowitz, Mathis, Troyanos, Prey, Fischer-Dieskau	LP: DG 2711 007 LP: DG 2740 108/2740 139 LP: DG 2740 202 LP: DG 2740 204/2740 222 LP: DG 415 5201 CD: DG 415 5202 CD: DG 429 8692/435 3942 Excerpts LP: DG 2537 023 CD: DG 423 1152/427 7122 CD: DG 429 8002/429 8222 Overture LP: DG 2535 229 LP: DG 2536 383/2721 181
Vienna 1975	VPO Vienna Opera Chorus Kanawa, Freni, Ewing, Prey, Fischer-Dieskau	VHS Video: DG 072 4033 Laserdisc: DG 072 4031

Le Nozze di Figaro K492: Excerpts

Salzburg July 1967	VPO Vienna Opera Chorus Watson, Grist, Mathis, Berry, Wixell	CD: Curcio-Hunt OPV 025

Le Nozze di Figaro K492: Excerpt (Non più andrai)

Vienna September 1950	VPO Schöffler	78: Decca K 23305 LP: Decca LXT 2554/LXT 2685 LP: Decca 414 4531

Le Nozze di Figaro K492: Excerpt (Aprite un po' quegli occhi)

Vienna March 1981	VPO Taddei	LP: Teletheater 29.402 Böhm's last public appearance

Le Nozze di Figaro K492, Overture

Dresden 1939	Dresden Staatskapelle	78: Electrola DB 4692 LP: Electrola 1C 137 53514-9M
Berlin 1952	Berlin RO	LP: Melodram MEL 218

Die Zauberflöte K620

Vienna May 1955	VPO Vienna Opera Chorus Güden, Lipp, Simoneau, Berry, Schöffler, Böhme,	LP: Decca LXT 5085-7/SXL 2215-7 LP: Decca GOM 501-3/GOS 501-3 CD: Decca 414 3622 Excerpts LP: Decca LW 5343 LP: Decca ADD 218/SDD 218 LP: Decca VIV 50 LP: Decca 417 1781 CD: Classical Collection CD3 CLC-4015
Berlin June 1964	BPO RIAS Choir Lear, Peters, Wunderlich, Hotter, Fischer-Dieskau	LP: DG SLPM 138 981-3 LP: DG 2709 017 LP: DG 2720 058 LP: DG 2740 207/2740 222 LP: DG 2740 108 CD: DG 419 5662 CD: DG 429 8772/435 3952 Excerpts LP: DG 136 440/136 527 LP: DG 2537 003 CD: DG 429 8002/429 8252 Overture LP: DG 2535 229/2535 602 LP: DG 2721 181

Die Zauberflöte K620: Excerpt (Dies Bildnis ist bezaubernd schön)

Vienna September 1950	VPO Dermota	LP: Decca LXT 2685 45: Decca 45-71116 LP: Telefunken 642.233 LP: Decca ECS 812

Nicolai

The Merry Wives of Windsor, Overture

Berlin March 1936	BPO	78: Electrola DB 4444 LP: Electrola 1C 137 54095-9 LP: EMI RLS 768 CD: EMI CF 3000.122

SALZBURGER FESTSPIELE 1953

URAUFFÜHRUNG
(17. AUGUST 1953)

DER PROZESS

NACH DEM ROMAN VON FRANZ KAFKA

NEUN BILDER IN ZWEI TEILEN
VON BORIS BLACHER UND HEINZ VON CRAMER

MUSIK VON
GOTTFRIED VON EINEM

DIRIGENT:
KARL BÖHM

INSZENIERUNG:
OSCAR FRITZ SCHUH

BÜHNENBILD UND KOSTÜME:
CASPAR NEHER

ORCHESTER:
DIE WIENER PHILHARMONIKER

Pfitzner

Symphony in C op 46

Dresden 1940	Dresden Staatskapelle	78: Electrola DB 5618-5619 LP: Electrola E 60 802 LP: Electrola 1C 137 53508-13M
Dresden November 1942	Dresden Staatskapelle	LP: Urania URLP 7044 CD: Fonoteam CD 74808
Vienna May 1969	VPO	CD: Memories HR 4159

Prokofiev

Peter and the Wolf

Vienna October 1974	VPO K-H.Böhm (German) Gingold (English) Richard (French) De Filippo (Italian)	LP: DG 2530 587 (German) LP: DG 2530 588 (English) LP: DG 2543 200 (German) CD: DG 413 3502 (German) CD: DG 413 3512 (English) CD: DG 413 3522 (French) CD: DG 419 1652 (Italian)

Puccini

La Fanciulla del West: Excerpt (Ch' ella mi creda)

Dresden 1940	Dresden Staatskapelle Sung in German	78: Electrola DB 5620 LP: Rococo 5233 LP: Electrola 1C 137 53514-19M

Turandot: Excerpt (Tu che di gel sei cinta)

Vienna March 1949	VPO Schwarzkopf	78: Columbia LB 85 45: Columbia SEL 1575 LP: EMI RLS 763

Reger

Variations on a theme of Mozart

Dresden 1938	Dresden Staatskapelle	78: Electrola DB 4480-4483/8345-8348 auto LP: Electrola 1C 137 53508-13M
Berlin 1956	BPO	LP: DG LPM 18 375 LP: DG 2548 103

Reznicek

Donna Diana, Overture

Dresden 1939	Dresden Staatskapelle	78: Electrola DB 4560 LP: Electrola 1C 137 53514-19M

Rossini

Il Barbiere di Siviglia

Vienna April 1966	VPO Vienna Opera Chorus Grist, Konetzni, Wunderlich, Kunz, Wächter, Czerwenka Sung in German	LP: Teatro Dischi TD 502-3 CD: Myto MCD 91752 Teatro Dischi incorrectly dated 1964

Saint-Saëns

Le Carnaval des animaux

Vienna October 1974	VPO Aloys and Alfons Kontarsky K-H.Böhm (German) Gingold (English) Richard (French) De Filippo (Italian)	LP: DG 2530 587 (German) LP: DG 2530 588 (English) LP: DG 2530 731 (French) LP: DG 2721 131 (German) LP: DG 2536 173 (German) LP: DG 2543 200/2546 173 (German) CD: DG 413 3502 (German) CD: DG 413 3512 (English) CD: DG 413 3522 (French) CD: DG 419 1652 (Italian)

Schmidt

Notre Dame, Intermezzo

Vienna	VPO	78: HMV C 3975
March 1949		78: HMV DB 20400
		45: Electrola E 30039

Schoenberg

Pelleas und Melisande

Vienna	VPO	CD: DG 435 3232/435 3212
June 1969		

Schubert

Symphony No 1

Berlin May 1971	BPO	LP: DG 2530 216 LP: DG 2740 127 /2720 062 CD: DG 419 3182

Symphony No 2

Berlin May 1971	BPO	LP: DG 2530 216 LP: DG 2740 127 /2720 062 CD: DG 419 3182

Symphony No 3

Berlin November 1971	BPO	LP: DG 2530 526 LP: DG 2740 127 /2720 062 CD: DG 419 3182

Symphony No 4 "Tragic"

Berlin November 1971	BPO	LP: DG 2530 526 LP: DG 2740 127 /2720 062 CD: DG 419 3182

Symphony No 5

Dresden June 1942	Dresden Staatskapelle	LP: Discocorp IGI 365 CD: Fonoteam CD 74808
Vienna June 1954	VPO	LP: Decca LXT 2998/LXT 5381 LP: Decca ECM 536/ECS 536
Berlin February and March 1966	BPO	LP: DG 139 162 LP: DG 2740 127/2740 188 /2720 062 LP: DG 2543 201 CD: DG 419 3182
Vienna December 1979	VPO	LP: DG 2531 279/2531 373

Symphony No 6

Berlin November 1971	BPO	LP: DG 2530 422 LP: DG 2740 127 /2720 062 CD: DG 419 3182

Symphony No 8 "Unfinished"

Vienna 1940	VPO	78: Electrola DB 5588-5590 LP: Electrola 1C 137 53032-6M
Vienna June 1954	VPO	LP: Decca LXT 2824/LXT 2998/LXT 5381 LP: Decca LW 5257 LP: Decca ECM 536/ECS 536 LP: Decca ACL 86
Salzburg August 1957	VPO	LP: Longanesi periodici GCL 26 LP: Foyer FO 1033
Berlin February and March 1966	BPO	LP: DG 139 162 LP: DG 2740 127/2740 188/2720 062 LP: DG 2721 205/2726 502 LP: DG 2543 203/2543 506/2545 037 CD: DG 419 3182
Tokyo March 1975	VPO	LP: DG (Japan) F35G-20016 CD: DG (Japan) 92MG-0650-3
Vienna June 1977	VPO	LP: DG 2531 373

Symphony No 9 "Great"

Berlin June 1963	BPO	LP: DG LPM 18 877/SLPM 138 877 LP: DG 2740 127/2740 188/2720 062 LP: DG 2726 502 LP: DG 2543 202 CD: DG 419 3182 Rehearsal extract LP: DG 004 241 LP: DG 2562 382
Budapest November 1969	VPO	CD: Curcio-Hunt CONB 03
Tokyo March 1975	VPO	LP: DG (Japan) F35G- 20017 CD: DG (Japan) 92MG-0650-3
Dresden January 1979	Dresden Staatskapelle	LP: Eterna 827.157 LP: DG 2531 352 LP: DG 419 4841 CD: DG 419 4842

Rosamunde: Overture, Entr'acte in D, Entr'acte in B and Ballet in G

Berlin	BPO	LP: DG 2530 422
November 1971		LP: DG 2740 127/2740 188 /2720 062
		LP: DG 2726 502
		LP: DG 2535 398
		LP: DG 2535 634 (Overture only)
		LP: DG 2543 201/2545 037

Marche militaire in D D733

Dresden	Dresden	78: Electrola DB 5559
1939	Staatskapelle	LP: Electrola 1C 137 53505-7M

Schumann

Symphony No 4

Vienna	VPO	LP: DG 2531 279
November 1978		LP: DG 2543 203

Piano Concerto

Dresden	Dresden	78: Columbia (Germany) LWX 356-359
1942	Staatskapelle	LP: Electrola 1C 137 53505-7M
	Gieseking	

Smetana

The Bartered Bride, Overture

Dresden	Dresden	78: Electrola DB 5552
1939	Staatskapelle	LP: Electrola 1C 137 53514-19M

Johann Strauss

An der schönen blauen Donau, Waltz

Berlin February 1954	BPO	LP: Longanesi periodici GCL 60 Incorrectly labelled Berlin RO
Vienna September 1972	VPO	LP: DG 2530 316 LP: DG 2535 649 LP: DG 2543 204/2563 414 LP: DG 419 3381
Tokyo March 1975	VPO	LP: DG (Japan) 92MG-0752-5

Annen Polka

Vienna September 1972	VPO	LP: DG 2530 316 LP: DG 2721 205 LP: DG 2543 204 LP: DG 419 3381 CD: DG 413 4322
Tokyo March 1975	VPO	LP: DG (Japan) 92MG-0752-5

Emperor Waltz

Dresden 1939	Dresden Staatskapelle	78: Electrola DB 5560 LP: Electrola 1C 137 53514-19M
Berlin February 1954	BPO	LP: Longanesi periodici GCL 60 Incorrectly labelled Berlin RO
Vienna September 1972	VPO	LP: DG 2530 316 LP: DG 2543 204 LP: DG 419 3381
Tokyo March 1975	VPO	LP: DG (Japan) 92MG-0752-5

Die Fledermaus

Vienna November 1971	VPO Vienna Opera Chorus Janowitz, Holm, Windgassen, Kunz, Holecek, Wächter, Kmennt, Schenk	LP: Decca SET 540-1

Die Fledermaus, Overture

Dresden 1939	Dresden Staatskapelle	78: Electrola DB 4638 LP: Electrola 1C 137 53514-19M
Berlin February 1954	BPO	LP: Melodram MEL 218 LP: Longanesi periodici GCL 60 Incorrectly labelled Berlin RO
Tokyo March 1975	VPO	LP: DG (Japan) 92MG-0752-5 CD: DG (Japan) F35G-20017

Morgenblätter, Waltz

Vienna March 1949	VPO	78: HMV C 3938 LP: Victor LBC 1008

New Pizzicato Polka (Fürstin Ninette)

Vienna March 1949	VPO	78: HMV C 3975 78: HMV DB 11521 45: Electrola E 30 039 LP: Electrola 1C 147 30226-7M

Perpetuum mobile

Vienna October 1943	VPO	CD: DG 435 3352
Berlin February 1954	BPO	LP: Melodram MEL 218 LP: Longanesi periodici GCL 60 Incorrectly labelled Berlin RO
Vienna September 1972	VPO	LP: DG 2530 316 LP: DG 2721 205 LP: DG 2543 204 LP: DG 419 3381 CD: DG 413 4322
Tokyo March 1975	VPO	LP: DG (Japan) 92MG-0752-5

Persian March

Berlin February 1954	BPO	LP: Melodram MEL 218 LP: Longanesi periodici GCL 60 Incorrectly labelled Berlin RO

Rosen aus dem Süden, Waltz

Vienna March 1949	VPO	78: HMV C 3919 78: Electrola EH 1374 LP: Victor LBC 1008
Vienna September 1972	VPO	LP: DG 2530 316 LP: DG 2535 649/2543 204/2563 414 LP: DG 2721 205 LP: DG 419 3381 CD: DG 413 4322 CD: DG 435 3352
Tokyo March 1975	VPO	LP: DG (Japan) 92MG-0752-5

1001 Nacht (Indigo), Intermezzo

Dresden 1939	Dresden Staatskapelle	78: Electrola DB 4560 LP: Electrola 1C 147 30226-7M LP: Electrola 1C 137 53514-19M CD: Preiser 90090

Tritsch-Tratsch Polka

Berlin February 1954	BPO	LP: Melodram MEL 218 LP: Longanesi periodici GCL 60 **Incorrectly labelled Berlin RO**
Vienna September 1972	VPO	LP: DG 2530 316 LP: DG 2543 204/2563 414 LP: DG 419 3381 CD: DG 413 4322
Tokyo March 1975	VPO	LP: DG (Japan) 92MG-0752-5

Unter Donner und Blitz, Polka

Vienna September 1972	VPO	LP: DG 2530 316 LP: DG 2543 204 LP: DG 2721 205 LP: DG 419 3381 CD: DG 413 4322

Johann Strauss father

Radetzky March

Berlin February 1954	BPO	LP: Melodram MEL 218 LP: Longanesi periodici GCL 60 Incorrectly labelled Berlin RO

Josef Strauss

Sphärenklänge, Waltz

Vienna 1949	VPO	78: HMV C 4070 78: Electrola EH 1360 LP: Victor LBC 1008 LP: Turnabout THS 65066 CD: EMI CHS 764 2942/CDH 764 2992

Frauenherz, Polka-Mazurka

Vienna March 1949	VPO	HMV unpublished

Johann & Josef Strauss

Pizzicato Polka

Berlin February 1954	BPO	LP: Longanesi periodici GCL 60 Incorrectly labelled Berlin RO
Vienna September 1972	VPO	LP: DG 2530 316 LP: DG 2721 205 LP: DG 2543 204 LP: DG 419 3381 CD: DG 413 4322
Tokyo March 1975	VPO	LP: DG (Japan) 92MG-0752-5

Richard Strauss

Alpine Symphony

Dresden September 1957	Dresden Staatskapelle	LP: DG LPM 18 476 LP: DG 89 594 CD: DG 423 4882

Also sprach Zarathustra

Berlin April 1958	BPO	LP: DG LPEM 19 144/SLPEM 136 001 LP: DG 2535 494 LP: DG 2726 028 LP: DG 2543 206 LP: DG 415 6371 CD: DG 423 4882 Opening only CD: DG 419 6302/423 1352
Salzburg August 1962	BPO	LP: Melodram MEL 712 LP: Movimento Musica 01.060

Don Juan

Dresden 1938	Dresden Staatskapelle	78: Electrola DB 4625-6 LP: Electrola 1C 137 53508-13M
Berlin March 1950	Berlin RO	LP: Longanesi periodici GCL 51
Dresden September 1957	Dresden Staatskapelle	LP: DG LPE 17 105 CD: DG 423 4882
Berlin April 1963	BPO	LP: DG LPM 18 866/SLPM 138 866 LP: DG 2535 208 LP: DG 2726 028 LP: DG 2543 205 LP: DG 415 6371 CD: DG 427 2182

Festliches Präludium

Berlin April 1963	BPO	LP: DG LPM 18 866/SLPM 138 866 LP: DG 2535 208 LP: DG 2726 028 LP: DG 2543 205 CD: DG 423 4882

Ein Heldenleben

Dresden February 1957	Dresden Staatskapelle	LP: DG LPM 18 378 LP: DG 89 644 CD: DG 423 4882
Vienna June 1976	VPO	LP: DG 2530 781 LP: DG 2543 207 LP: DG 415 6371

Till Eulenspiegels lustige Streiche

Dresden 1940	Dresden Staatskapelle	78: Electrola DB 5621-2 LP: Electrola 1C 137 53505-13M
Berlin March 1950	Berlin RO	LP: Longanesi periodici GCL 51
Dresden September 1957	Dresden Staatskapelle	LP: DG LPE 17 105
Berlin April 1963	BPO	LP: DG LPM 18 866/SLPM 138 866 LP: DG 2535 208 LP: DG 2721 205/2726 028 LP: DG 2543 205 LP: DG 415 6371 CD: DG 423 4882/427 2182

Tod und Verklärung

Berlin March 1950	Berlin RO	LP: Longanesi periodici GCL 51 CD: Memories HR 4159
Vienna May 1963	VPO	CD: DG 435 3232/435 3212
Salzburg August 1972	Dresden	CD: DG 423 4882

Orchestral Songs: Morgen; Zueignung; Meinem Kinde; Winterweihe; Allerseelen

Frankfurt 1954	Hessischer Rundfunk Orchestra Linhard-Böhm	LP: Melodram MEL 218

4 letzte Lieder

Vienna June 1953	VPO Della Casa	LP: Decca LXT 2865 LP: Decca LW 5056 LP: Decca LXT 5403-6 LP: Decca ACL 318 LP: Decca BR 3100 LP: Decca ECM 778 LP: Decca 411 6601 CD: Decca 425 9592

Arabella

Salzburg August 1947	VPO Vienna Opera Chorus Reining, Della Casa, Anday, Patzak, Hotter, Hann	LP: Melodram MEL 101 CD: Melodram future release

Arabella: Excerpts (Aber der Richtige; Das war sehr gut, Mandryka)

Dresden 1942	Dresden Staatskapelle Teschemacher, Goltz, Ahlersmayer	LP: Eterna 821.084 LP: Acanta DE 23.280-1

Ariadne auf Naxos

Vienna June 1944	VPO Reining, Seefried, Noni, Lorenz, Kunz, Schöffler	LP: DG LPM 18 850-2 LP: Acanta DE 23.309-10 Excerpts LP: DG LPEM 19 477/SLPEM 136 477 LP: DG 88017 LP: DG 2535 746 LP: BASF 22.221229 LP: Acanta DE 23.280-1
Salzburg August 1954	VPO Della Casa, Seefried, Güden, Schock, Schöffler	LP: Melodram MEL 104
Munich September 1969	Bavarian Radio Orchestra Hillebrecht, Grist, Troyanos, Thomas, Fischer-Dieskau	LP: DG 2721 189
Salzburg August 1979	VPO Behrens, Schmidt, Gruberova, King, Berry	LP: Legendary LR 183

Ariadne auf Naxos: Excerpt (Ein Schönes war....Es gibt ein Reich)

Vienna December 1967	VPO Rysanek	CD: HRE Records HR 1005 CD: Hunt CDKAR 207

Capriccio

Munich	Bavarian RO	LP: DG 2709 038
April 1971	Janowitz, Troyanos,	LP: DG 2721 188
	Auger, Schreier,	LP: DG 419 0231
	Fischer-Dieskau,	CD: DG 419 0232
	Prey, Ridderbusch	

Capriccio: Excerpt (Kein andres, das mir so im Herzen loht)

Vienna	VPO	45: Decca 45-71116
September 1950	Dermota	LP: Decca LXT 2592
		LP: Everest 3202
		LP: Telefunken 642.233
		LP: EMI EX 769 7411
		CD: EMI CMS 769 7412

Capriccio: Excerpt (Ihr Streiter im Apoll)

Vienna	VPO	LP: Acanta DE 23280-1
1944	Schöffler	LP: Melodram MEL 084

Capriccio: Excerpt (Closing scene)

Vienna	VPO	LP: Acanta DE 23280-1
1944	Cebotari,	
	Neralcic	

Daphne

Vienna	VSO	LP: DG SLPM 138 956-7
June 1964	Vienna Opera Chorus	LP: DG 2707 019
	Güden, Little,	LP: DG 2721 190/2726 090
	Streich, King,	CD: DG 423 5792
	Wunderlich,	
	Schöffler	

Daphne: Excerpts (1. O wie gern blieb' ich hier; 2. Götter, Brüder im hohen Olymp; 3. Wind, spiele mit mir)

Dresden	Dresden	78: Electrola DB 4627 (3)
1938	Staatskapelle	78: Electrola DB 4628 (1 and 2)
	Teschemacher (1 & 3)	LP: Rococo 5233 (2)
	Ralf (2)	LP: Electrola 1C 137 53514-19M
		LP: Acanta DE 23.280-1 (1 and 2)
		CD: Preiser 89090 (1 and 3)

Opernhaus

Sonnabend, am 15. Oktober 1938, Anfang 6 Uhr

Außer Anrecht

Uraufführung

Daphne

Bukolische Tragödie in einem Aufzug von Joseph Gregor

Musik von Richard Strauß

Musikalische Leitung: Karl Böhm

Inszenierung: Max Hofmüller

Personen:

Peneios	Sven Nilsson
Gaea	Helene Jung
Daphne	Margarete Teschemacher
Leukippos	Martin Kremer
Apollo	Torsten Ralf
Erster Schäfer Adrast	Arno Schellenberg
Zweiter Schäfer Kleontes	Heinrich Tessmer
Dritter Schäfer	Hans Löbel
Vierter Schäfer	Erich Händel
Erste Magd	Angela Kolniak
Zweite Magd	Marta Rohs

Schäfer, Maskierte des bacchischen Aufzugs, Mägde

Ort: Bei der Hütte des Peneios am Flusse dieses Namens

Chöre: Karl Maria Pembaur

Tänze: Valeria Kratina

Sächsische Staatstheater
Opernhaus

Montag, am 24. Juni 1935

Anfang **6** Uhr

Außer Anrecht

Uraufführung

Die schweigsame Frau

Komische Oper in drei Aufzügen

Frei nach Ben Jonson von Stefan Zweig

Musik von Richard Strauß

Musikalische Leitung: Karl Böhm   Inszenierung: Josef Gielen

Personen:

Sir Morosus	Friedrich Plaschke
Seine Haushälterin	Helene Jung
Der Barbier	Matthieu Ahlersmeyer
Henry Morosus	Martin Kremer
Aminta, seine Frau	Maria Cebotari
Isotta ⎫	Erna Sack
Carlotta ⎬ Komödianten	Marion Hundt
Vanuzzi ⎬	Kurt Böhme
Farfallo ⎬	Ludwig Ermold
Morbio ⎭	Rudolf Schmalnauer

Chor der Komödianten und Nachbarn

Ort der Handlung:
Zimmer des Sir Morosus in einem Vorort Londons
Zeit: etwa 1780

Chöre: Karl Maria Pembaur / Tanz im dritten Akt: Werner Stammer

Bühnenbild: Adolf Mahnke   Einrichtung: Georg Brandt   Trachten: Leonhard Santo

Pausen nach dem ersten und zweiten Akt

Krank: Liesel von Schuch, Hermann Kutzschbach, Horst Falke

Sämtliche Plätze müssen vor Beginn der Vorstellung eingenommen werden

Textbücher sind für 1,00 R.M. vormittags an der Kasse und abends bei den Türschließern zu haben

Gekaufte Karten werden nur bei Änderung der Vorstellung zurückgenommen

Einlaß 5¼ Uhr   Anfang 6 Uhr   Ende geg. 9¾ Uhr

Elektra

Dresden October 1960	Dresden Staatskapelle Borkh, Schech, Madeira, Uhl, Fischer-Dieskau, Böhme	LP: DG LPM 18 690-1/SLPM 138 690-1 LP: DG 2707 011 LP: DG 2721 187 CD: DG 431 7372
Vienna December 1965	VPO Nilsson, Rysanek, Resnik, Wächter, Windgassen, Guthrie	LP: HRE Records HRE 314 CD: Legato SRO 833 <u>Ich kann nicht sitzen</u> CD: HRE Records HR 1005 CD: Hunt CDKAR 207
Vienna April and June 1981	VPO Rysanek, Ligendza, Varnay, Beirer, Fischer-Dieskau, Greindl	VHS Video: Decca 071.4003 Laserdisc: Decca 071.4001 <u>Scene Elektra-Klytemnestra</u> LP: Legendary LR 204

Elektra: Excerpts (1. Ich kann nicht sitzen; 2. Recognition scene; 3. Closing scene)

Munich August 1955	Bavarian State Orchestra Goltz, Rysanek, Schöffler	LP: Melodram MEL 085 (1) LP: Melodram MEL 084/MEL 094 (2) LP: Orfeo S120.8421 (3)

Elektra: Excerpts (Ah! Das Gesicht!..Ich kann nicht sitzen; Closing scene)

Vienna September 1975	VPO Nilsson, Rysanek	LP: Legendary LR 101

Die Frau ohne Schatten

Vienna November and December 1955	VPO Vienna Opera Chorus Rysanek, Goltz, Höngen, Hopf, Schöffler, Böhme	LP: Decca LXT 5180-4 LP: Decca GOM 554-7/GOS 554-7 CD: Decca 425 9812 Excerpts LP: Decca 414 1771
Vienna October 1977	VPO Vienna Opera Chorus Rysanek, Nilsson, Hesse, King, Berry, Wimberger	LP: HRE Records HRE 322 LP: DG 415 4721 CD: DG 415 4722

Die Frau ohne Schatten: Excerpts

Vienna November 1943	VPO Konetzni, Höngen, Ralf, J.Herrmann	LP: Ed Smith UORC 345

Die Frau ohne Schatten: Excerpt (Falke, du Wiedergefundener)

Dresden 1944	Dresden Staatskapelle Ralf	LP: Eterna 820.933 LP: Acanta DE 23.280-1

Die Frau ohne Schatten: Excerpt (Sie haben es mir gesagt)

Dresden 1944	Dresden Staatskapelle J.Herrmann	LP: BASF 72.221792 LP: Acanta DE 23.280-1

Die Frau ohne Schatten, Act 1 Symphonic Interlude

Dresden 1944	Dresden Staatskapelle	LP: Acanta DE 23.280-1

Der Rosenkavalier

Dresden December 1958	Dresden Staatskapelle Dresden Opera Choir Schech, Seefried, Streich, Böhme, Fischer-Dieskau, Francl	LP: DG LPM 18 570-3/SLPM 138 040-3 LP: DG 2711 001 LP: DG 2721 162 LP: DG 419 1201 <u>Excerpts</u> LP: DG LPM 18 656/SLPM 138 656 LP: DG LPEM 19 410/SLPEM 136 410 45: DG EPL 30644 LP: DG LPEM 19 477/SLPEM 136 477 LP: DG 2535 746/2537 013 LP: DG 410 8471/419 3371

Der Rosenkavalier: Excerpts (Mit ihren Augen voll Tränen; Ist ein Traum, kann nicht wirklich sein)

Dresden 1940	Dresden Staatskapelle Rethy, Höngen	78: Electrola DB 5617 LP: Electrola 1C 137 53514-19M

Der Rosenkavalier, Act 3 Waltz Sequence

Dresden 1938	Dresden Staatskapelle	78: Electrola DB 4557 LP: Electrola 1C 137 53514-19M
Berlin April 1963	BPO	LP: DG 2721 205/2726 028

Salome

Hamburg November 1970	Hamburg State Orchestra Jones, Dunn, Fischer-Dieskau, Cassilly, Ochman, Sotin, Moll	LP: DG 2707 052 LP: DG 2721 186 Closing scene LP: DG 2721 206
Vienna March 1974	VPO Stratas, Varnay, Beirer, Weikl, Ochman	VHS Video: DG 072 1093 Laserdisc: DG 072 1091

Salome: Excerpt (Closing scene)

New York April 1972	Metropolitan Opera Orchestra Nilsson	LP: DG 2530 260
Vienna December 1972	VPO Rysanek, Hopf, G.Hoffman	LP: Legendary LR 101

Salome, Dance of the 7 veils

Dresden 1938	Dresden Staatskapelle	78: Electrola DB 4639 LP: Electrola 1C 137 53514-19M LP: Acanta DE 23.280-1
Berlin April 1963	BPO	LP: DG LPM 18 866/SLPM 138 866 LP: DG 2535 208 LP: DG 2726 026 LP: DG 2543 205 CD: DG 423 4882

Die schweigsame Frau

Salzburg August 1959	VPO Güden, Milinkovic, Wunderlich, Prey, Hotter	LP: Opera Discs OD 1000-2 LP: Melodram MEL 105 CD: Melodram MEL 27071

Stravinsky

L'oiseau de feu, Suite

Salzburg August 1968	BPO	CD: Memories HR 4159
Tokyo March 1975	VPO	LP: DG (Japan) 92MG 0752-5 This set contains 2 separate versions of the work recorded live during the 1975 VPO tour

Tchaikovsky

Symphony No 4

London December 1977	LSO	LP: DG 2531 078 LP: DG 2740 248 LP: DG 2543 208

Symphony No 5

London May 1980	LSO	LP: DG 2532 005 LP: DG 2740 248 LP: DG 2560 098 CD: DG 427 8222

Symphony No 6 "Pathétique"

London December 1978	LSO	LP: DG 2531 212 LP: DG 2740 248 LP: DG 2543 209 LP: DG 419 6471

Capriccio italien (abridged)

Dresden 1938	Dresden Staatskapelle	78: Electrola DB 4632 LP: Electrola 1C 137 53505-7M

Verdi

Aida, Act 1 Prelude

Dresden 1939	Dresden Staatskapelle	78: Electrola DB 5558 LP: Electrola 1C 137 53505-7M

Macbeth

Vienna 1943	VPO Vienna Opera Chorus Höngen, Alsen, Ahlersmayer, Witt Sung in German	LP: Acanta DE 23.277-8 Excerpts LP: BASF 72.221792 LP: BASF 10.223205
Vienna April 1970	VPO Vienna Opera Chorus C.Ludwig, Milnes, Ridderbusch, Cossutta	LP: Morgan MORG 7001 CD: Legato LCD 143 CD: Foyer 2CF-2027 Excerpts CD: Hunt CDMP 457

Otello

Vienna 1944	VPO Vienna Opera Chorus Koneztni, Ralf, Schöffler Sung in German	CD: Myto MCD 92260 Excerpts LP: BASF 72.221792 LP: Acanta BB 23058

Otello: Excerpt (Già nella notte densa)

New York April 1972	Metropolitan Opera Orchestra Zylis-Gara, Corelli	LP: DG 2530 260

Otello: Excerpt (Sì per ciel marmoreo giuro!)

Dresden 1940	Dresden Staatskapelle Ralf, J.Herrmann Sung in German	78: Electrola DB 5620 LP: Rococo 5233 LP: Electrola 1C 137 53514-19M

Otello: Excerpts (Era la notte; Credo in un dio crudel)

Vienna September 1950	VPO Schöffler	78: Decca K 23145 LP: Decca LXT 2554 LP: Decca 414 4531

Wagner

Der fliegende Holländer

Bayreuth July 1971	Bayreuth Festival Chorus & Orchestra Jones, Wagner, Esser, Ek, Stewart, Ridderbusch	LP: DG 2709 040 LP: DG 2720 052/2740 140 LP: DG 413 2911 Excerpts LP: DG 2537 024 Overture LP: DG 2536 383 LP: DG 2721 113 CD: DG 413 8492

Der fliegende Holländer: Excerpts (Bleib', Senta; Was muss ich hören?)

New York January 1963	Metropolitan Opera Orchestra Rysanek, Konya	LP: Melodram MEL 658

Der fliegende Holländer, Overture

Dresden 1939	Dresden Staatskapelle	78: Electrola DB 5553-4 LP: Electrola 1C 137 53514-19M
Vienna March and June 1980	VPO	LP: DG 2531 288 LP: DG 2543 211 LP: DG 415 1821 LP: DG 419 0691 CD: DG 413 7332/419 0692

Götterdämmerung

Bayreuth July and August 1967	Bayreuth Festival Chorus & Orchestra Nilsson, Mödl, Dvorakova, Stewart, Windgassen, Neidlinger, Greindl	LP: Philips 6747 037/6747 049 CD: Philips 412 4882/420 3252 Excerpts LP: Philips 6575 503/6575 504 LP: Philips 6833 083

Lohengrin, Act 1 Prelude

Vienna VPO
March and
June 1980

LP: DG 2531 288
LP: DG 2543 211
LP: DG 415 1821
LP: DG 419 0691
CD: DG 413 7332/419 0692

Japanese sources also mention a recording of this work dated May 1965 with catalogue number DG (Japan) MG 1488

Lohengrin, Act 3 Prelude

Dresden Dresden
1939 Staatskapelle

78: Electrola DB 5554
LP: Electrola 1C 137 53514-19M

Vienna VPO
March and
June 1980

LP: DG 2531 288
LP: DG 2543 211
LP: DG 415 1821
LP: DG 419 0691
CD: DG 413 7332/419 0692

Lohengrin, Procession to the Minster

Dresden Dresden
1939 Staatskapelle
 Dresden Opera Chorus

78: Electrola DB 5551
LP: Electrola 1C 137 53514-19M

Lohengrin, Bridal Chorus

Dresden Dresden
1939 Staatskapelle
 Dresden Opera Chorus

78: Electrola DA 4456
LP: Electrola 1C 137 53514-19M

Die Meistersinger von Nürnberg, Act 3

Dresden Dresden
1938 Staatskapelle
 Dresden Opera Chorus
 Teschemacher, Jung,
 Ralf, Kremer,
 Nissen, S.Nilsson,
 Fuchs

78: HMV DB 4562-4576/8643-8657 auto
LP: Electrola E 80983-4
LP: Electrola 1C 137 53514-19M
Excerpts
LP: Electrola E 83 387-8
LP: Electrola 1C 181 30669-78M
LP: Electrola 1C 187 29225-6M

Die Meistersinger von Nürnberg, Excerpt (Was duftet doch der Flieder)

Dresden Dresden
1940 Staatskapelle
 J.Herrmann

78: Electrola DB 5623
LP: Electrola 1C 137 53514-19M

BAYREUTHER FESTSPIELE
MITTWOCH, 12. AUGUST 1964
RICHARD WAGNER
TRISTAN UND ISOLDE

DER BEGINN JEDES AKTES WIRD 15 MINUTEN VORHER MIT EINER FANFARE, 10 MINUTEN VORHER MIT ZWEI UND 5 MINUTEN VORHER MIT DREI FANFAREN ANGEKÜNDIGT. 1. AKT 16.00 UHR · 2. AKT 18.20 UHR · 3. AKT 20.40 UHR · ENDE GEGEN 21.50 UHR / NACH BEGINN DER AKTE KEIN EINLASS

MUSIKALISCHE LEITUNG · KARL BÖHM
REGIE UND INSZENIERUNG · WIELAND WAGNER
CHOREINSTUDIERUNG · WILHELM PITZ
TRISTAN · WOLFGANG WINDGASSEN
ISOLDE · BIRGIT NILSSON
KÖNIG MARKE · HANS HOTTER
KURWENAL · GUSTAV NEIDLINGER
BRANGÄNE · KERSTIN MEYER
MELOT · NIELS MÖLLER
HIRT · ERWIN WOHLFAHRT
SEEMANN · HERMANN WINKLER
STEUERMANN · HANNS HANNO DAUM

MASKE · WILLI KLOSE — BELEUCHTUNG PAUL EBERHARDT / ERICH HAGER — BÜHNENTECHNIK · REINHARD KRUMM — REGIEASSISTENZ · PETER LEHMANN — MUSIKALISCHE ASSISTENZ · ALFRED WALTER / CLAUS ROESSNER

Die Meistersinger von Nürnberg, Overture

Dresden 1939	Dresden Staatskapelle	78: Electrola DB 4698 LP: Electrola 1C 137 53514-19M
Tokyo March 1975	VPO	LP: DG (Japan) 92MG-0650-3 LP: DG (Japan) 92MG-0752-5 CD: DG (Japan) F35G-20017 <u>The 2 LP versions are of 2 different performances from the 1975 VPO tour</u>
Vienna November 1978 and March 1979	VPO	LP: DG 2531 214 LP: DG 2543 210 LP: DG 415 1821 LP: DG 419 0691 CD: DG 413 5512/419 0692

Die Meistersinger von Nürnberg, Act 3 Prelude

Berlin April 1936	BPO	78: Electrola EH 962 LP: Electrola 1C 137 54095-9 LP: EMI RLS 768 CD: EMI CDF 3000122

Parsifal, Prelude

Vienna November 1978 and March 1979	VPO	LP: DG 2531 214 LP: DG 2543 210 LP: DG 415 1821 LP: DG 419 0691 CD: DG 413 5512/419 0692

Das Rheingold

Bayreuth July 1966	Bayreuth Festival Orchestra Burmeister, Silja, Soukupova, Adam, Windgassen, Esser, Neidlinger, Talvela, Nienstedt, Böhme	LP: Philips 6747 037/6747 046 CD: Philips 412 4752/420 3252 <u>Excerpts</u> LP: Philips 6575 500/6575 504

Rienzi, Overture

Vienna November 1978 and March 1979	VPO	LP: DG 2531 214 LP: DG 2543 210 LP: DG 415 1821 CD: DG 413 5512

Siegfried

Bayreuth July 1966	Bayreuth Festival Orchestra Nilsson, Köth, Adam, Windgassen, Böhme, Soukupova, Neidlinger	LP: Philips 6747 037/6747 048 CD: Philips 412 4832/420 3252 Excerpts LP: Philips 6575 502/6575 504

Tannhäuser

Naples March 1956	San Carlo Chorus & Orchestra Rysanek, Nilsson, Lustig, Terkal, Cordes, Frick	CD: Melodram MEL 37073

Tannhäuser: Excerpts

Rome March 1950	Rome Opera Chorus & Orchestra Tebaldi, Beirer, Tagliabue, Christoff Beirer sings in German, the others in Italian	CD: Legato SRO 834

Tannhäuser, Overture

Dresden 1939	Dresden Staatskapelle	78: Electrola DB 5555-5556 LP: Electrola 1C 137 53514-19M
Vienna November 1978 and March 1979	VPO	LP: DG 2531 214 LP: DG 2543 210 LP: DG 415 1821 LP: DG 419 0691 CD: DG 413 5512/419 0692

Tannhäuser, Entry of the Guests

Dresden 1939	Dresden Staatskapelle Dresden Opera Chorus	78: Electrola DB 5551 LP: Electrola 1C 137 53514-19M

Tristan und Isolde

Bayreuth July 1962	Bayreuth Festival Chorus & Orchestra Nilsson, Meyer, Windgassen, Greindl, Wächter	LP: Melodram MEL 625
Bayreuth July and August 1966	Bayreuth Festival Chorus & Orchestra Nilsson, C.Ludwig, Windgassen, Talvela, Wächter	LP: DG SLPM 139 221-5 LP: DG 2713 001 LP: DG 2740 144 LP: Philips 6747 243 LP: DG 415 3951 CD: DG 419 8892 Excerpts LP: DG SLPEM 136 433 LP: DG 2535 243/2537 001 LP: DG 2721 206 Rehearsal extract (Act 3) LP: DG SLPM 139 221-5 LP: DG 2713 001 LP: DG 2740 144
Bayreuth August 1966	Bayreuth Festival Chorus & Orchestra Nilsson, C.Ludwig, Windgassen, Talvela, Wächter	CD: Frequenz CML 3 Excerpts CD: Curcio-Hunt OPV 16
Orange July 1973	Orchestre National New Philharmonia Chorus Nilsson, Hesse, Vickers, Rundgren, Berry	LP: HRE Records HRE 359 CD: Rodolphe RPC 32553-5

Tristan und Isolde: Excerpt (Sink' hernieder, Nacht der Liebe)

London June 1949	Philharmonia Flagstad, Shacklock, Svanholm	78: HMV DB 21112-21114/9521-9523 auto LP: Victor LM 1151 LP: Electrola 1C 147 01491-2M LP: EMI EX 29 10373/EX 29 12273 78 auto version may not have been published

Tristan und Isolde: Excerpt (Tristan! Geliebter!)

New York January 1960	Metropolitan Opera Orchestra Nilsson, Dalis, Vinay	CD: Melodram CDM 26519

Tristan und Isolde, Prelude and Liebestod

Vienna March and June 1980	VPO	LP: DG 2531 288 LP: DG 2543 211 LP: DG 415 1821 CD: DG 413 7332

Die Walküre

Bayreuth July and August 1967	Bayreuth Festival Orchestra Nilsson, Rysanek, Burmeister, King, Adam, Nienstedt	LP: Philips 6747 037/6747 047 CD: Philips 412 4752/420 3252 Excerpts LP: Philips 6575 501/6575 504/6833 083

Die Walküre: Excerpts Acts 2 and 3

Bayreuth August 1965	Bayreuth Festival Orchestra Nilsson, Rysanek, King, Adam, Talvela	CD: Legato SRO 833

Die Walküre: Excerpt (Siegmund! Sieh' auf mich!)

London June 1949	Philharmonia Flagstad, Svanholm	78: HMV DB 6962-6963 LP: Electrola E 60 619 LP: EMI HQM 1138 LP: Electrola 1C 147 01491-2M LP: EMI EX 29 10373/EX 29 12273

Weber

Der Freischütz

Vienna May 1972	VPO Vienna Opera Chorus Janowitz, Holm, King, Ridderbusch, Jungwirth, Wächter	CD: Hunt CDMP 457

Der Freischütz, Huntsmens' Chorus

Dresden 1939	Dresden Staatskapelle Dresden Opera Chorus	78: Electrola DA 4457 LP: Electrola 1C 137 53514-19M

Der Freischütz, Overture

Dresden 1938	Dresden Staatskapelle	78: Electrola DB 4561 LP: Electrola 1C 137 53514-19M

Euryanthe, Overture

Vienna May 1951	VPO	LP: Decca LXT 2633 LP: Decca LW 5002 LP: Decca ACL 28

Oberon, Overture

Dresden 1939	Dresden Staatskapelle	78: Electrola DB 5557 LP: Electrola 1C 137 53514-19M
Vienna May 1951	VPO	LP: Decca LXT 2633 LP: Decca LW 5002 LP: Decca ACL 28
Berlin 1952	Berlin RO	LP: Melodram MEL 218

Peter Schmoll, Overture

Vienna May 1951	VPO	LP: Decca LXT 2633 LP: Decca LW 5032 LP: Decca ACL 28

Preciosa, Overture

Vienna May 1951	VPO	LP: Decca LXT 2633 LP: Decca LW 5032 LP: Decca ACL 28

National Anthems

Japanese and Austrian national anthems

Tokyo March 1975	VPO	45: DG (Japan) DI 4005 Issued with LP set DG (Japan) 92MG-0752-5

Karl Böhm speaks

LP: DG LPM 18 728	Erzähltes Leben: the conductor talks about his life and career, with musical examples
LP: DG 004 241	Böhm rehearses Schubert 9 (Berlin 1963)
LP: DG 102 220	Böhm talks about recording Mozart's Don Giovanni in Prague
LP: DG 643 209	Böhm talks about Mozart and the Symphonies
LP: DG 2562 283	Böhm rehearses Schubert 9 (Berlin 1963); talks about Mozart and the Symphonies
LP: DG 2720 095	Böhm talks about the Mozart Operas, with musical examples
LP: DG 2810 032	Böhm talks about the Vienna Philharmonic (Special issue for the Philharmonic Ball 1974)

Böhm speaks in German throughout

Böhm: a postscript

The city of Vienna's ambivalent attitude towards its most honoured musicians, that combination of heartfelt admiration for the musical achievement and ruthless exposure to the intrigues of the city's musical politics, was no more strongly illustrated than in the case of Karl Böhm (1894-1981). Two short and stormy periods as Director of the State Opera did nothing to lessen the love which the Vienna Philharmonic Orchestra radiated when Böhm stood in front of them, whether in the pit at the Staatsoper, in the Musikverein, in Salzburg or elsewhere on tour.

I personally remember three occasions in particular when the music-making was transcended by the inner bond which must have existed: a concert at the 1972 Salzburg Festival consisting of Beethoven's "Pastoral" and Strauss "Heldenleben"; a performance of "Fidelio" in Vienna marking the Orchestra's 125th anniversary; and the momentous first production in Salzburg (1959) of the Strauss opera "Die schweigsame Frau" which this same conductor had introduced to the world some 24 years earlier in Dresden.

The Böhm magic had somehow grown out of a very down-to-earth and literal approach to music, and indeed certain critics found some of the early Decca LPs with the Vienna Philharmonic a shade prosaic. Yet the sound and style which Böhm in his maturity conjured from that orchestra could just as readily be conveyed to orchestras less familiar with his approach: one remembers those outstanding LSO concerts and Covent Garden appearances in the last years of his life.

Apart from the personal and professional ties with Richard Strauss, Böhm will certainly be remembered for his Mozart opera performances. His ideal "Figaro" and "Cosi" accompanied me through many years of opera-going, from my first visit to Salzburg in 1957 - "Figaro" with a dream cast which by now all my friends must know by heart - to Covent Garden in the late seventies, when his hand-picked soloists guaranteed that same authentic stamp that had been the Böhm trademark wherever he had conducted the operas.

The choice of records of Böhm in those works is wide, and all convey to a vivid degree his benevolent grasp of Mozartian bliss. Perhaps his ultimate monument should be the EMI studio "Così fan tutte" - master-minded by Walter Legge - or the live Salzburg version from a decade later on DG, or even that vital Bayreuth "Tristan und Isolde" from 1966.

Victor de Sabata
Discography

with valuable assistance from
Angelo Scottini

compiled by John Hunt

Introduction

Victor De Sabata (1892-1967) remains a less vivid figure to the modern record collector simply because the number of available issues is modest. However, his searching readings of a wide repertoire are gradually emerging in the CD format. These include the Callas "Tosca" (never, of course, absent from the catalogues) and live versions of Verdi's "Otello", "Falstaff" and the Requiem.

De Sabata was also a keen advocate of his contemporaries, men like Respighi and Ravel (he had conducted the first performance of "L'Enfant et les Sortilèges"). He may have been the first foreigner to record with the Berlin Philharmonic, and certainly re-vitalised the London Philharmonic when he came here just after the war for concerts and recordings.

Like Toscanini, De Sabata was a formidable presence and disciplinarian in rehearsal, yet eye-witnesses recall how for the performance itself he managed to unleash a great and unforgettable surge of spontaneity. Even the confines of the recording studio, especially when it was La Scala Milan on the occasion of that "Tosca" recording, could not dim his intensity.

Il M° Victor de Sabata, il tenore Max Lorenz e il soprano Gertrud Rünger nel «Tristano e Isotta» al Teatro Reale dell'Opera.

ROYAL ALBERT HALL
Manager: C. S. Taylor

BEETHOVEN CYCLE

SECOND CONCERT
THURSDAY, APRIL 24th, 1947, at 7.30

Overture, Leonora No. 3

Symphony No. 4 in B flat

INTERVAL

Symphony No. 7 in A

THE LONDON PHILHARMONIC ORCHESTRA
(Leader: Andrew Cooper)

Conductor:
VICTOR DE SABATA

Programme One Shilling

Barber

The School for Scandal, Overture

New York March 1951	NYPO	LP: Fonit Cetra DOC 33 CD: Nuova Era 2297

Beethoven

Symphony No 3 "Eroica"

London May 1946	LPO	78: Decca K 1507-13 LP: Decca 6BB 236-7 CD: Decca 425 9712

Symphony No 5

New York March 1950	NYPO	LP: Discocorp IGI 297 LP: Fonit Cetra LO 504 CD: Nuova Era 6316 CD: Melodram MEL 18008

Symphony No 6 "Pastoral"

Rome January and February 1947	Santa Cecilia Orchestra	78: HMV DB 6473-7/9154-8 auto LP: World Records SH 235

Symphony No 8

New York March 1951	NYPO	LP: Discocorp IGI 297 LP: Fonit Cetra DOC 33 CD: Nuova Era 6338

Berlioz

Le carnaval romain, Overture

London May 1946	LPO	78: Decca K 1552 LP: Decca 6BB 236-7 CD: Decca 425 9712
Salzburg August 1953	VPO	LP: Discocorp RR 202 LP: Melodram MEL 706 CD: Nuova Era 2319

Brahms

Symphony No 3: rehearsal extract of last movement

San Francisco February 1953	San Francisco Symphony Orchestra	CD: Nuova Era 2319

Symphony No 4

Berlin March and April 1939	BPO	78: Polydor 67490-5 78: Cetra OR 5001-6 LP: Decca (USA) DL 9516 LP: DG 88001 LP: DG 2535 812 CD: DG 423 7152

Violin Concerto

New York March 1950	NYPO Milstein	CD: Nuova Era 6316 CD: Melodram MEL 18008 CD: Hunt CD 735

Debussy

Jeux

Rome January and February 1947	Santa Cecilia Orchestra	78: HMV DB 6493-4 78: Victor M 1276 LP: Victor LM 1057 LP: HMV (Italy) QALP 178 LP: Rococo 2075 LP: EMI XLP 30118

Nuages et Fêtes (Nocturnes)

Rome January 1947	Santa Cecilia Orchestra	78: HMV DB 6706 (Nuages) 78: HMV DB 6870 (Fêtes)

Dukas

L'apprenti sorcier

New York March 1950	NYPO	LP: Fonit Cetra DOC 59 CD: Nuova Era 6350

Dvorak

Symphony No 9 "From the New World"

New York March 1950	NYPO	CD: Nuova Era 2297 CD: Hunt CD 735

Franck

Symphony in D minor

New York March 1950	NYPO	CD: Nuova Era 6350

ROMA - 14 DICEMBRE XIX
ORE 15,30 PRECISE
TRASMISSIONE DALLA BASILICA DI
S. MARIA DEGLI ANGELI ALLE TERME

MESSA DA REQUIEM

PER QUATTRO PARTI PRINCIPALI
(SOPRANO, MEZZOSOPRANO, TENORE, BASSO)
E CORO

MUSICA DI
GIUSEPPE VERDI

INTERPRETI:
MARIA CANIGLIA
EBE STIGNANI, BENIAMINO GIGLI
TANCREDI PASERO

DIRETTORE:
VICTOR DE SABATA

ORCHESTRE E CORI DELL'E.I.A.R.

ISTRUTTORE DEL CORO:
COSTANTINO COSTANTINI

150 PROFESSORI D'ORCHESTRA
250 CORISTI

Ghedini

Marinaresca e Baccanale

New York March 1950	NYPO	CD: Nuova Era 2219

Giordano

Andrea Chenier: Excerpts

Milan March 1949	La Scala Chorus & Orchestra Tebaldi, Silveri, Del Monaco	LP: Fonit Cetra DOC 42 CD: Myto MCD 90634

Glazunov

Scherzo and Troubadour's Serenade (From the Middle Ages)

Turin 1934 or 1935	EIAR Orchestra	78: Cetra 56548-9 78: Parlophone 60008-9 LP: Discocorp IGI 356

Kodaly

Dances of Galanta

Berlin April 1939	BPO	78: Polydor 67525-6 LP: Decca (USA) DL 9518 LP: DG LPEM 19078 LP: DG 88001 CD: Koch Legacy 3-7126-2

Mendelssohn

Nocturne and Scherzo (A Midsummer Night's Dream)

Vatican City June 1945	Santa Cecilia Orchestra	CD: Frequenz 061.007

Mossolov

Steel Foundry (Sawod)

Turin 1934 or 1935	EIAR Orchestra	78: Parlophone 60008 78: Decca (USA) 25510 78: Cetra 56548 LP: Discocorp IGI 356

Mozart

Requiem

Rome December 1941	EIAR Chorus and Orchestra Tassinari, Stignani, Tagliavini, Tajo	78: Polydor 68422-9 78: HMV DB 9541-8 78: SS 1001-8 LP: Cetra LPV 1001/LPC 55058 LP: DG 88005 DG 88005 incorrectly states that recording made April 1939 in Berlin

BASILICA DI SANTA MARIA DEGLI ANGELI ALLE TERME
ROMA - 5 DICEMBRE 1941-XX

REQUIEM

PER QUATTRO PARTI PRINCIPALI
(SOPRANO, MEZZOSOPRANO, TENORE, BASSO)
E CORO

MUSICA DI
WOLFANGO AMEDEO MOZART

INTERPRETI:
PIA TASSINARI, EBE STIGNANI
FERRUCCIO TAGLIAVINI, ITALO TAJO

DIRETTORE:
VICTOR de SABATA

ORCHESTRE E CORI DELL'E.I.A.R
ISTRUTTORI DEL CORO:
COSTANTINO COSTANTINI E BRUNO ERMINERO
COADIUVATI DA MARCELLO TOMMASETTI E GENNARO D'ANGELO

160 PROFESSORI D'ORCHESTRA - 300 CORISTI

ASOCIACIÓN WAGNERIANA
DE BUENOS AIRES
Santa Fe 1145 - T. A. 41 - Plaza 6296

XXXVIª TEMPORADA DE CONCIERTOS

3
CONCIERTOS SINFONICOS DE ABONO

DIRECTOR

VICTOR DE SABATA

LUNES 5, 12 y 19 de Julio a las 21.30 horas

en el

GRAN REX

1948

Corrientes 857 — Buenos Aires

Puccini

La Bohème: Excerpts

Milan December 1949	La Scala Chorus & Orchestra Carosio, Noni, Poggi, Silveri, Siepi	CD: Myto MCD 90634

Tosca

Milan August 1953	La Scala Chorus & Orchestra Callas, Gobbi, Di Stefano	LP: Columbia 33CX 1094-5 LP: EMI SLS 825 CD: EMI CDC 747 1758 Excerpts LP: Columbia 33CX 1725/33CX 1784/33CX 1893 45: Columbia SEL 1526/1530/1543/1569 LP: EMI SLS 825/SLS 5104

Tosca: Excerpt (Vissi d'arte)

Milan April 1953	La Scala Orchestra Tebaldi	CD: Nuova Era 2319

Rachmaninov

Rhapsody on a theme of Paganini

New York March 1950	NYPO Rubinstein	LP: Discocorp IGI 297 CD: Nuova Era 2232

Ravel

Bolero

New York March 1950	NYPO	LP: Fonit Cetra DOC 59 CD: Nuova Era 2219

Ma mère l'oye: Excerpts

Vatican City June 1945	Santa Cecilia Orchestra	CD: Frequenz 061.007
New York March 1950	NYPO	CD: Nuova Era 2219

La Valse

Salzburg August 1953	VPO	LP: Fonit Cetra DOC 59 CD: Nuova Era 2219

Respighi

I fontane di Roma

Rome January 1947	Santa Cecilia Orchestra	78: HMV DB 6448-9 78: Victor DM 1337 LP: Victor LM 1057 LP: HMV (Italy) QALP 178/QALP 10413 LP: EMI XLP 30118 LP: EMI Italiana 3C 061 01051

Feste Romane

Berlin April 1939	BPO	78: Polydor 67510-13 78: Cetra OR 5015-8 LP: Discocorp IGI 356 CD: Koch Legacy 3-7126-2

I pini di Roma

New York March 1950	NYPO	LP: Discocorp IGI 297 CD: Nuova Era 2232

Bernburger Str. 22   PHILHARMONIE   Bernburger Str. 22

Sonntag, den 12. Januar 1936, vormittags 11½ Uhr
Montag, den 13. Januar 1936, abends 8 Uhr

6. Philharmonisches Konzert

Leitung: **Victor de Sabata**
(von der Mailänder Scala)

Solist: **Helge Roswaenge**

I.
Quattro pezzi . . . . G. Frescobaldi-Ghedini
   Toccata   (1620)

II.
Arie für Tenor
  „Laß mir meinen stillen Kummer" . . W. A. Mozart
           Helge Roswaenge

III.
„J pini di Roma", sinfonische Dichtung . . . . O. Respighi

IV.
3 Lieder mit Orchester . . . . R. Strauß
  a) Morgen   b) Freundliche Vision   c) Zueignung
           Helge Roswaenge

—— P a u s e ——

V.
Sinfonie Nr. 5 e-moll, op. 95
 „Aus der Neuen Welt" . . . . A. Dvorak
   Adagio — Allegro molto
   Largo — Piu mosso, Tempo I
   Scherzo
   Allegro con brio

PHILHARMONIE, Montag, den 3. Februar 1936, abends 8 Uhr:
7. Philharmonisches Konzert
Leitung: Willem Mengelberg (Amsterdam)
Beethoven: Egmont-Ouvert. · Dopper: Chaconne · Tschaikowsky: Sinf. Nr. 5
Öffentliche Voraufführung: Sonntag, den 2. Februar 1936, vormittags 11½ Uhr

Rossini

Il Barbiere di Siviglia

Milan April 1952	La Scala Chorus & Orchestra Gatta, Valletti, Bechi, Rossi-Lemeni	LP: Rococo 1019 LP: Hope Records HOPE 225

William Tell, Overture

Rome February 1948	Santa Cecilia Orchestra	78: HMV DB 6880-1 LP: HMV (Italy) QALP 10413 LP: EMI Italiana 3C 061 01051

De Sabata

Juventus, Symphonic Poem

Turin 1934 or 1935	EIAR Orchestra	78: Parlophone 60006-7 LP: Discocorp IGI 357

Schumann

Piano Concerto

New York March 1951	NYPO Arrau	LP: Discocorp IGI 297 LP: Fonit Cetra DOC 33 CD: Nuova Era 6338 CD: Curcio-Hunt CON 019

Sibelius

Symphony No 1

New York March 1950	NYPO	LP: Discocorp IGI 297 CD: Nuova Era 2210

En Saga

London May 1946	LPO	78: Decca AK 1504-6 LP: Decca 6BB 236-7

Valse triste

London May 1946	LPO	78: Decca AK 1504 LP: Decca 6BB 236-7 CD: Decca 425 9712

Richard Strauss

Dance of the Seven Veils (Salome): rehearsal extract

San Francisco February 1953	San Francisco Symphony Orchestra	CD: Nuova Era 2319

Tod und Verklärung

Berlin April 1939	BPO	78: Polydor 67516-8 78: Cetra OR 5012-4 LP: DG 88002 CD: DG 423 7152
Salzburg August 1953	VPO	LP: Melodram MEL 706 CD: Nuova Era 2210

Stravinsky

Le chant du rossignol

Stockholm September 1947	Stockholm PO	LP: Fonit Cetra DOC 59 CD: Nuova Era 2319

Feux d'artifices

Turin 1934 or 1935	EIAR Orchestra	78: Parlophone 60009 78: Cetra 56549 78: Decca (USA) 25510 LP: Discocorp IGI 356
Vatican City June 1945	Santa Cecilia Orchestra	CD: Frequenz 061.007

Operntheater

Sonntag den 7. Juni 1936
Bei aufgehobenem Abonnement

AÏDA

Oper in vier Akten

Text von A. Ghislanzoni, für die deutsche Bühne bearbeitet von J. Schanz

Spielleitung: Hans Duhan   Musik von Giuseppe Verdi   Dirigent: . . .

Der König	Nicola Zec
Amneris, seine Tochter	Kerstin Thorborg
Aïda, äthiopische Sklavin	Maria Nemeth
Radames, Anführer der Leibwache	
Ramphis, Oberpriester	Ludwig Hofmann
Amonasro, König von Äthiopien und Vater Aïdas .	Alexander Sved
Ein Bote	Ernst Kurz
Stimme der Priesterin	Ilona Hajmassy

Priester, Priesterinnen, Minister, Hauptleute, Soldaten, Sklaven, gefangene Äthiopier, Volk

Die Handlung spielt in Theben und Memphis zur Zeit der Herrschaft der Pharaonen

Choreographie und Einstudierung der Tänze: Toni Birkmeyer, ausgeführt von Frl. Pfundmayr, Hrn. Willy Fränzl, Toni Birkmeyer und dem Corps de Ballet

In Szene gesetzt von Hans Duhan

. . . „Radames" Jussy Björling von der kgl. Oper in Stockholm a. G.

. . . Dirigent: Victor de Sabata vom Scalatheater in Mailand a. G.

Nach dem zweiten Akt eine größere Pause

Das offizielle Programm nur bei den Billeteuren erhältlich, Preis 50 Groschen — Garderobe frei

Kassen-Eröffnung vor 7 Uhr   Anfang 7½ Uhr   Ende 11 Uhr

Während der Vorspiele und der Akte bleiben die Saaltüren zum Parkett, Parterre und den Galerien geschlossen. Zuspätkommende haben daher nur während der Pausen Einlaß finden.

Opernteater

Donnerstag den 6. Juni 1935

FEST-KONZERT

unter Leitung von

Maestro Victor de Sabata

PROGRAMM:

1. ROSSINI . . . . Ouvertüre zu „Wilhelm Tell"
2. FRESCOBALDI (1583—1644) . . Toccata
3. IGNOTO DEL XVI SECOLO . . a) Villanella, b) Passo mezzo e Mascherata
4. CATALANI (1854—1893) . . . . . A sera
5. VICTOR DE SABATA . . . . . Juventus, Poema Sinfonico

GRÖSSERE PAUSE

6. MOZART . . . . Serenata notturna in drei Sätzen für vier Orchester
7. RAVEL . . . . Ma Mère l'Oye a) Petit Poucet, b) Entretien de la Belle et de la Bête, c) Laideronnette, Princesse des Pagodines
8. MOSSOLOW . . . . Fonderie d'acier (Eisengießerei), Maschinenmusik
9. WAGNER . . . . Ouvertüre zu „Tannhäuser"

Das Staatsopernorchester

Das offizielle Programm nur bei den Billetteuren erhältlich. Preis 50 Groschen — Garderobe frei

Kassen-Eröffnung vor 7 Uhr   **Anfang 7½ Uhr**   **Ende vor 10 Uhr**

Nach Beginn des Konzertes bleiben die Saaltüren zum Parkett, Parterre und den Galerien geschlossen. Zuspätkommende können daher nur während der Pausen Einlaß finden.

Der Kartenverkauf findet heute statt für obige Vorstellung und für

Freitag   den 7. Othello. „Othello" Hr. **Gotthelf Pistor** vom Deutschen Opernhaus in Berlin a. G. Dirigent: Hr. **Victor de Sabata** a. G. Im Abonnement I. Gruppe (Anfang **7** Uhr)

Samstag   den 8. Das Rheingold. „Wotan" Hr. Kammersänger **Friedrich Schorr** von der Metropolitan Opera in New York a. G. Im Abonnement I. Gruppe (Anfang **7½** Uhr)

Weiterer Spielplan:

Sonntag   den 9. Festvorstellung: Die Fledermaus. „Eisenstein" Hr. **Karl Ziegler** a. G. „Alfred" Hr. **Basso Argyris** a. G. (Anfang **7½** Uhr)

Montag   den 10. Die Walküre. „Siegmund" Hr. Kammersänger **Richard Schubert** a. G. „Wotan" Hr. Kammersänger **Friedrich Schorr** von der Metropolitan Opera in New York a. G. (Anfang **7** Uhr)

Kartenverkauf für alle Bundestheater an den Tageskassen: I., Bräunerstraße 14, an Werktagen von 9—18·30 Uhr (am Vorstellungstage selbst nur bis 16·30 Uhr und an der Abendkassa), an Sonn- u. Feiertagen von 9—17 Uhr. Telephonische Bestellungen von Sitzen (mit Ausnahme der Gänsesitze) ausschließlich unter der Telephon-Nummer R-28-3-20

„Elbemühl" Wien IX.

Verdi

Aida: Excerpts (Celeste Aida and fragments from Acts 2 and 3)

Vienna June 1936	VPO Vienna Opera Chorus Nemeth, Björling, Sved, Zec <u>Björling appears to sing in Swedish, Nemeth in Hungarian and the rest in German</u>	LP: Teletheater 762.3589

Aida, Prelude

Berlin   BPO   78: Polydor 68395
April 1939   LP: DG 88002
                                         CD: Koch Legacy 3-7126-2

Falstaff

Milan   La Scala   LP: Ed Smith UORC 111
June 1951   Chorus & Orchestra   LP: Discocorp IGI 288
                      Tebaldi, Noni,   LP: Fonit Cetra LO 14
                      Elmo, Canali,   LP: Foyer FO 1039
                      Valletti, Stabile,   CD: Nuova Era 2220-1
                      Silveri   <u>Also issued on Estro Armonico label</u>

Macbeth

Milan   La Scala   LP: FWR 655
December 1952   Chorus & Orchestra   LP: Opera Viva JLT 3
                      Callas, Penno,   LP: Estro Armonico EA 005
                      Mascherini, Tajo   LP: BJR Records BJR 117
                                                    LP: MRF Records MRF 61
                                                    LP: Discocorp IGI 287
                                                    LP: Fonit Cetra LO 10
                                                    LP: Turnabout THS 65131-3
                                                    CD: Movimento Musica 051.022
                                                    CD: Nuova Era 2202-3
                                                    CD: Hunt CDLSMH 34027
                                                    CD: Legendary 1003
                                                    <u>Excerpts</u>
                                                    LP: Opera Viva JLT 1
                                                    LP: Gemma WK 1001
                                                    LP: Legendary LR 148/LR 157
                                                    LP: Gioielli della lirica GML 38
                                                    CD: Opera Italiana OP 1-11

Otello: Excerpt (Fuoco di gioia)

Vienna June 1935	VPO Vienna Opera Chorus Sung in German	LP: Teletheater 643.333 AG

La Traviata, Preludes Acts 1 and 3

Rome February and March 1948	Santa Cecilia Orchestra	78: HMV DB 6855 LP: EMI XLP 30118

I Vespri Siciliani, Overture

Vatican City June 1945	Santa Cecilia Orchestra	CD: Frequenz 061.009
Rome February 1947	Santa Cecilia Orchestra	78: HMV DB 6444 LP: HMV (Italy) QBLP 5038/QALP 10413 LP: EMI XLP 30118 LP: EMI Italiana 3C 061 01051
Salzburg August 1953	VPO	LP: Discocorp RR 202 LP: Melodram MEL 706 CD: Nuova Era 2319

Requiem

Milan January 1951	La Scala Chorus & Orchestra Tebaldi, Rankin, Prandelli, Rossi-Lemeni	LP: Discocorp RR 202 LP: Fonit Cetra DOC 32 CD: Nuova Era 6346-7 CD: Hunt CDSLMH 34046
Milan June 1954	La Scala Chorus & Orchestra Schwarzkopf Dominguez, Siepi, Di Stefano	LP: Columbia 33CX 1195-6 LP: Pathé 100 9373 Libera me CD: EMI CDM 763 6572/CMS 763 7902

Requiem: Excerpts

Rome December 1940	Rome Opera Chorus & Orchestra	LP: Ed Smith EJS 359 CD: Hunt CDSLMH 34046

Società Veneziana Concerti Sinfonici

STAGIONE 1932   SABATO **26 Marzo 1932 X°**

Teatro "La Fenice"

Ore 21.15 precise

VI. CONCERTO ORCHESTRALE

diretto dal Maestro **VICTOR DE SABATA**

Programma

1. Mussorgsky M. — UNA NOTTE SUL MONTE CALVO - *Poema sinfonico* (*Prima esecuz. a Venezia*)

2. Martucci G. — NOVELLETTA

3. Coppola P. — DUE DANZE (*Prima esecuz. a Venezia*)

4. Berlioz E. — MARCIA UNGHERESE

---

5. Strauss R. — UNA VITA D'EROE, *Poema sinfonico*

6. Wagner R. — LA CAVALCATA DELLE VALCHIRIE

BÜHNENFESTSPIELE BAYREUTH

MONTAG, DEN 14. AUGUST 1939

TRISTAN UND ISOLDE

Musikalische Leitung: Victor de Sabata

Inszenierung: Heinz Tietjen

Bühnenbild und Trachten: Emil Preetorius

Chöre: Friedrich Jung

Isolde	Germaine Lubin
Tristan	Karl Buschmann
Marke	Josef v. Manowarda
Kurwenal	Jaro Prohaska
Brangäne	Margarete Klose
Hirt	Gustav Rödin
Melot	Fritz Wolff
Junger Seemann	Benno Arnold
Steuermann	Edwin Heyer

1. Akt: Zur See auf dem Verdeck von Tristans Schiff während der Überfahrt von Irland nach Kornwall
2. Akt: In der Königlichen Burg Markes in Kornwall / 3. Akt: Tristans Burg in Bretagne

Technische Leitung und Beleuchtung: Paul Eberhardt · Kostümwesen: Kurt Palm

Beginn: 1. Aufzug 16 Uhr   2. Aufzug: 18.15 Uhr   3. Aufzug: 20.30 Uhr

Das Fotografieren während der Aufführung ist untersagt

Wagner

Götterdämmerung: Excerpt (Starke Scheite schichtet mir dort)

New York March 1951	NYPO Farrell	LP: Discocorp BWS 512 LP: Fonit Cetra DOC 33 CD: Hunt CD 512 CD: Nuova Era 6337

Die Meistersinger von Nürnberg, Prelude

New York March 1951	NYPO	LP: Discocorp BWS 512 LP: Fonit Cetra DOC 33 CD: Hunt CD 512 CD: Nuova Era 6337

Parsifal, Prelude

Vatican City June 1945	Santa Cecilia Orchestra	CD: Frequenz 061.007 <u>Incorrectly labelled Good Friday Music</u>
New York March 1951	NYPO	LP: Discocorp BWS 512 LP: Fonit Cetra DOC 33 CD: Hunt CD 512 CD: Nuova Era 6337

Parsifal, Good Friday Music

New York March 1951	NYPO	LP: Discocorp BWS 512 LP: Fonit Cetra DOC 33 CD: Nuova Era 6337

Tristan und Isolde

Milan December 1951	La Scala Chorus & Orchestra Grob-Prandl, Cavelti, Lorenz, S.Nilsson, S.Björling	LP: Fonit Cetra LO 73 CD: Nuova Era 2347-9

Tristan und Isolde: Excerpts

Milan March 1947	La Scala Orchestra Flagstad, Cavelti, Beyron, Frantz, Schöffler	LP: Ed Smith ANNA 1052
Milan April 1948	La Scala Chorus & Orchestra Flagstad, Anday, Lorenz, Weber, Schöffler	LP: Ed Smith UORC 260 LP: Discocorp IGI 347 <u>Liebestod</u> LP: Rococo 5380 <u>Act 3 Prelude</u> LP: Acanta 40.23502

Tristan und Isolde: Excerpt (Wohin nun Tristan scheidet)

Bayreuth July 1939	Bayreuth Festival Orchestra Lorenz	LP: Acanta 40.23502

Tristan und Isolde, Prelude and Liebestod

Berlin April 1939	BPO	78: Polydor 67496-8 LP: DG LPEM 19393 LP: DG 88002 CD: Koch Legacy 3-7126-2 <u>Prelude only</u> LP: DG 2700 703/2721 113
New York March 1951	NYPO Farrell	LP: Discocorp BWS 512 LP: Fonit Cetra DOC 33 CD: Hunt CD 512 CD: Nuova Era 6337

Die Walküre, Ride of the Valkyries

London May 1946	LPO	78: Decca K 1561-2 LP: Decca 6BB 236-7 CD: Decca 425 9712

Wolf-Ferrari

Il Segreto di Susanna, Overture; Il quattro rusteghi, Act 2 Intermezzo

Rome February 1948	Santa Cecilia Orchestra	78: HMV DB 6786 LP: HMV (Italy) QALP 10413 LP: EMI XLP 30118

PHILHARMONISCHE KONZERTE
76. SAISON 1935/36

Freitag, den 1. Mai 1936, präzise **8** Uhr abends
im Großen Musikvereins-Saale

Außerordentliches Konzert

zugunsten der Wohlfahrtseinrichtungen der Wiener Philharmoniker

Dirigent: **Maestro VICTOR de SABATA**

*

PROGRAMM:

R. Strauß . . . . Don Quixote. Phantastische Variationen über ein Thema ritterlichen Charakters, op. 35
Bratschen-Solo: **Ernst Moravec**
Cello-Solo: **Richard Krotschak**

M. Ravel . . . . Bolero für großes Orchester

A. Dvořák . . . . . Symphonie Nr. 5 E-moll, op. 95 „Aus der neuen Welt"
1. Adagio — Allegro molto
2. Largo
3. Scherzo: Molto vivace
4. Allegro con fuoco

*

Streichinstrumente: Ateliers Anton Poller — Karl Haudek
(Gegründet 1840 von Gabriel Lemböck)

In diesen Konzerten spielten Liszt, Rubinstein, Bülow,
Brahms und alle lebenden Meister stets nur
Bösendorfer-Klaviere

THE PHILHARMONIC-SYMPHONY SOCIETY
1842 OF NEW YORK 1878
CONSOLIDATED 1928

1950   ONE HUNDRED NINTH SEASON   **1951**

Conductor: DIMITRI MITROPOULOS
Guest Conductors: BRUNO WALTER, GEORGE SZELL,
VICTOR DE SABATA, LEONARD BERNSTEIN
Associate Conductor: FRANCO AUTORI
For Young People's Concerts: IGOR BUKETOFF

CARNEGIE HALL

4932nd and 4933rd Concerts

THURSDAY EVENING, MARCH 22, 1951, at 8:45
FRIDAY AFTERNOON, MARCH 23, 1951, at 2:30

Under the Direction of

VICTOR DE SABATA

WAGNER PROGRAM

Prelude to *Die Meistersinger*

*A Siegfried Idyl

*Prelude and Love-Death, *Tristan und Isolde*

INTERMISSION

Prelude to Act I, *Parsifal*

Good Friday Spell, *Parsifal*

Overture to *Tannhäuser*

ARTHUR JUDSON, BRUNO ZIRATO, Managers
THE STEINWAY is the Official Piano of The Philharmonic-Symphony Society
*COLUMBIA AND ‡VICTOR RECORDS

Hans Knappertsbusch Discography

with valuable assistance from
Heyko Reysen

compiled by John Hunt

HANS KNAPPERTSBUSCH

HANS KNAPPERTSBUSCH was born in Elberfeld. He first studied philosophy, but in 1908 turned his attention to music, and studied at the Cologne Conservatory under Fritz Steinbach and Otto Lohse.

In 1911 he began his career as a conductor at Mulheim in the Ruhr; in 1912 he went to Bochum, and from 1913 to 1918 he was conductor and opera director at Elberfeld. In 1918 he was appointed to the Leipzig Opera, then to Dessau.

In 1922 he succeeded Bruno Walter as Generalmusikdirektor of the Bavarian State Opera in Munich, a position he held until 1936, when he found he was no longer *persona grata* with the Nazis. From 1932 to 1935 he was artistic director of the Munich Summer Opera Festivals, and has also conducted at the Salzburg and Zürich Festivals.

Strauss and Wagner are Knappertsbusch's great loves; and it was as a Strauss conductor that he introduced himself to London when he conducted *Salome* at Covent Garden in 1937.

At post-war Bayreuth his reading of *Parsifal* has been considered one of the finest ever heard. He has also conducted *The Ring*, and in 1955 was in charge of the new *Der fliegende Holländer*.

In 1954 he returned to the Munich Opera as its chief conductor; a naturally modest man who hates taking curtain calls, he was persuaded to make a brief solo appearance in front of the curtain at the Prinzregenten Theatre, and the ovation he received after his *Meistersinger* left no one in doubt as to the affection in which he is held by the Bavarians.

From the Decca Book of Opera

SALZBURGER KONZERT-ZYKLUS 1940
der
Wiener Philharmoniker

Samstag, den 13. Juli 1940, im Festspielhaus, um 20 Uhr
KNAPPERTSBUSCH
L. v. Beethoven: Leonore 3 / A. Bruckner: Symphonie Nr. 7

Mittwoch, den 17. Juli 1940, im Mozarteum, um 20 Uhr
DR. BÖHM
W. Jerger: Salzburger Hof- u. Barockmusik / W. A. Mozart: Violinkonzert A-dur, Solist: W. SCHNEIDERHAN
P. J. Tschaikowsky: Symphonie Nr. 4

Freitag, den 19. Juli 1940, im Hof der erzb. Residenz, um 20.30 Uhr
Serenade der Bläservereinigung der Wiener Philharmoniker
L. v. Beethoven: Rondino / G. Rossini: Quartett für Flöte, Klarinette, Fagott und Horn
R. Strauß: Serenade op. 7 für 13 Bläser / W. A. Mozart: Serenade für 13 Bläser (K. V. 361)

Samstag, den 20. Juli 1940, im Festspielhaus, um 20 Uhr
FRANZ LEHAR dirigiert eigene Werke
Mitwirkend: E. RETHY (Sopran), Staatsoper Wien / M. WITTRISCH (Tenor), Staatsoper Berlin

Dienstag, den 23. Juli 1940, im Mozarteum, um 20 Uhr
KNAPPERTSBUSCH
O. Respighi: Antiche Danse / R. Schumann: Klavierkonzert, Solist: E. v. SAUER
L. v. Beethoven: Symphonie Nr. 7

Donnerstag, den 25. Juli 1940, im Mozarteum, um 20 Uhr
KNAPPERTSBUSCH
Wiener Musik

Freitag, den 26. Juli 1940, im Hof der erzb. Residenz, um 20.30 Uhr
Serenade Schneiderhan-Quartett und
Bläservereinigung der Wiener Philharmoniker
L. v. Beethoven: Septett / Fr. Schubert: Oktett

Samstag, den 27. Juli 1940, im Festspielhaus, um 20 Uhr
KNAPPERTSBUSCH
R. Wagner: Eine Faust-Ouverture / Siegfried Idyll / 3 Wesendonck Lieder (Träume — Schmerzen — Treibhaus)
Tristan Vorspiel und Liebestod / Siegfrieds Rheinfahrt / Tannhäuser-Ouverture
Solistin: G. RUNGER, Staatsoper Berlin

EINTRITTSPREISE:
Festspielhaus und Mozarteum RM 10.— bis RM 2.— / Serenaden: Sitzplätze RM 2.—, Stehplätze RM 1.—

KARTENVERKAUF: **VORAUSBESTELLUNGEN:**
bei der Bayernbank, Salzburg, Makartplatz ab 4. Juli   Kartenbüro der Salzburger Festspiele

Bach

Orchestral Suite No 3

Vienna   VPO   LP: Private issue (USA) P 1017
June 1944

Violin Concerto in A minor

Vienna   VPO   LP: Private issue (USA) P 1017
June 1944   Schneiderhan

Beethoven

Symphony No 3 "Eroica"

Berlin 1942	BPO	78: Electrola DB 7666-71 LP: Private issue (USA) P 1005
Munich December 1953	Munich PO	LP: Rococo 2067 LP: Fonit Cetra LO 512 <u>Fonit Cetra incorrectly dated 1950</u>
Vienna February 1962	VPO	LP: Seven Seas K20C 78 CD: Memories HR 4171-3

Symphony No 5

Berlin April 1956	BPO	CD: Chaconne CHCD 1001 CD: Seven Seas KICC 2026 CD: Hunt CD 723
Dresden 1956	Dresden Staatskapelle	LP: Private issue (USA) P 1012-3 LP: Seven Seas K20C 58 <u>Incorrectly dated 1961</u>

Symphony No 6 "Pastoral"

Dresden 1961	Dresden Staatskapelle	LP: Private issue (USA) P 1012-3 LP: Seven Seas K20C 76

Symphony No 7

Berlin November 1929	Berlin Staatskapelle	78: Parlophone E 11103-7/15211-5 auto 78: Odeon O 6775-9/U 10048-52 auto LP: Electrola 1C 053 28932M LP: Toshiba GR 2305

Symphony No 8

Berlin January 1952	BPO	LP: Movimento Musica 08.001 CD: Hunt CD 723
Hamburg March 1960	NDR Orchestra	LP: Private issue (USA) P 1011 LP: Discocorp RR 375 LP: Seven Seas K20C 57 CD: Seven Seas KICC 2028

Piano Concerto No 3

Hamburg March 1962	NDR Orchestra Foldes	LP: Longanesi periodici GCL 64 LP: Laudis (Japan) RCL 3322 Pianist incorrectly named as Arrau

Piano Concerto No 4

Vienna April 1954	VPO Curzon	LP: Decca LXT 2948 LP: Decca ECS 752
Vienna May 1962	VPO Backhaus	LP: Baton 1002 CD: Seven Seas KICC 2028

Piano Concerto No 5 "Emperor"

Vienna June 1957	VPO Curzon	LP: Decca LXT 5391/SXL 2002 LP: Decca SPA 334 CD: Decca 421 6162
Munich December 1959	Bavarian State Orchestra Backhaus	LP: Longanesi periodici GCL 64 LP: Laudis (Japan) RCL 3320 CD: Foyer CDS 16008 Lausis and Foyer incorrectly date this as Berlin 1953
Hamburg March 1960	NDR Orchestra Badura-Skoda	LP: Discocorp RR 483 LP: Replica RPL 2476 CD: Music and Arts 241

Fidelio

Munich 1961	Bavarian State Chorus & Orchestra Jurinac, Stader, Dickie, Peerce, Ernster, Guthrie, Neidlinger	LP: Westminster XWN 3319/WST 319 LP: World Records SOC 104-6 LP: Westminster S 1003 CD: MCA Classics MCAD2 9809

Leonore No 3, Overture

Salzburg July-August 1938	VPO	LP: Melodram MEL 711 Incorrectly dated 1949
Munich 1961	Bavarian State Orchestra	Westminster unpublished
Vienna May 1962	VPO	CD: Memories HR 4171-3

Brahms

Symphony No 1

Dresden Date uncertain	Dresden Staatskapelle	LP: Private issue (USA) P 1012-3 LP: Seven Seas K20C 53

Symphony No 2

Berlin December 1943	BPO	LP: Discocorp RR 536 Also published on LP by Melodiya
Geneva June 1948	Suisse Romande Orchestra	78: Decca K 1906-10
Munich October 1956	Munich PO	LP: Private issue (USA) P 1014 LP: Discocorp IGI 388 LP: Seven Seas K20C 54
Dresden November 1959	Dresden Staatskapelle	CD: Music and Arts KICC 2021

Symphony No 3

Berlin 1942-1944	BPO	LP: Private issue (USA) P 1003 LP: Discocorp IGI 383 CD: Seven Seas KICC 2022
Salzburg July 1955	VPO	LP: Seven Seas K20C 55/K17C 9484
Dresden November 1956	Dresden Staatskapelle	CD: Hunt CD 724

Symphony No 4

Cologne May 1953	WDR Orchestra	LP: Private issue (USA) P 1004 LP: Discocorp RR 543 LP: Seven Seas K20C 56 CD: Seven Seas KICC 2023

Piano Concerto No 2

Vienna October 1957	VPO Curzon	LP: Decca LXT 5434 LP: Decca ECM 571/ECS 571

Alto Rhapsody

Vienna June 1957	VPO Akademiechor West	LP: Decca LXT 5394 LP: Decca ECS 701 CD: Decca (Germany) 2894.308792

Haydn Variations (St Antoni Chorale)

Vienna June 1957	VPO	LP: Decca LXT 5394 LP: Decca ECS 701 CD: Decca (Germany) 2894.308792

Academic Festival Overture

Vienna June 1957	VPO	LP: Decca LXT 5394 LP: Decca BR 3063 LP: Decca ECS 701 CD: Decca (Germany) 2894.308792

Tragic Overture

Vienna June 1957	VPO	LP: Decca LXT 5394 LP: Decca ECS 701 CD: Decca (Germany) 2894.308792

Bruckner

Symphony No 3

Vienna   VPO   LP: Decca LXT 2967
April 1954   LP: Decca ECM 553/ECS 553
                                                   CD: Decca (Japan) K35Y 1013

Munich   Bavarian   CD: Music and Arts CD 257
October 1954   State Orchestra

Hamburg   NDR Orchestra   LP: Discocorp RR 496
March 1962

Symphony No 4 "Romantic"

Berlin   BPO   LP: Discocorp IGI 383
March 1944   CD: Music and Arts CD 249

Vienna   VPO   LP: Decca LXT 5065-6
March 1955   LP: Decca ECM 511/ECS 511

Vienna   VPO   CD: Nuova Era NE 2205
April 1964

Symphony No 5

Vienna June 1956	VPO	LP: Decca LXT 5255-6 LP: Decca ECM 530/ECS 530
Munich March 1959	Munich PO	LP: Movimento Musica 02.008

Symphony No 7

Salzburg August 1949	VPO	LP: Melodram MEL 711 LP: Discocorp RR 209 CD: Music and Arts CD 209 CD: Hunt CD 712
Cologne May 1963	WDR Orchestra	LP: Seven Seas K19C 18-19/K17C 9479-80 Orchestra incorrectly named as Munich PO
Baden-Baden Date uncertain	SDR Orchestra	LP: Private issue (USA) P 1010 First movement only

Symphony No 8

Berlin January 1951	BPO	CD: Hunt CD 711 CD: Seven Seas KICC 2027
Munich 1955	Bavarian State Orchestra	CD: Music and Arts CD 266
Vienna October 1961	VPO	LP: Discocorp IGI 375 CD: Memories HR 4171-3 Austrian Radio has suggested that the date of this performance should be 1958
Munich January 1963	Munich PO	LP: Westminster S 235 CD: MCA Classics MCAD 29825 Also published on LP by World Records

Symphony No 9

Berlin January 1950	BPO	LP: Melodram MEL 216 LP: Longanesi periodici GCL 56 LP: Laudis (Japan) RCL 3312 CD: Music and Arts CD 219 CD: Foyer CDS 16004 Melodram incorrectly labelled Berlin RO
Munich February 1958	Bavarian State Orchestra	LP: Seven Seas K20C 52 CD: Hunt CD 710

Sociedad Filarmónica de Bilbao

DOS CONCIERTOS EXTRAORDINARIOS

LOS DIAS 22 Y 23 DE MAYO DE 1943

EN EL TEATRO BUENOS AIRES

Orquesta Filarmónica de Berlín

BAJO LA DIRECCION DEL MAESTRO

HANS KNAPPERTSBUSCH

Día 22, a las SIETE de la tarde
Día 23, a las ONCE Y CUARTO de la mañana

Operntheater

Im Abonnement　　　Freitag den 19. März 1937　　　II. Gruppe

Zum ersten Male:

DER SCHMUCK DER MADONNA
(I Gioielli della Madonna)

Volksoper in drei Akten. Worte von C. Zangarini und E. Golisciani. Deutsche Übersetzung von Hans Liebstoeckl. Musik von Ermanno Wolf-Ferrari.

Spielleitung: Erich v. Wymetal a. G.　　　　　Musikalische Leitung: * * *

Gennaro, Schmied	Norbert Ardelli a. G.	Totonno, ein junger Mann aus dem Volke		Emmerich Godin
Carmela, seine Mutter	Kerstin Thorborg	Erster } Mönch		Georg Monthy
Maliella	Margit Bokor	Zweiter		Alfred Muzzarelli
Rafaele, Führer der „Bravi"	Alfred Jerger	Pazzariello		Adolph Nemeth
Biaso, Schreiber	Hermann Gallos	Erstes }		Betty Kodidek
Ciccillo } Bravi	Georg Maikl	Zweites } Mädchen		Steffi Klinger
Rocco	Karl Ettl	Drittes }		Gretl Enders
Stella	Luise Helletsgruber	Eine junge Bäuerin		Mimi Wessely
Concetta	Rona Hajmassey	Erster } Moraspieler		Albert Piffl
Serena	Dora With	Zweiter		Johann Hahn
Grazia, genannt „die Blondine"	Maria Schindler	Erster } Bravo		Viktor Maiwald
		Zweiter		Franz Polcar

Kinderchor: Wiener Sängerknaben

Volk, Verkäufer, Bravi, einzelne charakteristische Typen usw.

Die Handlung spielt in Neapel — Zeit: Erste Hälfte des 19. Jahrhunderts

I. Akt: Eine Piazzetta am Meere — II. Akt: Der Garten im Hause der Carmela — III. Akt: Die Höhle der Bravi in der Umgebung von Neapel

* * * Musikalische Leitung: Generalmusikdirektor **Hans Knappertsbusch** a. G.

In Szene gesetzt von Erich v. Wymetal

Choreographie und Einstudierung des Tanzes im III. Akt: Willy Fränzl

ausgeführt von den Damen Schiender, Drapal, Pokorny, Szakal, Fiedler, Feix A., Graf, Klima, Opek, Leibenfrost, Stanitz, Swiezinski, den Herren Binder, Pokorny, Raimund, Weinrich, Pichler, Kaiser, Nowak, Kloss, Jandosch, Wondrak, Kres, Kaiser H.

Bühnenbilder: Robert Kautsky — Kostüme: Ladislaus Czettel

Der im Orchester zur Verwendung kommende Flügel ist von der Firma L. Bösendorfer beigestellt Elektrische Musikwiedergabe-Einrichtung durchgeführt von Ing. Hermann May, mit Lautsprecher und Verstärker der Firma Czeija, Nißl & Co., Wien

Nach dem zweiten Akt eine größere Pause

Das offizielle Programm nur bei den Billetteuren erhältlich. Preis 50 Groschen — Garderobe frei

Kassen-Eröffnung vor 6½ Uhr　　　Anfang 7 Uhr　　　Ende 10 Uhr

Während der Vorspiele und der Akte bleiben die Saaltüren zum Parkett, Parterre und den Galerien geschlossen. Zuspätkommende können daher nur während der Pausen Einlaß finden.

Telephonische Bestellungen von Sitzen, R-28-320 (ausgenommen Sitzparterre) zum Preise von S 4.— aufwärts werden für folgende Vorstellungen entgegengenommen.

Der Kartenverkauf findet heute statt für obige Vorstellung und für

Sonntag　　den 20. Rigoletto. „Herzog" Jussi Björling von der kgl. Oper in Stockholm a. G. im Abonnement II. Gruppe (Anfang 7½ Uhr)

Sonntag　　den 21. Nachmittags 2½ Uhr: Rigoletto. „Herzog" Norbert Ardelli a. G. Sondervorstellung der Österreichischen Kunststelle für „Theater der Werksgemeinschaften". Beschränkter Kartenverkauf

Franckenstein

Variations on a theme by Meyerbeer

Berlin	Berlin	78: Polydor 66120-1
1924	Staatskapelle	

Glinka

Russlan and Ludmilla, Overture

Berlin	Grosses	78: Parlophone R 1631/A 3766
April 1933	Sinfonie-Orchester	78: Odeon O 11875
	(Staatskapelle)	

Handel

Concerto Grosso op 6 no 5

Berlin	BPO	LP: Discocorp RR 536
March 1944		CD: Seven Seas KICC 2021

Haydn

Symphony No 88

Vienna December 1962	VPO	CD: Seven Seas KICC 2025

Symphony No 92 "Oxford"

Berlin 1924	Berlin Staatskapelle	78: Polydor 66344-6/69783-5 auto

Symphony No 94 "Surprise"

Berlin September 1928	Berlin Staatskapelle	78: Parlophone E 10844-6 78: Odeon O 6695-7 LP: Private issue (USA) P 1009
Berlin 1942	BPO	78: Electrola DB 5671-3
Berlin February 1950	BPO	LP: Longanesi periodici GCL 62 LP: Laudis (Japan) RCL 3301 CD: Seven Seas KICC 2022

Symphony No 100 "Military"

Berlin April 1933	Grosses Sinfonie-Orchester (Staatskapelle)	78: Parlophone R 1537-40 78: Odeon O 11848-51 78: Victor M 199 LP: Private issue (USA) P 1008

Komzak

Badner Madln, Waltz

Vienna 1942	VPO	78: Electrola DB 7710 Incorrectly labelled BPO
Munich March 1955	Bavarian State Orchestra	CD: Melodram MEL 18033 Orchestra incorrectly named as Munich PO Also published on CD as private issue for Friends of the Munich Prinzregenten- theater
Vienna October 1957	VPO	LP: Decca LXT 5420/SXL 2016 LP: Decca BR 3043 LP: Telefunken ND 760

Lanner

Die Schönbrunner, Waltz

Munich March 1955	Bavarian State Orchestra	CD: Melodram MEL 18033 Orchestra incorrectly named as Munich PO; Also published on CD as private issue for Friends of Munich Prinzregententheater

Liszt

Les Préludes

Berlin 1942	BPO	78: Electrola DB 5691-2 LP: Electrola 1C 137 54095-9 LP: EMI RLS 768 CD: EMI CDF 3000122

Mazeppa

Berlin April 1933	Grosses Sinfonie-Orchester (Staatskapelle)	78: Parlophone R 1579-81 78: Odeon O 11897-9 78: Decca (USA) 20082-4

Lortzing

Undine, Overture

Berlin April 1933	Grosses Sinfonie-Orchester (Staatskapelle)	78: Parlophone E 11253 78: Odeon O 6842 LP: Private issue (USA) P 1008

Mahler

Kindertotenlieder

Berlin April 1956	BPO West	CD: Hunt CD 710 CD: Seven Seas KICC 2026

Mendelssohn

Calm Sea and Prosperous Voyage, Overture

Berlin April 1933	Grosses Sinfonie-Orchester (Staatskapelle)	78: Parlophone 78: Odeon

Meyerbeer

Les Huguenots: Excerpt (Gloire au grand Dieu vengeur)

Berlin May 1929	Berlin Chorus and Staatskapelle Sung in German	78: HMV C 1681

Mozart

Symphony No 39

Berlin October 1929	Berlin Staatskapelle	78: Parlophone E 11003-5/15202-4 auto 78: Odeon O 6735-7 LP: Private issue (Japan) P 1006

Symphony No 40

Vienna 1941	VPO	LP: HKV (Japan) TY 3

Clarinet Concerto

Berlin 1952	Berlin RO Bürkner	LP: Melodram MEL 216
Berlin March 1956	BPO Bürkner	LP: Longanesi periodici GCL 48
Munich January 1962	Munich PO Schröder	LP: Private issue (USA) P 1006 LP: Seven Seas K20C 77

6 German Dances K509

Berlin 1933	Grosses Sinfonie-Orchester (Staatskapelle)	78: Parlophone R 1561 78: Odeon O 11862 LP: Private issue (USA) P 1006

6 German Dances K600

Berlin 1933	Grosses Sinfonie-Orchester (Staatskapelle)	78: Parlophone R 1562 78: Odeon O 11863

Münchner Philharmoniker

Herkules-Saal / Residenz

Mittwoch, 15. Januar 1964 / 20 Uhr
Donnerstag, 16. Januar 1964 / 20 Uhr

Leitung:

Hans Knappertsbusch

Richard Strauss: Tod und Verklärung

Anton Bruckner: 3. Symphonie d-moll

WAGNER

Die Meistersinger von Nürnberg

THE MASTERSINGERS OF NUREMBERG

Hans Sachs	Paul Schoeffler (Bass-Baritone)
Veit Pogner	Otto Edelmann (Bass)
Kunz Vogelgesang	Hugo Meyer-Welfing (Tenor)
Konrad Nachtigall	Wilhelm Felden (Bass)
Sixtus Beckmesser	Karl Dönch (Baritone)
Fritz Kothner	Alfred Poell (Baritone)
Balthasar Zorn	Erich Majkut (Tenor)
Ulrich Eisslinger	William Wergnick (Tenor)
Augustin Moser	Hermann Gallos (Tenor)
Hermann Ortel	Harald Pröglhöf (Bass)
Hans Foltz	Ljubomir Pantscheff (Bass)
Hans Schwarz	Franz Bierbach (Bass)
Walther von Stolzing	Günther Treptow (Tenor)
David	Anton Dermota (Tenor)
Eva	Hilde Gueden (Soprano)
Magdalene	Else Schürhoff (Soprano)
Night watchman	Harald Pröglhöf (Bass)

with The Vienna State Opera Chorus and
The Vienna Philharmonic Orchestra
conducted by Hans Knappertsbusch

LXT 2659-64

Also available with each act coupled separately
Act I: LXT 2646-7; Act II: LXT 2566-8; Act III: LXT 2648-50

A libretto has been published giving the German text as sung on the records with a line-by-line literal English prose translation. This book is at the moment reprinting and if copies are not in stock at the bookstall we shall be pleased to receive orders direct, to be fulfilled as soon as supplies are again available.

THE DECCA RECORD COMPANY LTD 1-3 BRIXTON ROAD LONDON SW9

Nicolai

The Merry Wives of Windsor, Overture

Berlin 1950	BPO	CD: Hunt CD 723
Vienna February 1960	VPO	LP: Decca LXT 5594/SXL 2239 LP: London (USA) STS 15045

Pfitzner

Palestrina, Act 1 Prelude

Berlin 1942	BPO	78: Electrola DB 7677

Rossini

William Tell, Overture

Munich 1928-29	Bavarian State Orchestra	78: Homochord 4-8942

Schmidt

Variations on a Hussar's Song

Vienna October 1957	VPO	CD: DG 435 3282/435 3212

Schubert

Symphony No 8 "Unfinished"

Berlin January 1950	BPO	LP: Melodram MEL 216 CD: Chaconne CHCD 1001 Melodram incorrectly states Berlin RO

Symphony No 9 "Great"

Vienna October 1957	VPO	CD: DG 435 3282/435 3212
Munich January 1959	Munich PO	LP: Hans-Knappeertsbusch-Gesellschaft (Japan) HK 1001

Marche militaire in D (orch. Weingartner)

Munich March 1955	Bavarian State Orchestra	CD: Melodram MEL 18033 Orchestra incorrectly named as Munich PO; Also published on CD as private issue for Friends of Munich Prinzregententheater

Schumann

Symphony No 4

Dresden April 1956	Dresden Staatskapelle	LP: Seven Seas K20C 57 CD: Hunt CD 724 CD: Fonoteam CD 74802
Vienna December 1962	VPO	CD: Seven Seas KICC 2025 CD: Memories HR 4171-3

Johann Strauss

Accelerations, Waltz

Berlin February 1928	Berlin Staatskapelle	78: Electrola EH 123 78: Victor 56025
Vienna October 1957	VPO	LP: Decca LXT 5420/SXL 2016 LP: Decca SPA 73

Annen Polka

Munich March 1955	Bavarian State Orchestra	CD: Melodram MEL 18033 Orchestra incorrectly named as Munich PO; also published on CD as private issue for Friends of the Munich Prinzregententheater
Vienna October 1957	VPO	LP: Decca LXT 5420/SXL 2016 45: Decca CEP 577/Decca (Germany) VD 661 LP: Telefunken ND 760 LP: Decca SPA 73

Bei uns z' Haus', Waltz

Berlin 1933	Berlin Staatskapelle	78: Parlophone R 1804 78: Odeon O 11864 78: Decca (USA) 20302

Donauweibchen, Waltz

Berlin February 1928	Berlin Staatskapelle	78: Electrola EH 118 78: Victor 50008

Egyptian March

Munich March 1955	Bavarian State Orchestra	CD: Melodram MEL 18033 Orchestra incorrectly named as Munich PO; also published on CD as private issue for Friends of the Munich Prinzregententheater

Die Fledermaus, Overture

Berlin September 1928	Grosses Sinfonie-Orchester (Staatskapelle)	78: Odeon O 6663/U 10043

Freut euch des Lebens, Waltz

Berlin February 1928	Berlin Staatskapelle	78: Electrola EH 119 78: Victor 50009

Kusswalzer

Berlin 1933	Grosses Sinfonie-Orchester (Staatskapelle)	78: Parlophone R 1675 78: Odeon O 11865

Leichtes Blut, Polka

Vienna January 1942	VPO	78: Electrola DA 4487 LP: Electrola 1C 147 30226-7M CD: DG 435 3352 CD: Preiser 90116/90090 CD: EMI CHS 764 2942/CDH 764 2992
Vienna October 1957	VPO	LP: Decca LXT 5420/SXL 2016 45: Decca CEP 577/Decca (Germany) VD 661 LP: Decca SPA 73

Rosen aus dem Süden, Waltz

Munich March 1955	Bavarian State Orchestra	CD: Melodram MEL 18033 Orchestra incorrectly named as Munich PO; also published on CD as private issue for Friends of the Munich Prinzregententheater

Tales from the Vienna Woods, Waltz

Berlin February 1928	Berlin Staatskapelle	78: HMV C 1828 78: Electrola EH 120
Munich March 1955	Bavarian State Orchestra	CD: Melodram MEL 18033 Orchestra incorrectly named as Munich PO; also published on CD as private issue for Friends of the Munich Prinzregententheater
Vienna October 1957	VPO	LP: Decca LXT 5420/SXL 2016 LP: Telefunken ND 760 CD: DG 435 3352

Tritsch-Tratsch Polka

Vienna October 1957	VPO	LP: Decca LXT 5420/SXL 2016 45: Decca CEP 577/Decca (Germany) VD 661 LP: Decca BR 3063 LP: Decca SPA 73

1001 Nacht, Intermezzo

Munich March 1955	Bavarian State Orchestra	CD: Melodram MEL 18033 Orchestra incorrectly named as Munich PO; also published on CD as private issue for Friends of the Munich Prinzregententheater

Johann & Josef Strauss

Pizzicato Polka

Vienna January 1942	VPO	78: Electrola DA 4487 CD: Preiser 90116 CD: EMI CHS 764 2942/CDH 764 2992

Johann Strauss father

Radetzky March

Vienna October 1957	VPO	LP: Decca LXT 5420/SXL 2016 45: Decca CEP 577/Decca (Germany) VD 661 LP: Decca BR 3063 LP: Telefunken ND 760

Richard Strauss

Don Juan

Paris May 1956	Paris Conservatoire Orchestra	LP: Decca LXT 5239 LP: Telefunken AJ 641.939

Elektra: Excerpts (Agamemnon! Wo bist du, Vater?; Orest! Es rührt sich niemand)

Vienna September 1936	VPO Pauly	LP: Teletheater 762.3589

Intermezzo, Waltz Sequence

Berlin September 1928	Berlin Staatskapelle	78: Parlophone E 10894 78: Odeon O 6788

Der Rosenkavalier

Vienna November 1955	VPO Vienna Opera Chorus Reining, Güden, Jurinac, Terkal, Böhme, Poell	LP: Hans-Knappertsbusch-Gesellschaft (Japan) HK 1012-5
Munich September 1957	Bavarian State Chorus & Orchestra Schech, Köth, Töpper, Edelmann, Fehenberger, Peter	LP: Discocorp IGI 482 LP: Melodram MEL 102

Der Rosenkavalier: Excerpts (Kann mich auch an ein Mädel erinnern; Heut' oder morgen)

Zürich 1949	Tonhalle Orchestra Reining	LP: Decca LX 3021 LP: Preiser PR 9829 CD: Preiser 90083

Der Rosenkavalier: Excerpts (Mir ist die Ehre widerfahren; Hab' mir's gelobt)

Vienna April 1936	VPO Lehmann, Schumann, Hadrabova	LP: Ed Smith EJS 332 LP: Teletheater 762.3589

Der Rosenkavalier: Excerpt (Leopold, wir gehn!)

Vienna September 1936	VPO Sterneck, Paalen, Gallos	LP: Teletheater 762.3589

Der Rosenkavalier: Fragments

Vienna June 1937	VPO Konetzni, Bokor, Novotna	LP: Ed Smith EJS 332

Salome, Dance of the 7 Veils

Berlin September 1928	Berlin Staatskapelle	78: Parlophone E 10894 78: Odeon O 6788

Till Eulenspiegels lustige Streiche

Berlin September 1928	Berlin Staatskapelle	78: Odeon O 6772-3

Tod und Verklärung

Paris May 1956	Paris Conservatoire Orchestra	LP: Decca LXT 5239 LP: Telefunken AJ 641.939
Dresden November 1959	Dresden Staatskapelle	CD: Fonoteam CD 74802
Vienna December 1962	VPO	CD: Seven Seas KICC 2025 CD: Memories HR 4171-3

Suppé

Poet and Peasant, Overture

Berlin February 1932	Grosses Sinfonie-Orchester (Staatskapelle)	78: Homochord Catalogue number uncertain

Tchaikovsky

The Nutcracker, Suite

Vienna February 1960	VPO	LP: Decca LXT 5594/SXL 2239 LP: Telefunken ND 760 LP: London (USA) STS 15045 Excerpts LP: Decca 414 0771

Verdi

Aida, Grand March

Vienna September 1940	VPO	78: Electrola DB 5608 CD: Preiser 90116

Wagner

Der fliegende Holländer

Bayreuth July 1955	Bayreuth Festival Chorus & Orchestra Varnay, Schärtel, Windgassen, Traxel, Uhde, Weber	LP: Discocorp IGI 319 LP: Fonit Cetra LO 51 LP: Melodram MEL 550 CD: Music and Arts CD 319 CD: Hunt CDLSMH 34021 <u>Wie aus der Ferne</u> LP: Melodram MEL 094

Der fliegende Holländer: Excerpt (Die Frist ist um)

Vienna June 1958	VPO London	LP: Decca LXT 5478/SXL 2068 LP: Decca ADD 143/SDD 143 LP: Decca 414 6101

Der fliegende Holländer, Overture

Berlin 1928	BPO	78: Polydor 66830 78: Cetra OR 5112-3 LP: DG LPEM 19601
Vienna May 1953	VPO	LP: Decca LXT 2822 LP: Decca LW 5106 LP: Decca ACL 22 LP: Decca ECM 672/ECS 672
Munich November 1962	Munich PO	LP: Westminster XWN 19055/WST 17055 LP: Westminster MCA 1413

Götterdämmerung

Bayreuth August 1951	Bayreuth Festival Chorus & Orchestra Varnay, Mödl, Siewert, Schwarzkopf, Aldenhoff, Uhde, Weber, Pflanzl	Decca unpublished
Munich September 1955	Bavarian State Chorus & Orchestra Nilsson, Rysanek, Malaniuk, Aldenhoff, Uhde, Frick	LP: Melodram MEL 425
Bayreuth August 1956	Bayreuth Festival Chorus & Orchestra Varnay, Madeira, Browenstijn, Windgassen, Uhde, Greindl, Neidlinger	LP: Melodram MEL 569 Excerpts CD: Music and Arts CD 319
Bayreuth August 1957	Bayreuth Festival Chorus & Orchestra Varnay, Ilosvay, Grümmer, Windgassen, Uhde, Neildlinger, Greindl	LP: Discocorp IGI 292 LP: Fonit Cetra LO 61 LP: Melodram MEL 579 CD: Music and Arts CD 256 CD: Laudis LCD 44013/LCD 154020
Bayreuth July 1958	Bayreuth Festival Chorus & Orchestra Varnay, Madeira, Grümmer, Windgassen, Wiener, Andersson, Greindl	LP: Melodram MEL 589 CD: Hunt CDLSMH 34044

Götterdämmerung, Dawn and Siegfried's Rhine Journey

Vienna January 1942	VPO	78: Electrola DB 5699 CD: Preiser 90116
Vienna June 1956	VPO	LP: Decca LXT 5255 LP: Decca LXT 5249/SXL 2074 LP: Decca LW 5320 LP: Decca SDD 426 LP: Decca GOS 581-2 CD: Decca 414 6252
Berlin November 1959	Berlin Staatskapelle	LP: Private issue (USA) P 1015 LP: Discocorp RR 535 CD: Music and Arts CD 257 CD: Seven Seas KICC 2030 Seven Seas incorrectly dated 1951

Götterdämmerung, Siegfried's Funeral Music

Vienna January 1942	VPO	CD: Preiser 90116 Previously unpublished Electrola recording
Vienna June 1956	VPO	LP: Decca LXT 5255 LP: Decca LXT 5249/SXL 2074 LP: Decca LW 5320 LP: Decca BR 3063 LP: Decca SDD 426 LP: Decca GOS 581-2 CD: Decca 414 6252
Berlin November 1959	Berlin Staatskapelle	LP: Discocorp RR 535 CD: Music and Arts CD 257 CD: Seven Seas KICC 2030 Seven Seas incorrectly dated 1951

Götterdämmerung, Brünnhilde's Immolation

Hamburg March 1963	NDR Orchestra C.Ludwig	LP: Discocorp RR 535 CD: Nuova Era 013.6304 CD: Seven Seas KICC 2030

Lohengrin, Act 1 Prelude

Zürich December 1947	Tonhalle Orchestra	78: Decca K 1709
Munich November 1962	Munich PO	LP: Westminster XWN 19055/WST 17055 LP: Westminster MCA 1413

Lohengrin, Act 3 Prelude

London January 1948	LPO	78: Decca K 1820-1

Lohengrin: Excerpt (Einsam in trüben Tagen)

Vienna May 1956	VPO Flagstad	LP: Decca LXT 5249 LP: Decca LXT 6042/SXL 6042 LP: Decca SDD 212 LP: Decca ECS 826 LP: Decca GRV 11

Lohengrin: Excerpt (Heil, König Heinrich!...Elsa! Hast du mich vernommen?)

Vienna December 1936	VPO Vienna Opera Chorus Teschemacher, Kötter, Alsen	LP: Teletheater 762.3589

Die Meistersinger von Nürnberg

Vienna September 1950 (Act 2) and September 1951 (Acts 1 and 3)	VPO Vienna Opera Chorus Güden, Schürhoff, Treptow, Dermota, Schöffler, Dönch, Edelmann	78: Decca K 28385-92/53046-53 auto (Act 2) LP: Decca LXT 2560-1 (Act 2) LP: Decca LXT 2646-7 (Act 1) LP: Decca LXT 2648-50 (Act 3) LP: Decca LXT 2659-64 LP: Decca GOM 535-9 Preludes Acts 1 and 3 78: Decca K 28573-4 LP: Decca LW 5038 Excerpts 78: Decca K 1731 LP: Decca LXT 5544 LP: Decca LW 5082/LW 5101/LW 5103 LP: Decca BR 3089 LP: Decca ECS 812 LP: Decca 414 4531
Bayreuth August 1952	Bayreuth Festival Chorus & Orchestra Della Casa, Unger, Malaniuk, Hopf, Edelmann, Böhme, Pflanzl	LP: Melodram MEL 522 CD: Hunt CDLSMH 34040 Excerpts from Meistersinger on Gioielli della lirica LP GML 37 are labelled Bayreuth 1952 but actually derive from a 1949 Munich performance conducted by Jochum
Bayreuth July 1960	Bayreuth Festival Chorus & Orchestra Grümmer, Schärtel, Windgassen, Stolze, Greindl, Adam, Schmitt-Walter	LP: Melodram MEL 602 LP: Melodram MEL 46103

Die Meistersinger von Nürnberg: Excerpt (Guten Abend, Meister)

Zürich June 1947	Tonhalle Orchestra Reining, Schöffler	78: Decca X 312 LP: Decca LX 3021 LP: Preiser PR 9829 CD: Preiser 90083

Die Meistersinger von Nürnberg: Excerpt (O Sachs, mein Freund!)

Zürich June 1947	Tonhalle Orchestra Reining, Schöffler	Decca unpublished

Die Meistersinger von Nürnberg: Excerpts (Was duftet doch der Flieder; Wahn, Wahn, überall Wahn)

Vienna June 1958	VPO London	LP: Decca LXT 5478/SXL 2068 45: Decca CEP 601/SEC 5032 LP: Decca ADD 143/SDD 143 LP: Decca 414 6101

Die Meistersinger von Nürnberg, Act 1 Prelude

Berlin 1928	BPO	78: Polydor 66698 78: Cetra RR 8031 78: Decca CA 8018 LP: DG LPEM 19601 LP: DG 88031
Geneva 1948	Suisse Romande Orchestra	78: Decca K 1905 LP: London (USA) T 5124
Berlin November 1959	Berlin Staatskapelle	LP: Discocorp RR 388
Munich November 1962	Munich PO	LP: Westminster XWN 19055/WST 17055 LP: Westminster MCA 1413
Hamburg March 1963	NDR Orchestra	CD: Nuova Era 013.6304

Die Meistersinger von Nürnberg, Act 3 Prelude

Berlin 1928	BPO	78: Polydor 66678 LP: DG LPEM 19601 LP: DG 88031
London January 1948	LPO	78: Decca AK 2209-10
Hamburg March 1963	NDR Orchestra	CD: Nuova Era 013.6304

Die Meistersinger von Nürnberg, Dance of the Apprentices

Berlin 1928	BPO	78: Polydor 66075 LP: DG LPEM 19601/LPEM 19078 LP: DG 88031
London January 1948	LPO	78: Decca AK 2209-10

Die Meistersinger von Nürnberg, Entry of the Masters

London January 1948	LPO	78: Decca AK 2209-10

BAYREUTHER FESTSPIELE
DIENSTAG, 25. JULI 1961
PARSIFAL · EIN BÜHNEN-
WEIHFESTSPIEL VON
RICHARD WAGNER

DER BEGINN JEDES AKTES WIRD 15 MINUTEN VORHER MIT EINER FANFARE, 10 MINUTEN VORHER MIT ZWEI UND 5 MINUTEN VOR-HER MIT DREI FANFAREN ANGEKÜNDIGT 1. AKT 16.00 UHR · 2. AKT 18.50 UHR · 3. AKT 21.00 UHR · ENDE GEGEN 22.20 UHR / NACH BEGINN DER AKTE KEIN EINLASS

AMFORTAS · GEORGE LONDON / TITUREL
LUDWIG WEBER / GURNEMANZ · HANS HOTTER / PARSIFAL · JESS THOMAS / KUNDRY
IRENE DALIS / KLINGSOR · GUSTAV NEIDLINGER / ERSTER GRALSRITTER · NIELS
MOELLER / ZWEITER GRALSRITTER · THEO
ADAM / KNAPPEN · CLAUDIA HELLMANN
RUTH HESSE · GERHARD STOLZE · GEORG
PASKUDA / KLINGSORS ZAUBERMÄDCHEN
GUNDULA JANOWITZ · ANJA SILJA · CLAUDIA HELLMANN · DOROTHEA SIEBERT · RITA
BARTOS · RUTH HESSE / MUSIKALISCHE
LEITUNG · HANS KNAPPERTSBUSCH / REGIE
UND INSZENIERUNG · WIELAND WAGNER
CHOREINSTUDIERUNG · WILHELM PITZ
CHOREOGRAPHIE · GERTRUD WAGNER
KOSTÜM · KURT PALM / MASKE · WILLI
KLOSE / AUSSTATTUNGSLEITUNG · JOHANNES DREHER / BÜHNENTECHNIK · REINHARD
KRUMM / BELEUCHTUNG · JAKOB SCHLOSSSTEIN / REGIEASSISTENZ · MANFRED HUBRICHT – PETER LEHMANN / MUSIKALISCHE
ASSISTENZ · MAXIMILIAN KOJETINSKY
HERBERT VOCKS – ROBERT KUPPELWIESER
DAS FESTSPIELORCHESTER / DER FESTSPIELCHOR

Parsifal

Bayreuth August 1951	Bayreuth Festival Chorus & Orchestra Mödl, Windgassen, London, Weber, Uhde, Van Mill	LP: Decca LXT 2651-6 LP: Decca GOM 504-8 CD: Teldec 9031.760472
Bayreuth July 1956	Bayreuth Festival Chorus & Orchestra Mödl, Vinay, Greindl, Fischer-Dieskau, Blankenheim, Hotter	LP: Melodram MEL 563 LP: Fonit Cetra LO 79 CD: Hunt CDLSMH 34035
Bayreuth July 1958	Bayreuth Festival Chorus & Orchestra Crespin, Beirer, Wächter, Hines, Blankenheim, Greindl	LP: Melodram MEL 583
Bayreuth August 1960	Bayreuth Festival Chorus & Orchestra Crespin, Beirer, Stewart, Greindl, Neidlinger, Ward	LP: Melodram MEL 018/MEL 603 Excerpts LP: Rodolphe RP 12445-6 CD: Rodolphe RPC 32445-6
Bayreuth August 1962	Bayreuth Festival Chorus & Orchestra Dalis, Thomas, London, Hotter, Neidlinger, Talvela	LP: Philips AL 3475-9/SAL 3475-9 LP: Philips 6747 242/6747 250 LP: Philips 6723 001 CD: Philips 416 3902
Bayreuth August 1964	Bayreuth Festival Chorus & Orchestra Ericson, Vickers, Stewart, Hotter, Neidlinger, Hagenau	LP: Melodram MEL 643 CD: Hunt CDLSMH 34051

Parsifal, Act 3

Berlin 1943	Städtische Oper Chorus & Orchestra Larcen, Hartmann, Weber, Reinmar	LP: Acanta DE 23.036 Excerpts LP: Acanta 40.23502

Parsifal: Excerpts (Amfortas Scenes)

Bayreuth August 1954	Bayreuth Festival Chorus & Orchestra Hotter	LP: Melodram MEL 643

Parsifal: Opening, up to and including first scene of Amfortas (Recht so! Habt Dank!)

Bayreuth August 1959	Bayreuth Festival Orchestra Mödl, Wächter, Hines	CD: Hunt CDKAR 219 Inadvertently included in a performance conducted by Karajan in 1961 in Vienna with singers named as Höngen, Wächter and Hotter

Parsifal: Excerpt (Transformation Scene, Act 1)

Berlin 1928	BPO	78: Polydor 66700 LP: DG LPEM 19601 LP: DG 88031 LP: DG 2721 113
Vienna June 1950	VPO Vienna Opera Chorus	78: Decca K 28359-60 LP: Decca LX 3036

Parsifal: Excerpt (Flower Maidens' Scene, Act 2)

Vienna September 1950	VPO Vienna Opera Chorus Treptow	78: Decca K 28443 LP: Decca LX 3036 LP: Decca LXT 2644

Parsifal: Excerpt (Ich sah das Kind)

Vienna June 1956	VPO Flagstad	LP: Decca LXT 5249 LP: Decca SDD 212 LP: Decca ECS 826 LP: Decca GRV 11 CD: Decca 414 6252

Parsifal, Act 1 Prelude

Berlin 1943	Städtische Oper Orchestra	LP: Acanta DE 23.036 CD: Seven Seas KICC 2023
Vienna June 1950	VPO	78: Decca K 28359-60 LP: Decca LX 3036
Munich November 1962	Munich PO	LP: Westminster XWN 19055/WST 17055 LP: Westminster MCA 1413

Das Rheingold

Bayreuth August 1951	Bayreuth Festival Orchestra Brivkalne, Siewert, Malaniuk, Schwarzkopf, Fritz, Windgassen, Kuen, S.Björling, Pflanzl	Decca unpublished
Bayreuth August 1957	Bayreuth Festival Orchestra Grümmer, Ilosvay, Milinkovic, Kuen, Suthaus, Hotter, Neidlinger, Greindl	LP: Discocorp IGI 292 LP: Fonit Cetra LO 58 LP: Melodram MEL 576 CD: Music and Arts CD 253 CD: Laudis LCD 34010/LCD 154021
Bayreuth July 1958	Bayreuth Festival Orchestra Grümmer, Ilosvay, Gorr, Konya, Uhl, Saeden, Fritz, Adam, Greindl	LP: Melodram MEL 586 CD: Hunt CDLSMH 34041

Rienzi, Overture

Vienna 1940	VPO	78: Electrola DB 5607-8 CD: Preiser 90116
London January 1948	LPO	78: Decca K 1820-1 LP: Private issue (USA) P 1009
Vienna June 1950	VPO	78: Decca K 28361-2 LP: Decca LX 3034
Munich November 1962	Munich PO	LP: Westminster XWN 19055/WST 17055 LP: Westminster MCA 1413

Siegfried

Bayreuth August 1951	Bayreuth Festival Orchestra Varnay, Siewert, Lipp, Aldenhoff, Kuen, S.Björling, Pflanzl, Dalberg	Decca unpublished
Bayreuth August 1957	Bayreuth Festival Orchestra Varnay, Ilosvay, Hollweg, Aldenhoff, Kuen, Hotter, Neidlinger	LP: Discocorp IGI 292 LP: Fonit Cetra LO 60 LP: Fonit Cetra DOC 49 LP: Melodram MEL 578 CD: Music and Arts CD 255 CD: Laudis LCD 44012/LCD 154021
Bayreuth July 1958	Bayreuth Festival Orchestra Varnay, Ilosvay, Siebert, Stolze, Windgassen, Hotter, Andersson, Greindl	LP: Melodram MEL 588 CD: Hunt CDLSMH 34043

Siegfried: Excerpt (Forest Murmurs)

Vienna June 1950	VPO Lechleitner	78: Decca K 28442 LP: Decca LX 3034 LP: Decca LXT 2644

Siegfried Idyll

Salzburg August 1949	VPO	LP: Melodram MEL 711
Vienna April 1955	VPO	LP: Decca LXT 5065 LP: Decca ECM 563/ECS 563
Munich November 1962	Munich PO	LP: Westminster XWN 19055/WST 17055 LP: Westminster MCA 1413
Hamburg March 1963	NDR Orchestra	CD: Seven Seas KICC 2030 Incorrectly labelled WDR Orchestra Cologne 1953

Tannhäuser, Overture

Munich	Munich PO	LP: Westminster XWN 19055/WST 17055
November 1962		LP: Westminster MCA 1413

Tannhäuser, Venusberg Music

Berlin	BPO	78: Polydor 66701-2
1928		78: Brunswick 90298-9
		LP: DG LPEM 19601
		LP: DG 88031
		LP: DG 2721 113

Tannhäuser, Overture and Venusberg Music

London	LPO	78: Decca AK 2211-3
January 1948		LP: London (USA) LPS 42
Vienna	VPO	LP: Decca LXT 2822
May 1953		LP: Decca LW 5106
		LP: Decca ACL 22
		LP: Decca ECM 672/ECS 672

Tannhäuser, Entry of the Guests

Berlin	BPO	78: Polydor 66702
1928		78: Brunswick 90299
		78: Decca LY 6047
		<u>Decca label states Berlin-Charlottenburg</u>
		<u>Opera Orchestra, possibly because that</u>
		<u>issue coupled the work with Tannhäuser</u>
		<u>Overture played by the Charlottenburg</u>
		<u>Orchestra conducted by Gürlitt</u>

Tannhäuser: Excerpts (Dich teure Halle; Allmächt'ge Jungfrau)

Zürich	Tonhalle Orchestra	LP: Decca LX 3021
1949	Reining	LP: Preiser PR 9829
		CD: Preiser 90083

Tannhäuser: Excerpt (Inbrunst im Herzen)

Vienna	VPO	78: Electrola DB 7602
January 1942	Lorenz	LP: Electrola 1C 147 29154-5M
		CD: Preiser 90116

Tristan und Isolde

Munich July 1950	Bavarian State Chorus & Orchestra Braun, Klose, Treptow, Frantz, Schöffler, Peter	LP: Discocorp IGI 345 LP: Documents OP 7542-6 LP: Movimento Musica 05.002 CD: Laudis LCD 44009

Tristan und Isolde: Excerpt (Weh, ach wehe, dies zu dulden)

Vienna September 1959	VPO Nilsson, G.Hoffman	LP: Decca LXT 5559/SXL 2184 LP: Decca JB 58

Tristan und Isolde: Excerpts (Entartet Geschlecht; Wie sorgt' ich schlecht... to end Act 1)

Zürich June 1947	Zürich Opera Chorus & Orchestra Flagstad, Cavelti, Lorenz	LP: Ed Smith ANNA 1025

Tristan und Isolde, Act 3 Prelude

Berlin 1942	Berlin Staatskapelle	LP: Private issue Munich Nationaltheater

Tristan und Isolde, Prelude and Liebestod

Vienna September 1959	VPO Nilsson	LP: Decca LXT 5559/SXL 2184 LP: Decca JB 58 LP: Decca BR 3063 (Prelude only) LP: Decca SDD 426 (Prelude only) LP: Decca GRV 24 (Liebestod only) CD: Decca 414 6252 CD: Decca 433 3332/433 3402
Hamburg March 1963	NDR Orchestra C.Ludwig	CD: Nuova Era 013.6304

Tristan und Isolde, Prelude and Liebestod (orchestral version)

Berlin November 1959	Berlin Staatskapelle	LP: Discocorp RR 535 CD: Seven Seas KICC 2030
Munich November 1962	Munich PO	LP: Westminster XWN 19055/WST 17055 LP: Westminster MCA 1413

Operntheater

Im Abonnement Mittwoch den 22. April 1936 I. Gruppe

Der Rosenkavalier

Komödie für Musik in drei Aufzügen von Hugo von Hofmannsthal
Musik von Richard Strauß

Spielleitung: Dr. Lothar Wallerstein   Dirigent: **

Feldmarschallin Fürstin Werdenberg	Lotte Lehmann*	Ein Friseur	Adolph Nemeth
Der Baron Ochs auf Lerchenau	**	Dessen Gehilfe	Max. Leidenfrost
Octavian, genannt Quinquin, ein junger Herr aus großem Haus	Eva Hadrabova	Eine adelige Witwe	Fritzi Berthold
		Drei adelige Waisen	Molly Jonas / Marie Mathias / Rosa Brunnbauer
Herr von Faninal, ein reicher Neugeadelter	Viktor Madin	Eine Modistin	Rosa Braun
Sophie, seine Tochter	Elisabeth Schumann	Ein Tierhändler	Anton Arnold
Jungfer Marianne Leitmetzerin, die Duenna	Henne Michalsky	Ein Wirt	Georg Maikl
Valzacchi, ein Intrigant	William Wernigk	Vier Lakaien der Marschallin	Leopold Männling / Franz Rouland / Hermann Reich / Franz Szlezak
Annina, seine Begleiterin	Bella Paalen		
Ein Polizeikommissär	Karl Ettl		Charles Verständig / Ferd. Schmalzer
Der Haushofmeister bei der Feldmarschallin	Rolf Telasko	Fünf Kellner	Johann Hahn / Heinrich Berthold / Karl Amry
Der Haushofmeister bei Faninal	Richard Tomel		
Ein Notar	Alfred Muzzarelli	Ein Arzt	Heinrich Berthold
Ein Sänger	Kolomann v. Pataky	Leopold, Diener des Barons	Fritz Birkmeyer
Ein Gelehrter	Alexander Bichler	Ein kleiner Mohr	Grete Mikocki
Ein Flötist	Ludwig Berlit		

Ein kleiner Neger, Lakaien, Läufer, Heiducken, Küchenpersonal, Gäste, Musikanten, Kutscher, zwei Wächter, vier kleine Kinder, verschiedene verdächtige Gestalten.

* Ehrenmitglied — In Wien, in den ersten Jahren der Regierung Maria Theresias
In Szene gesetzt von Dr. Lothar Wallerstein
Bühnenbilder: Alfred Roller

** „Baron Ochs" Kammersänger **Berthold Sterneck** vom Nationaltheater in München a. G.
** Dirigent: **Hans Knappertsbusch** a. G.

Nach dem zweiten Aufzug eine größere Pause.
Das offizielle Programm nur bei den Billeteuren erhältlich. Preis 30 Groschen — Garderobe frei

Kassa-Eröffnung um 6½ Uhr   Anfang 7 Uhr   Ende nach 10½ Uhr

Während der Vorspiele und der Akte bleiben die Saaltüren zum Parkett, Parterre und den Galerien geschlossen. Zuspätkommende können daher nur während der Pausen Einlaß finden.

Der Kartenverkauf findet heute statt für obige Vorstellung und für:
Donnerstag den 23. Der liebe Augustin. Bei aufgehobenem Stammsitz-Abonnement. Ballettpreise (Anfang 7½ Uhr)
Freitag den 24. Neu einstudiert und inszeniert: Der Corregidor. „Frasquita" Kammersängerin **Jarmila Novotna** a. G. Dirigent: **Bruno Walter** a. G. Im Abonnement I. Gruppe. Erhöhte Preise (Anfang 7½ Uhr)

Weiterer Spielplan:
Samstag den 25. Manon (Massenet) Im Abonnement I. Gruppe. Bei aufgehobenem Stammsitz-Abonnement (Anfang 7½ Uhr)
Sonntag den 26. Der Ring des Nibelungen. Dritter Tag: Götterdämmerung. Dirigent: **Hans Knappertsbusch** a. G. (Anfang 5 Uhr)

STAATSOPER WIEN

Freitag, den 30. Juni 1944

Preise II

DER RING DES NIBELUNGEN

Ein Bühnenfestspiel für drei Tage und einen Vorabend
von Richard Wagner

Dritter Tag:

Götterdämmerung

In drei Aufzügen und einem Vorspiel

Musikalische Leitung: Hans Knappertsbusch

Spielleitung: Erich v. Wymetal

Personen der Handlung.

Siegfried	Dr. Julius Pölzer *Staatsoper München*
Brünnhilde	Helena Braun *Staatsoper München*
Gutrune	Daga Söderqvist
Hagen	Herbert Alsen
Gunther	Carl Kronenberg *Staatsoper München*
Alberich	Adolf Vogel
Waltraute	Elisabeth Höngen
Die drei Nornen	Else Schürhoff / Elena Nikolaidi / Daniza Jlitsch
Die drei Rheintöchter	Esther Réthy / Aenne Michalsky / Elena Nikolaidi
Die drei Mannen	Egyd Toriff / Karl Ettl / Roland Neumann

Bühnenbilder und Kostüme nach Entwürfen von Alfred Roller

Nach jedem Aufzug eine größere Pause

Anfang 16 Uhr   Ende 21 Uhr

Das Publikum wird gebeten, sich vor Beginn der Vorstellung beim Erscheinen unserer verwundeten Frontsoldaten in der Mitteiloge von den Plätzen zu erheben.

Bei Fliegeralarm Ruhe bewahren! Es ist Vorsorge getroffen, daß alle Besucher Platz in den Luftschutzräumen finden. Richtungspfeile beachten! Die Sitzplätze ohne Hast verlassen und allen Anordnungen der Luftschutzorgane Folge leisten!

Die Walküre

Bayreuth August 1951	Bayreuth Festival Orchestra Varnay, Rysanek, Malaniuk, Treptow, S.Björling, Van Mill	Decca unpublished
Bayreuth * August 1956	Bayreuth Festival Orchestra Varnay, Milinkovic, Brouwenstijn, Windgassen, Hotter, Greindl	LP: Melodram MEL 567
Bayreuth August 1957	Bayreuth Festival Orchestra Varnay, Nilsson, Milinkovic, Vinay, Hotter, Greindl	LP: Discocorp IGI 292 LP: Fonit Cetra LO 59 LP: Fonit Cetra DOC 48 LP: Melodram MEL 577 CD: Music and Arts CD 254 CD: Laudis LCD 44011/LCD 154021
Bayreuth July 1958	Bayreuth Festival Orchestra Varnay, Rysanek, Gorr, Vickers, Hotter, Greindl	LP: Melodram MEL 587 CD: Hunt CDLSMH 34042

Die Walküre, Act 1

Vienna October 1957	VPO Flagstad, Svanholm, Van Mill	LP: Decca LXT 5429-30/SXL 2074-5 LP: Decca GOS 581-2 LP: Decca GRV 26 CD: Decca 425 9632

Die Walküre: Excerpts (Der Männer Sippe; Du bist der Lenz)

Vienna	VPO	LP: Decca LXT 5249
May 1956	Flagstad	LP: Decca ADD 212/SDD 212
		LP: Decca GRV 11

Die Walküre: Excerpt (Wotan's Farewell and Magic Fire Music)

Vienna	VPO	LP: Decca LXT 5478/SXL 2068
June 1958	London	LP: Decca ADD 143/SDD 143
		LP: Decca SDD 426
		LP: Decca 414 6101
		CD: Decca 414 6252

Die Walküre, Ride of the Valkyries

Berlin	BPO	78: Polydor 66705
1928		78: Decca CA 8036
		LP: DG LPEM 19601
		LP: DG 88001
Vienna	VPO	LP: Decca LXT 2822
May 1953		LP: Decca LW 5106
		LP: Decca ACL 22
		LP: Decca ECM 672/ECS 672

Wesendonk-Lieder

Vienna	VPO	LP: Decca LXT 5249
May 1956	Flagstad	LP: Decca LW 5302
		LP: Decca ADD 212/SDD 212
		LP: Decca ECS 826
		LP: Decca GRV 11
		CD: Decca 414 6242
		<u>2 songs only</u>
		LP: Decca LXT 6042/SXL 6042

Weber

Euryanthe, Overture

Cologne May 1962	WDR Orchestra	LP: Discocorp RR 543 CD: Seven Seas KICC 2023

Der Freischütz, Overture

Munich December 1928	Bavarian State Orchestra	78: Homochord 4-8941

Invitation to the Dance (orch. Berlioz)

Berlin 1942	BPO	78: Electrola DB 7647
Munich March 1955	Bavarian State Orchestra	CD: Melodram MEL 18033 <u>Orchestra incorrectly named as Munich PO; also published on CD as private issue for Friends of the Munich Prinzregententheater</u>
Vienna February 1960	VPO	LP: Decca LXT 5594/SXL 2239 LP: London (USA) STS 15045

Wolf

Italian Serenade (arr. Reger)

Berlin BPO LP: Discocorp RR 496
September 1952

Wolf-Ferrari

Der Schmuck der Madonna: Excerpts (Schon lange lieb' ich dich...nun ist die Beute dort; Oeffne, du Holde, öffne mir dein Fenster; Im Staube lag ich dort)

Vienna VPO LP: Teletheater 762.3596-7
March 1937 Bokor, Ardelli,
  Jerger, Maikl, Ettl

Ziehrer

Weaner Madl'n, Waltz

Vienna VPO 78: Electrola EH 1299
1940   LP: Private issue (USA) P 1008
    CD: Preiser 90116

Wiener Bürger, Waltz

Vienna VPO LP: Decca LXT 5420/SXL 2016
October 1957 LP: Decca BR 3043

Knappertsbusch on film

Vienna 1939
Mozart Eine kleine Nachtmusik/VPO
Movements 1, 2 and 4
Knappertsbusch does not actually appear

Berlin 1943
Beethoven Choral Symphony/BPO/Kittel Choir
Concluding bars of last movement
Deutsche Wochenschau

Berlin 1944
Beethoven Eroica Symphony/BPO
Extract from last movement
Deutsche Wochenschau

Bayreuth 1959
Wagner Parsifal/Bayreuth Festival Orchestra
Transformation Music from Act 1

Vienna 1963
Wagner Siegfried Idyll/VPO
ORF

Vienna 1963
Wagner Die Walküre Act 1/concert performance
Watson/Uhl/Greindl/VPO
ORF

Hans Knappertsbusch: Unpublished recordings

Many additional Knappertsbusch recordings exist in the archives of Bavarian and Austrian Radio and in tape copies in the possession of private collectors. This list is confined to known recordings of works which do not feature in the discography of published recordings.

Bach	Brandenburg Concerto No 3 (Vienna 1944)
Beethoven	Coriolan (Vienna 1954 and Hamburg 1960) Consecration of the House (Munich 1963) Symphony 2 (Bremen 1952 and Vienna 1962)
Berger	Rondo giocoso (Salzburg 1950)
Brahms	Double Concerto (Munich 1959) Piano Concerto 1 (Berlin 1950)
Cornelius	Barbier v.Bagdad Overture (Munich 1953)
Mozart	Le Nozze di Figaro (Vienna 1942) Symphony 41 (Vienna 1941)
Pfitzner	Scherzo (RAI 1951 and Munich 1957)
Reger	Mozart Variations (Vienna 1944)
Respighi	Ancient Airs & Dances (Munich 1958)
Schubert	Overture in Italian Style (RAI 1951)
Schumann	Cello Concerto (Berlin 1952)
Sibelius	Violin Concerto (Berlin 1952)
R.Strauss	Bürger als Edelmann (Munich 53/Salzburg 50) Don Quixote (Munich 1958)
Trapp	Concerto for Orchestra (Mun 54/Berlin 56)
Uhl	4 Caprices (Vienna 1949)

Knappertsbusch: a postscript

One's first impression when hearing "Parsifal" in Bayreuth is bound to be of the immensity of its scope, aided as one is by the glow and breadth of the Bayreuth acoustic. But when, as in my case in 1961, the conductor was Hans Knappertsbusch (1888-1965), one enters a world of even vaster timelessness.

It would be beside the point to say that I never "saw" Knappertsbusch - those were the days when the audience still observed the rule (actually going beyond what Wagner had requested) of no applause, so that the conductor did not appear onstage at the end. And how the singers must have enjoyed being able to leave the theatre without those interminable curtain calls !

It is the same when we listen to Kna's other Wagner recordings: applause seems out of place after the deathly cavalcade of "Götterdämmerung" or the neurotic doom of "Der fliegende Holländer" have passed before us. And in the case of that latter work, anyone who is prone to seasickness will surely feel uneasy when Kna unleashes the storm of the Overture.

As for his recordings of other repertoire, the listener is literally grabbed by the character and individuality exuded by every bar of his Haydn 88 and 94, the provocatively broad Beethoven 8 from Hamburg or the recently published DG edition of Schubert 9 - a real "performance" if ever there was one, full of risk-taking abandon. And who has produced such a mightily exuberant "Academic Festival Overture" (Decca) ? Kna's was certainly not a light touch in the accepted sense of that term, yet his Johann Strauss repertoire, fortunately well documented with recordings, brims over with lilting enjoyment.

This is all conducting on the grandest scale, and it does seem incredible (or credible, if one equates much commercial recording in a studio with compromises leading to mediocrity) that at the start of Decca's stereo era and their project to record the major music-dramas of Wagner, they should gradually have dropped Knappertsbusch from their roster in favour of a conductor with a "marketable" image.

Tullio Serafin
Discography

with valuable assistance from
Angelo Scottini

compiled by John Hunt

Introduction

You only have to survey the list of eminent singers who passed through the hands of Tullio Serafin (1878-1968) to realise his importance in the history of operatic performance. That list of over 150 famous names starts with Battistini and Schaliapin, takes in Muzio and Ponselle on the way, and then concludes with Christoff, Gobbi, Callas, Tebaldi and Sutherland !

Serafin not only conducted but also prepared, with meticulous attention to detail, every aspect of works of every style and period. His vast knowledge of vocal capabilities enabled him, for example, to nurse Maria Callas through the trauma of alternating roles as diverse as Elvira ("I Puritani") and Isolde. Callas herself stated that "Serafin was the first great conductor I worked with. He was my mentor. He knew me before my marriage and between him and me there were always very strong links".

The modern listener, perhaps used to the point-making of some of today's high-powered maestri, may find Serafin's conducting a trifle less colourful. His concern was to relate all the parts of a performance to the vocal line, and to mould the orchestral structure so as to assist in bringing out the opera's expression (meaning) with the utmost clarity.

It was not just Italian music, but key works from the French, German and Russian repertory which he advocated and performed in the pre-war period, second only to Toscanini in his tireless activity on both sides of the Atlantic (Serafin's discography includes tantalising fragments of his conducting at the Metropolitan Opera).

Tullio Serafin's name features prominently in lists of highly recommended operatic recordings even in this CD era. Apart from the half-dozen operas which he conducted for Callas, there are versions of "La Traviata", "Otello", "La Bohème" and "Madama Butterfly" which still appear on many a reviewer's short-list. And the recital discs which he conducted for Maria Callas and Jon Vickers remain object lessons not just by virtue of their vocal contribution.

Salzburger Festspiele 1939

1. AUGUST BIS 8. SEPTEMBER

OPER:

W. A. Mozart:

Die Entführung aus dem Serail

Dirigent: Karl Böhm. Regie: Wolf Völker
Mitwirkend: Irma Beilke, Maria Cebotari, Salvatore Baccaloni, Helge Roswaenge, Richard Sallaba

W. A. Mozart:

Don Giovanni

Dirigent: Clemens Krauß. Regie: Wolf Völker
Mitwirkend: Maria Cebotari, Hilde Konetzni, Elisabeth Rethberg, Anton Dermota, Virgilio Lazzari, Ezio Pinza, Ludwig Weber
In italienischer Sprache

W. A. Mozart:

Le Nozze di Figaro

Dirigent: Hans Knappertsbusch
Regie: Guido Salvini
Mitwirkend: Angelica Cravcenco, M. Reining, Eszther Rethy, Martha Rohs, Giuseppe Nessi, Ezio Pinza, Gino del Signore, Mariano Stabile
In italienischer Sprache

Carl Maria v. Weber:

Der Freischütz

Dirigent: Hans Knappertsbusch
Regie: Heinrich Strohm
Mitwirkend: Tijana Lemnitz, Elisabethe Rutgers, Herbert Alsen, Paul Schöffler, Michael Bohnen, Franz Völker

Giuseppe Verdi:

Falstaff

Dirigent: Tullio Serafin. Regie: Guido Salvini
Mitwirkend: Angelica Cravcenco, Augusta Oltrabella, Franca Somigli, Mita Vasari, Piero Biasini, Mariano Stabile, Gino del Signore, Alfio Tedesco, Virgilio Lazzari
In italienischer Sprache

Richard Strauß:

Der Rosenkavalier

Dirigent: Karl Böhm. Regie: Erich v. Wymetal
Mitwirkend: Hilde Konetzni, Elisabeth Rethberg, Martha Rohs, Eszther Rethy, Fritz Krenn, Helge Roswaenge

Gioachino Rossini:

Il Barbiere di Siviglia

Dirigent: Tullio Serafin. Regie: Guido Salvini
Mitwirkend: Margherita Carosio, Salvatore Baccaloni, Luigi Fort, Ezio Pinza, Mariano Stabile
In italienischer Sprache

SCHAUSPIEL:

William Shakespeare:

Viel Lärm um Nichts

Regie: Heinz Hilpert
Mitwirkend: Eva Lissa, A. Salloker, Ewald Balser, Hans Brausewetter, P. Dahlke, Alfred Neugebauer, Albin Skoda
In der Felsenreitschule

Molière:

Der Bürger als Edelmann

mit der Musik von Richard Strauß
Mitwirkend: Elisabeth Flickenschildt, Eva Lissa, Hans Moser
Regie: Heinz Hilpert

KONZERT:

9 ORCHESTERKONZERTE

der Wiener Philharmoniker

Dirigenten: Karl Böhm, Edwin Fischer, Hans Knappertsbusch, Clemens Krauß, Willem Mengelberg, Richard Strauß, Tullio Serafin

Karten und Auskünfte bei allen Reisebüros oder bei der Direktion der Salzburger Festspiele

Salzburg – Festspielhaus

Bellini

Norma

Milan April and May 1954	La Scala Chorus & Orchestra Callas, Stignani, Filippeschi, Rossi-Lemeni	LP: Columbia 33CX 1179-81 LP: Angel 3517/6037 LP: EMI SLS 5115 LP: EMI EX 29 00663 CD: EMI CDC 747 3048 Excerpts LP: EMI SLS 5057/5104 45: Columbia SEL 1536/SEL 1550/SEL 1586
Rome June 1955	RAI Rome Chorus & Orchestra Callas, Stignani, Del Monaco, Modesti	LP: Opera Vivia JLT 6 LP: Discophilia KS 22-24 LP: Fonit Cetra LAR 28 LP: Replica 2416-8 LP: Melodram MEL 017 CD: Fonit Cetra CDC 4 CD: Hunt CDLSMH 34029 Excerpts LP: Gioielli della lirica GML 03 CD: Di Stefano GDS 1201
Milan September 1960	La Scala Chorus & Orchestra Callas, C.Ludwig, Corelli, Zaccaria	LP: Columbia 33CX 1766-8/SAX 2412-4 LP: Angel 3615 LP: EMI SLS 5186 CD: EMI CMS 763 0002 Excerpts LP: EMI ASD 3908

Norma: Excerpt (O rimembranza)

Buenos Aires June 1949	Teatro Colon Orchestra Callas, Barbieri	LP: HRE Records HRE 373 CD: Melodram MEL 36513

Norma, Overture

London April 1961	Philharmonia	LP: HMV ALP 1898/ASD 466 LP: EMI CFP 110 CD: EMI CDZ 762 6092

I Puritani

Milan March 1953	La Scala Chorus & Orchestra Callas, Di Stefano, Panerai, Rossi-Lemeni	LP: Columbia 33CX 1058-60 LP: Angel 3502 LP: EMI SLS 5140 LP: EMI EX 29 08743 CD: EMI CDC 747 3088 Excerpts LP: EMI SLS 856/SLS 5057/SLS 5104 45: Columbia SEL 1550/SEL 1554 CD: EMI CDM 769 5432
Palermo 1961	Teatro Massimo Chorus & Orchestra Sutherland, G.Raimondi, Zanasi, Mazzoli	LP: Melodram MEL 460

I Puritani: Excerpt (Ah! per sempre)

Naples Date uncertain	San Carlo Orchestra Taddei	LP: Preiser PR 9832 CD: Preiser 90020 Conductor named on CD as Rapalo

La Sonnambula: Excerpts (1. Come per me sereno; 2. Ah non credea; 3. Ah! non giunge!)

Milan June 1955	La Scala Orchestra Callas	LP: Penzance Records 15 LP: Morgan MOR 5401 LP: FWR 644 (1)/FWR 656 (2 and 3) LP: HRE Records HRE 263 (3) LP: EMI ASD 3535 LP: EMI 2C 165 54178-88 CD: EMI CDC 747 2822/CDS 749 4532

La Sonnambula: Excerpts

London February 1960	Covent Garden Orchestra Sutherland Lazzari, Rouleau	CD: Myto MCD 90529

Bizet

Carmen: Excerpt (Je dis que rien ne m'épouvante)

Rome	Rome Opera Orchestra	LP: RCA LSC 2504/SB 2156
1960	Moffo	LP: RCA (Germany) 26.41207

Boito

Mefistofele

Rome	Santa Cecilia	LP: Decca LXT 5487-9/SXL 2094-6
June 1956	Chorus & Orchestra	LP: Decca GOS 591-3
	Tebaldi,	Excerpts
	Del Monaco, Siepi	LP: Decca LXT 5568/SXL 2195

Mefistofele: Excerpts (Sediam sovra quel sasso; Il giardino, cavaliere illustre e saggio; Morte di Margherita; Morte di Faust)

Rome	Santa Cecilia	LP: Decca SET 558
June 1956	Chorus & Orchestra	Morte di Faust
	Tebaldi,	LP: Decca GRV 14
	Di Stefano, Siepi	

Mefistofele: Excerpt (L'altra notte)

Watford	Philharmonia	LP: Columbia 33CX 1231
September 1954	Callas	45: Columbia SEL 1581
		LP: EMI SLS 869
		LP: EMI ASD 3824
		LP: EMI 2C 165 54178-88
		CD: EMI CDC 747 2882/CDS 749 4532

Catalani

La Wally: Excerpt (Ebben? Ne andrò lontana)

Watford	Philharmonia	LP: Columbia 33CX 1231
September 1954	Callas	LP: EMI SLS 869
		LP: EMI ASD 3824
		LP: EMI 2C 165 54178-88
		CD: EMI CDC 747 2882/CDS 749 4532

Cherubini

Medea

Milan September 1957	La Scala Chorus & Orchestra Callas, Scotto, Pirazzini, Picchi, Modesti	LP: Columbia 33CX 1618-20/SAX 2290-2 LP: Ricordi OS 101-3 LP: DG 2728 001 LP: Everest 327 LP: Fonit Cetra DOCL 201 CD: EMI CMS 763 6252 Excerpts LP: Everest 7437

Medea: Excerpt (Dei tuoi figli)

Milan June 1955	La Scala Orchestra Callas	LP: Columbia 33CX 1540 LP: EMI ASD 3535 LP: EMI 2C 165 54178-88 CD: EMI CDC 747 2822/CDS 749 4532

Cilea

Adriana Lecouvreur: Excerpts (Io sono l'umile ancella; Poveri fiori)

Watford September 1954	Philharmonia Callas	LP: Columbia 33CX 1231 45: Columbia SEL 1581 LP: EMI SLS 869 LP: EMI ASD 3824 LP: EMI 2C 165 54178-88 CD: EMI CDC 747 2822/CDS 749 4532

Adriana Lecouvreur: Excerpt (Ecco il monologo)

Naples Date uncertain	San Carlo Orchestra Taddei	LP: Preiser PR 9832 CD: Preiser 90020 Conducted named on CD as Rapalo

L'Arlesiana: Excerpt (E' la solita storia)

Rome 1962	Rome Opera Orchestra Vickers	LP: RCA LM 2741/LSC 2741 LP: RCA RB 6577/SB 6577 LP: RCA LSB 4106

L'Arlesiana: Excerpt (Come due tizzi accesi)

Naples Date uncertain	San Carlo Orchestra Taddei	LP: Preiser PR 9832 CD: Preiser 90020 Conductor named on CD as Rapalo

Cimarosa

Il matrimonio segreto, Overture

Florence 1939	Maggio Musicale Orchestra	78: HMV DB 4326

Delibes

Lakmé: Excerpt (Bell Song)

Watford September 1954	Philharmonia Callas	LP: Columbia 33CX 1231 LP: EMI SLS 5018/SLS 5057 LP: EMI ASD 3824 LP: EMI 2C 165 54178-88 CD: EMI CDC 747 2882/CDS 749 4532
Rome 1960	Rome Opera Orchestra Moffo	LP: RCA LM 2504/LSC 2504/SB 2156 LP: RCA (Germany) 26.41207

Donizetti

Don Pasquale, Overture

London April 1961	Philharmonia	LP: HMV ALP 1898/ASD 466 LP: EMI CFP 110 CD: EMI CDZ 762 6092

L'Elisir d'amore

Milan 1959	La Scala Chorus & Orchestra Carteri, Alva, Taddei, Panerai	LP: Columbia 33CX 1649-50/SAX 2298-9 LP: Angel 6001 LP: EMI Italiana 3C 163 00863-4

La Favorite: Excerpt (Vien, Leonora, a piedi tuoi)

Naples Date uncertain	San Carlo Orchestra Taddei	LP: Preiser PR 9832 CD: Preiser 90020 Conductor named on CD as Rapalo

Linda di Chamounix

Naples 1959	San Carlo Chorus & Orchestra Stella, Barbieri, Valletti, Cappecchi, Modesti, Taddei	LP: Philips A 00423-5 L LP: Philips 6706 005 Excerpts LP: Philips GBL 5519 LP: Preiser PR 9832

Linda di Chamounix, Overture

London April 1961	Philharmonia	LP: HMV ALP 1898/ASD 466 LP: EMI CFP 110 CD: EMI CDZ 762 6092

Lucia di Lammermoor

Florence February 1953	Maggio Musicale Chorus & Orchestra Callas, Di Stefano, Gobbi, Arié	LP: Columbia 33CX 1131-2 LP: Angel 3503/6032 CD: EMI CMS 769 9802 Excerpts 45: Columbia SEL 1522 LP: Columbia 33CX 1385
Rome June 1957	RAI Rome Chorus & Orchestra Callas, Fernandi, Panerai, Modesti	LP: HRE Records HRE 221 LP: Replica RPL 2419-21 Excerpts LP: BJR Records BJR 133 CD: Melodram MEL 26014
London February 1959	Covent Garden Chorus & Orchestra Sutherland, Gibin, Shaw, Rouleau	LP: HRE Records HRE 342 CD: Di Stefano GDS 21017 Excerpts CD: Myto MCD 91545
London March 1959	Philharmonia Chorus & Orchestra Callas, Tagliavini, Cappuccilli, Ladysz	LP: Columbia 33CX 1723-4/SAX 2316-7 LP: EMI SLS 5086 LP: EMI EX 29 08763 CD: EMI CDS 747 4408

Flotow

Martha: Excerpt (M'apparì)

Rome	Rome Opera	LP: RCA LM 2741/LSC 2741
1962	Orchestra	LP: RCA RB 6577/SB 6577
	Vickers	LP: RCA LSB 4106

Giordano

Andrea Chenier: Excerpt (La mamma morta)

Watford	Philharmonia	LP: Columbia 33CX 1231
September 1954	Callas	LP: EMI SLS 869
		LP: EMI ASD 3824
		LP: EMI 2C 165 54178-88
		CD: EMI CDC 747 2882/CDS 749 4532

Andrea Chenier: Excerpt (Come un bel dì di maggio)

Rome	Rome Opera	LP: RCA LM 2741/LSC 2741
1962	Orchestra	LP: RCA RB 6577/SB 6577
	Vickers	LP: RCA LSB 4106

Andrea Chenier: Excerpt (Un dì all' azzurro spazio)

Rome	Rome Opera	LP: RCA LM 2741/LSC 2741
1962	Orchestra	LP: RCA RB 6577/SB 6577
	Vickers	LP: RCA LSB 4106
Turin	Turin SO	LP: Morgan MOR 6301
1963	Di Stefano	

Fedora, Act 2 Intermezzo

Rome	Santa Cecilia	78: HMV (Italy) S 10539
1942	Orchestra	

Gounod

Faust: Excerpt (Ah, je ris!)

Rome	Rome Opera	LP: RCA LM 2504/LSC 2504/SB 2156
1960	Orchestra	LP: RCA (Germany) 26.41207
	Moffo	

Faust: Excerpt (Vous qui faites l'endormie)

Milan	Milan SO	LP: HMV ALP 1074
1952	Rossi-Lemeni	LP: EMI Italiana 3C 053 03249

Leoncavallo

I Pagliacci

Milan	La Scala	LP: Columbia 33CX 1211-2
June 1954	Chorus & Orchestra	LP: Angel 3527/3528
	Callas, Di Stefano,	LP: EMI SLS 819
	Monti, Gobbi,	CD: EMI CDC 747 9818
	Panerai	Excerpt
		LP: EMI SLS 5104

I Pagliacci: Excerpts (Vesti la giubba; No! Pagliaccio non son)

Rome	Rome Opera	LP: RCA LM 2741/LSC 2741
1962	Orchestra	LP: RCA RB 6577/SB 6577
	Vickers	LP: RCA LSB 4106

Mascagni

L'Amico Fritz, Intermezzo

London April 1961	Philharmonia	LP: HMV ALP 1898/ASD 466 LP: EMI CFP 110

Cavalleria Rusticana

Milan August 1953	La Scala Chorus & Orchestra Callas, Canali, Di Stefano, Panerai	LP: Columbia 33CX 1182-1 LP: Angel 3509/3528 LP: EMI SLS 819 CD: EMI CDC 747 9818 Excerpts 45: Columbia SEL 1549 LP: EMI SLS 856
Rome 1960	Santa Cecilia Chorus & Orchestra Simionato, Satre, Del Monaco, MacNeil	LP: Decca LXT 5613-5/LXT 5643-4 LP: Decca SXL 2253-5/SXL 2281-2 LP: Decca GOS 588-9 Excerpts LP: Decca LXT 6012/SXL 6012 Intermezzo LP: Decca VIV 19

Isabeau

San Remo January 1962	San Remo SO Pobbe, Ferraro Rola	LP: Fonit Cetra LPC 55034 LP: Ed Smith EJS 430 Excerpts LP: Fonit Cetra LPS 24 /LPC 55078

Meyerbeer

Le pardon de Ploërmel: Excerpt (Ombre légère)

Watford September 1954	Philharmonia Callas Sung in Italian	LP: Columbia 33CX 1231 LP: EMI ASD 3824 LP: EMI SLS 5018/SLS 5057 LP: EMI 2C 165 54178-88 CD: EMI CDC 747 2882/CDS 749 4532
Rome 1960	Rome Opera Orchestra Moffo Sung in Italian	LP: RCA LM 2504/LSC 2504/SB 2156 LP: RCA (Germany) 26.41207

Les Huguenots

Milan June 1956	RAI Milan Chorus & Orchestra Pastori, Cavalieri, Lauri-Volpi, Tozzi, Zaccaria, Taddei	LP: Replica RPL 2401-3

ROYAL OPERA HOUSE
COVENT GARDEN

LA SONNAMBULA

Monday, 31st October, 1960

Monday, 31st October, 1960

The 175th performance at the Royal Opera House of

LA SONNAMBULA

OPERA IN TWO ACTS

Music by Vincenzo Bellini

(Property of G. Ricordi & Co.)

Libretto by Felice Romani

Scenery and costumes by Filippo Sanjust

Conductor — TULLIO SERAFIN

Producer — ENRICO MEDIOLI

CHARACTERS IN ORDER OF APPEARANCE

LISA, proprietress of the village inn	JENIFER EDDY
ALESSIO, a villager	DAVID KELLY
AMINA, Teresa's foster-daughter	JOAN SUTHERLAND
TERESA, proprietress of the mill	NOREEN BERRY
NOTARY	ROBERT BOWMAN
ELVINO, a young farmer	AGOSTINO LAZZARI
COUNT RODOLFO, lord of the Castle	DAVID WARD

Mozart

Don Giovanni: Excerpts

New York December 1932	Metropolitan Opera Chorus & Orchestra Ponselle, Müller, Fleischer, Schipa, Pinza, Lazzari	LP: Ed Smith UORC 2162

Pietri

Maristella: Excerpt (Io conosco un giardino)

Turin 1963	Turin SO Di Stefano	LP: Morgan MOR 6301

Ponchielli

La Gioconda: Excerpt (Cielo e mar)

Rome 1962	Rome Opera Orchestra Vickers	LP: RCA LM 2741/LSC 2741 LP: RCA RB 6577/SB 6577 LP: RCA LSB 4106

Puccini

La Bohème

Rome July 1959	Santa Cecilia Chorus & Orchestra Tebaldi, D'Angelo, Bergonzi, Siepi, Bastianini, Corena	LP: Decca LXT 5542-3/SXL 2170-1 LP: Decca D5 D24 LP: Decca 411 8681 CD: Decca 411 8682 CD: Decca 425 5342 <u>Excerpts</u> LP: Decca LXT 5608/SXL 2248 LP: Decca BR 3061 LP: Decca JB 11/GRV 17 CD: Decca 421 3012/430 8412

La Bohème: Excerpt (Sì, mi chiamano Mimì)

Watford September 1954	Philharmonia Callas	LP: Columbia 33CX 1204 45: Columbia SEL 1546 LP: EMI ALP 3799 LP: EMI 2C 165 54178-88 CD: EMI CDC 747 9662/CDS 749 4532
Rome 1960	Rome Opera Orchestra Moffo	LP: RCA LM 2504/LSC 2504 LP: RCA (Germany) 26.41207 LP: RCA LSB 4106

La Bohème: Excerpt (Donde lieta uscì)

Watford September 1954	Philharmonia Callas	LP: Columbia 33CX 1204 LP: EMI SLS 5057 LP: EMI ALP 3799 LP: EMI 2C 165 54178-88 CD: EMI CDC 747 9662/CDS 749 4532

Madama Butterfly

Rome
July 1958

Santa Cecilia
Chorus & Orchestra
Tebaldi, Cossotto,
Bergonzi, Sordello

LP: Decca LXT 5468-70/SXL 2054-6
LP: Decca D4 D3
LP: Decca 411 6341
CD: Decca 411 6432
CD: Decca 425 5312
Excerpts
LP: Decca LXT 5575/SXL 2202
LP: Decca BR 3023/SWL 8004
45: Decca CEP 619
LP: Decca JB 32
CD: Decca 417 7332
CD: Decca 421 3122/421 8732
CD: Decca 430 8412

Madama Butterfly: Excerpt (Un bel dì)

Watford
September 1954

Philharmonia
Callas

LP: Columbia 33CX 1204
45: Columbia SEL 1546
LP: EMI ALP 3799
LP: EMI 2C 165 54178-88
CD: EMI CDC 747 9662/CDS 749 4532

Madama Butterfly: Excerpt (Con onor muore)

Watford
September 1954

Philharmonia
Callas

LP: Columbia 33CX 1204
LP: EMI SLS 5057
LP: EMI ALP 3799
LP: EMI 2C 165 54178-88
CD: EMI CDC 747 9662/CDS 749 4532

Gianni Schicchi: Excerpt (O mio babbino caro)

Watford
September 1954

Philharmonia
Callas

LP: Columbia 33CX 1204
45: Columbia SEL 1546
LP: EMI SLS 5104
LP: EMI ALP 3799
LP: EMI 2C 165 54178-88
CD: EMI CDC 747 9662/CDS 749 4532

Manon Lescaut

Milan
July 1957

La Scala
Chorus & Orchestra
Callas, Di Stefano,
Calabrese

LP: Columbia 33CX 1583-5
LP: Angel 3564/6089
LP: EMI RLS 737
LP: EMI EX 29 00413
CD: EMI CDC 747 3938
Excerpts
LP: EMI SLS 856/SLS 5104
CD: EMI CDM 769 5423

Manon Lescaut: Excerpt (In quelle trine morbide)

Watford	Philharmonia	LP: Columbia 33CX 1204
September 1954	Callas	45: Columbia SEL 1546
		LP: EMI ALP 3799
		LP: EMI 2C 165 54178-88
		CD: EMI CDC 747 9662/CDS 749 4532

Manon Lescaut: Excerpt (Sola perduta abandonata)

Watford	Philharmonia	LP: Columbia 33CX 1204
September 1954	Callas	LP: EMI SLS 5057
		LP: EMI ALP 3799
		LP: EMI 2C 165 54178-88
		CD: EMI CDC 747 9662/CDS 749 4532

Manon Lescaut, Intermezzo

Rome	Santa Cecilia	LP: HMV (Italy) S 10517
1942	Orchestra	

Suor Angelica

Rome	Rome Opera	LP: HMV ALP 1577
1958	Orchestra	LP: EMI SLS 5066
	De Los Angeles	
	Barbieri	

Suor Angelica: Excerpt (Senza mamma)

Watford	Philharmonia	LP: Columbia 33CX 1204
September 1954	Callas	LP: EMI ALP 3799
		LP: EMI 2C 165 54178-88
		CD: EMI CDC 747 9662/CDS 749 4532

Tosca

Naples	San Carlo	LP: Philips A 00463-4 L
1957	Chorus & Orchestra	LP: Philips 6720 007
	Stella, Poggi,	Excerpts
	Taddei	LP: Philips 695 032 KL
		LP: Preiser PR 9832

Tosca: Excerpt (Recondita armonia)

Rome	Rome Opera	LP: RCA LM 2741/LSC 2741
1962	Orchestra	LP: RCA RB 6577/SB 6577
	Vickers	LP: RCA LSB 4106

Turandot

Milan July 1957	La Scala Chorus & Orchestra Callas, Fernandi, Schwarzkopf, Zaccaria	LP: Columbia 33CX 1555-7 LP: Angel 3571 LP: EMI RLS 741 CD: EMI CDC 747 9718 <u>Excerpts</u> LP: Columbia 33CX 1792 LP: EMI SLS 5104 CD: EMI CDM 763 6572/CMS 763 7902

Turandot: Excerpt (In questa reggia)

Watford September 1954	Philharmonia Callas	LP: Columbia 33CX 1204 45: Columbia SEL 1533 LP: EMI SLS 5107 LP: EMI ALP 3799 LP: EMI 2C 165 54178-88 CD: EMI CDC 747 9662/CDS 749 4532

Turandot: Excerpts (Signore ascolta; Tu che di gel sei cinta)

Watford September 1954	Philharmonia Callas	LP: Columbia 33CX 1204 45: Columbia SEL 1533 LP: EMI ALP 3799 LP: EMI 2C 165 54178-88 CD: EMI CDC 747 9662/CDS 749 4532
Rome 1960	Rome Opera Orchestra Moffo	LP: RCA LM 2504/LSC 2504/SB 2156 LP: RCA (Germany) 26.41207

Turandot: Excerpt (In questa reggia....to end Act 2)

Buenos Aires May 1949	Teatro Colon Chorus & Orchestra Callas, Del Monaco	LP: Rodolphe RP 22413-5 CD: Rodolphe RPC 22413-5

Turandot: Fragments from Act 3

Buenos Aires May 1949	Teatro Colon Chorus & Orchestra Callas, Del Monaco	LP: Legendary LR 111/LR 156

Robbiani

Anna Karenina, Prelude and "Gli amanti"

Rome 1942	Rome SO	78: HMV (Italy) S 10517

Rossini

Armida

Florence April 1952	Maggio Musicale Chorus & Orchestra Callas, F.Albanese, G.Raimondi, Filippeschi, Salvarezza, Ziliani	LP: FWR 657 LP: Penzance 24 LP: Morgan MOR 5202 LP: Hope Records 224 LP: CLS Records MDP 016 LP: Fonit Cetra LO 39 LP: CLS Records CLS 22030 LP: Melodram MEL 463 CD: Melodram MEL 26024 Excerpts LP: FWR 656 LP: Legendary LR 150 CD: Foyer CDS 15001

Il Barbiere di Siviglia

Milan 1951	Milan SO De Los Angeles, Monti, Bechi, Rossi-Lemeni	LP: HMV ALP 1022-4 LP: HMV (Italy) QALP 10001-3 Excerpts 45: HMV 7ER 5038

Il Barbiere di Siviglia: Excerpt (Una voce poco fa)

Watford September 1954	Philharmonia Callas	LP: Columbia 33CX 1231 LP: EMI SLS 5018/SLS 5104 LP: EMI ASD 3824 LP: EMI 2C 165 54178-88 CD: EMI CDC 747 2882/CDS 749 4532
Turin 1963	Turin SO Simionato	LP: Morgan MOR 6301

Il Barbiere di Siviglia, Overture

Florence 1950	Maggio Musicale Orchestra	78: HMV C 4136 45: RCA ERAB 1
Rome 1964	Rome Opera Orchestra	LP: DG LPEM 19 395/SLPEM 136 395 LP: DG 135 015 LP: DG 2535 365/2548 171

Il Barbiere di Siviglia, Storm music

Rome 1964	Rome Opera Orchestra	LP: DG LPEM 19 395/SLPEM 136 395 LP: DG 135 015 LP: DG 2535 365/2548 171

La Cenerentola, Overture

London April 1961	Philharmonia	LP: HMV ALP 1898/ASD 466 LP: EMI CFP 110 CD: EMI CDZ 762 6092/CDZ 767 2552

La donna del lago

Florence May 1958	Maggio Musicale Chorus & Orchestra Carteri, Companeez, Valletti, Washington	LP: Ed Smith EJS 253 LP: CLS Records ARPCL 32038

La gazza ladra, Overture

Rome 1964	Rome Opera Orchestra	LP: DG LPEM 19 395/SLPEM 136 395 LP: DG 2535 365/2548 171

William Tell, Overture

Rome 1964	Rome Opera Orchestra	LP: DG LPEM 19 395/SLPEM 136 395 LP: DG 2535 365/2548 171

William Tell: Excerpts (1. Piccola marcia dei pastori e danza; 2. Passo a sei)

Rome 1942	Santa Cecilia Orchestra	78: HMV (Italy) S 10509 (1) 78: HMV (Italy) S 10519 (2)

William Tell: Excerpt (Sois immobile)

Milan 1952	Milan SO Rossi-Lemeni Sung in Italian	LP: HMV ALP 1074

L'Italiana in Algeri, Overture

Rome 1942	Santa Cecilia Orchestra	78: HMV C 4012 78: HMV (Italy) S 10519

Mosè

Naples 1957	San Carlo Chorus & Orchestra Danieli, Filippeschi, Rossi-Lemeni, Taddei	LP: Philips A 00393-5 LP: Philips 6700 013 Excerpts LP: Philips GBL 5519

La scala di seta, Overture

Rome 1964	Rome Opera Orchestra	LP: DG LPEM 19 395/SLPEM 136 395 LP: DG 2535 365/2548 171

Semiramide, Overture

Rome	Rome Opera	LP: DG LPEM 19 395/SLPEM 136 395
1964	Orchestra	LP: DG 2535 365/2548 171

Semiramide: Excerpt (Bel raggio lusinghier)

Rome	Rome Opera	LP: RCA LM 2504/LSC 2504/SB 2156
1960	Orchestra	LP: RCA (Germany) 26.41207
	Moffo	

Tancredi: Excerpt (Di tanti palpiti)

Turin	Turin SO	LP: Morgan MOR 6301
1963	Simionato	

La boutique fantasque, arr. Respighi: Excerpt

Rome	Santa Cecilia	78: HMV (Italy) S 10525
1942	Orchestra	

La boutique fantasque, arr. Respighi: Selection

Rome	Santa Cecilia	78: HMV C 3910-12
1949	Orchestra	

Samson et Dalila, Bacchanale

Florence	Maggio Musicale	45: RCA ERAB 1
1950	Orchestra	

Spontini

La Vestale: Excerpts (Tu che invoco; O nume tutelar; Caro oggetto)

Milan	La Scala	LP: Columbia 33CX 1540
June 1955	Orchestra	LP: EMI ASD 3535
	Callas	LP: EMI 2C 165 45178-88
		CD: EMI CDC 747 2822/CDS 749 4532

Deems Taylor

Peter Ibbetson

New York	Metropolitan Opera	LP: Ed Smith UORC 143
December 1933	Chorus & Orchestra	Excerpts (dated March 1934)
	Bori, Swarthout,	LP: Ed Smith EJS 187
	Johnson, Tibbett	

"HIS MASTER'S VOICE"
RECORD LIBRARY SERIES

No. 444

UN BALLO IN MASCHERA
(The Masked Ball)
(VERDI)

ORIGINAL ITALIAN TEXT
with the
ENGLISH SINGING VERSION

Two Shillings and Sixpence

GREATEST ARTISTS  FINEST RECORDING

The Hallmark of Quality

THE GRAMOPHONE COMPANY, LTD., HAYES, MIDDLESEX

The Full Glory of Italian Opera

BROUGHT TO LIFE ON THIS MAGNIFICENT LONG PLAYING RECORDING OF

Donizetti's
Lucia di Lammermoor

Lucia - **MARIA MENEGHINI CALLAS**
Edgardo - **GIUSEPPE DI STEFANO**
Enrico Asthon - **TITO GOBBI**
Raimondo - RAFFAELE ARIE
Arturo - VALIANO NATALI
Alisa - ANNA MARIA CANALI
Normanno - GINO SARRI

ORCHESTRA AND CHORUS OF "MAGGIO MUSICALE FIORENTINO"
Chorus Master: ANDREA MOROSINI
conducted by **TULLIO SERAFIN**
33CX1131-2

AVAILABLE MID-MARCH

COLUMBIA

33⅓ R.P.M. LONG PLAYING RECORDS

COLUMBIA GRAPHOPHONE COMPANY LIMITED, RECORD DIVISION, 8-11 GREAT CASTLE STREET, LONDON, W.1.

Verdi

Aida

Rome July 1946	Rome Opera Chorus & Orchestra Caniglia, Stignani, Gigli, Bechi, Pasero	78: HMV DB 6392-6411/9131-9150 auto LP: HMV (Italy) QALP 10010-3 LP: World Records SH 153-5 LP: EMI Italiana 3C 153 00686-8 CD: EMI CHS 763 3312 <u>Excerpts</u> 45: HMV 7ER 5037 LP: EMI EX 29 10753 CD: EMI CDH 761 0522
Naples March 1953	San Carlo Chorus & Orchestra Tebaldi, Stignani, Penno, Savarese, Neri	LP: Edizione lirica EL 006
Milan August 1955	La Scala Chorus & Orchestra Callas, Barbieri, Tucker, Gobbi, Zaccaria	LP: Columbia 33CX 1318-20 LP: Angel 3525 LP: EMI SLS 5108 CD: EMI CDS 749 0308 <u>Excerpts</u> LP: Columbia 33CX 1376/33CX 1681 LP: EMI SLS 5104

Aida, Prelude

London February 1959	Philharmonia	LP: Columbia 33CX 1684/SAX 2324 LP: EMI MFP 2059 CD: EMI CDZ 762 6092

Aroldo

Florence 1953	Maggio Musicale Chorus & Orchestra Stella, Penno, Protti	CD: Melodram MEL 27014

Un Ballo in maschera

Rome June 1943	Rome Opera Chorus & Orchestra Caniglia, Barbieri, Gigli, Bechi	78: HMV DB 9075-9091 LP: HMV (Italy) QALP 10057-8 LP: World Records SH 131-2 LP: EMI Italiana 3C 153 17086-7 LP: Angel 6026 CD: EMI CHS 769 9932 <u>Excerpts</u> CD: EMI CDH 761 0522

Un Ballo in maschera: Excerpt (Eri tu)

Naples Date uncertain	San Carlo Orchestra Taddei	LP: Preiser PR 9832 CD: Preiser 90020 <u>Conductor on CD named as Rapalo</u>

Don Carlo: Excerpt (Io t' ho perduta)

Rome	Rome Opera	LP: RCA LM 2741/LSC 2741
1962	Orchestra	LP: RCA RB 6577/SB 6577
	Vickers	LP: RCA LSB 4106

Don Carlo: Excerpt (O Carlo, ascolta!)

Naples	San Carlo Orchestra	LP: Preiser PR 9832
Date uncertain	Taddei	CD: Preiser 90020
		Conductor on CD named as Rapalo

I Due Foscari

Venice	La Fenice	LP: Fonit Cetra LO 67
December 1957	Chorus & Orchestra	
	Gencer, Picchi,	
	Guelfi	

Ernani: Excerpt (Noi fratelli in tal momento)

| Milan | La Scala | LP: Columbia 33CX 1376 |
| June 1955 | Chorus & Orchestra | 45: Columbia SEL 1571 |

Falstaff

Chicago	Chicago Opera	LP: HRE Records HRE 282
October 1958	Chorus & Orchestra	
	Tebaldi, Moffo,	
	Simionato, Canali,	
	Gobbi, Misciano,	
	MacNeil	

Falstaff: Excerpts

Milan	RAI Milan	LP: Gioielli della lirica GML 46
November 1958	Chorus & Orchestra	
	Carteri, Barbieri,	
	Canali, Moffo, Alva,	
	Taddei, Colombo	

La Forza del destino

Milan	La Scala	LP: Columbia 33CX 1258-60
August 1954	Chorus & Orchestra	LP: Angel 3531/6088
	Callas, Nicolai,	LP: EMI SLS 5120
	Tucker, Tagliabue,	CD: EMI CDC 747 5818
	Rossi-Lemeni	Excerpts
		LP: Columbia 33CX 1502/33CX 1681
		LP: EMI SLS 5104
		Overture
		45: Columbia SEL 1536

La Forza del destino, Overture

London	RPO	LP: Columbia 33CX 1684/SAX 2324
February 1959		LP: EMI MFP 2059
		CD: EMI CDZ 762 6092

Giovanna d'Arco, Overture

London	Philharmonia	LP: Columbia 33CX 1684/SAX 2324
February 1959		LP: EMI MFP 2059

I Lombardi: Excerpts (1. O Signore, del tetto natio; 2. Gerusalemma)

Milan	La Scala	LP: Columbia 33CX 1376
June 1955	Chorus & Orchestra	45: Columbia SEL 1571 (1)

Nabucco, Overture

London	Philharmonia	LP: Columbia 33CX 1684/SAX 2324
February 1959		LP: EMI MFP 2059
		CD: EMI CDZ 762 6092

Nabucco: Excerpt (Và, pensiero)

Milan	La Scala	LP: Columbia 33CX 1376
June 1955	Chorus & Orchestra	45: Columbia SEL 1571

Otello

Rome	Rome Opera	LP: RCA LD 6155/LDS 6155
1960	Chorus & Orchestra	LP: RCA SER 5646-8
	Rysanek, Vickers,	LP: RCA AGL3-1969
	Gobbi	LP: RCA VL 43546
		CD: RCA GD 81969
		Excerpts
		LP: RCA LM 2741/LSC 2741
		LP: RCA RB 6577/SB 6577
		LP: RCA GL 42167
Rome	Rome Opera	LP: Legendary LR 177
December 1962	Chorus & Orchestra	
	Zeani, McCracken,	
	Gobbi	

Otello, Act 1

Turin	EIAR Chorus and	LP: Ed Smith UORC 132
1939	Orchestra	
	Sanizo, Merli,	
	De Francheschi	

Otello: Excerpt (Fuoco di gioia)

Milan	La Scala	LP: Columbia 33CX 1376
June 1955	Chorus & Orchestra	45: Columbia SEL 1571

Rigoletto

Rome 1946	Rome Opera Chorus & Orchestra Pagliughi, Gobbi, Filippeschi	VHS Video: Historic Opera SL 1056 LP (soundtrack): MDP Records MDP 003 <u>An actress mimes to Pagliughi' voice in the film version</u>
Milan September 1955	La Scala Chorus & Orchestra Callas, Gobbi, Di Stefano, Zaccaria	LP: Columbia 33CX 1324-6 LP: Angel 3537 LP: EMI SLS 5018 LP: EMI EX 29 09283 CD: EMI CDS 747 4698 Excerpts LP: Columbia 33CX 1582/33CX 1681 45: Columbia SEL 1656/SEL 1659/SEL 1676 LP: EMI SLS 856/SLS 5057/SLS 5104 CD: EMI CDM 769 5432

La Traviata

Milan September 1955	La Scala Stella, Gobbi, Di Stefano	LP: Columbia 33CX 1555-7 Excerpts LP: Columbia 33CX 1376 45: Columbia SEL 1566 <u>Preludes to Acts 1 and 3 were also recorded in June 1955 as well as September sessions</u>
Florence May 1956	Maggio Musicale Chorus & Orchestra Tebaldi, Savarese, Filacuridi	LP: Fonit Cetra DOC 73
Rome June and October 1959	Rome Opera Chorus & Orchestra De Los Angeles, Del Monte, Sereni	LP: HMV ALP 1780-2/ASD 359-61 LP: Angel 3628 LP: EMI SLS 5097 CD: EMI CDS 749 5782

La Traviata, Preludes Acts 1 and 3

London February 1959	RPO	LP: Columbia 33CX 1864/SAX 2324 LP: EMI MFP 2059 CD: EMI CDZ 762 6092

Il Trovatore

Naples January 1951	San Carlo Chorus & Orchestra Callas, Elmo, Lauri-Volpi, Silveri, Tajo	LP: Ed Smith UORC 304 LP: FWR 654 LP: Fonit Cetra LO 29 LP: Discocorp RR 473 CD: Melodram MEL 26001 Excerpts LP: HRE Records HRE 219 LP: Anna Records 1040
Milan 1962	La Scala Chorus & Orchestra Stella, Cossotto, Bergonzi, Vinco, Bastianini	LP: DG LPM 18 835-7/SLPM 138 835-7 LP: DG 2709 011/2740 197 LP: DG 2728 008 CD: Excerpts LP: DG LPEM 19 277/SLPEM 136 277 LP: DG 2537 015 LP: DG 415 4451

Il Trovatore: Excerpt (Ah sì ben mio)

Rome 1962	Rome Opera Orchestra Vickers	LP: RCA LM 2741/LSC 2741 LP: RCA RB 6577/SB 6577 LP: RCA LSB 4106

Il Trovatore: Excerpts (Vedi le fosche; Or co' dadi)

Milan June 1955	La Scala Chorus & Orchestra	LP: Columbia 33CX 1376 45: Columbia SEL 1566

Les Vêpres siciliennes

Palermo January 1957	Teatro Massimo Chorus & Orchestra Stella, Filippeschi, Taddei, Ladysz Sung in Italian	LP: HRE Records HRE 346 Excerpts LP: Ed Smith UORC 338 Excerpts dated 1955

Les Vêpres siciliennes, Overture

London February 1959	RPO	LP: Columbia 33CX 1684/SAX 2324 LP: EMI MFP 2059 CD: EMI CDZ 762 6092

Les Vêpres siciliennes: Excerpt (Mercè, dilette amiche)

Watford September 1954	Philharmonia Callas Sung in Italian	LP: Columbia 33CX 1231 LP: EMI SLS 5018/SLS 5057 LP: EMI ASD 3824 LP: EMI 2C 165 54178-88 CD: EMI CDC 747 2882/CDS 749 4532

Les Vêpres siciliennes: Excerpt (In braccio alle dovizie)

Naples Date uncertain	San Carlo Orchestra Taddei Sung in Italian	LP: Preiser PR 9832 CD: Preiser 90020 Conductor on CD named as Rapolo

Requiem

Rome 1939	Rome Opera Chorus & Orchestra Caniglia, Stignani, Gigli, Pinza	78: HMV DB 6210-6219/8984-8993 auto LP: World Records SH 103-4 LP: EMI Italiana 3C 153 00671-2 LP: Angel 6050 CD: EMI CDH 763 3412 CD: Nuova Era HMT 90001
Rome 1959	Rome Opera Chorus & Orchestra Vartenissian, Cossotto, Fernandi, Christoff	LP: HMV ALP 1775-6/ASD 353-4 LP: EMI Italiana 3C 153 01461-2 LP: EMI SXDW 3055 LP: Electrola 1C 137 01461-2

Wolf-Ferrari

Il Segreto di Susanna, Overture

London April 1961	Philharmonia	LP: HMV ALP 1898/ASD 466 LP: EMI CFP 110

Clemens Krauss
Discography

compiled by John Hunt

CLEMENS KRAUSS

KRAUSS, PERHAPS the greatest of all Strauss conductors, was born in Vienna in March 1893, and died in Mexico City in May 1954. When only ten, he joined the choir of the Imperial Chapel in Vienna, and later attended the Conservatory of his native city.

While still in his teens he became choral conductor and coach at Brunn, where he conducted his first opera, *Zar und Zimmermann*, in January 1913. Then followed seasons at Stettin and Graz, where he was heard by Franz Schalk, who was then the chief conductor at the Vienna Opera; Schalk invited Krauss back to Vienna to become his assistant. From 1924 to 1929 he was director of the Frankfurt Opera; in 1929 he was invited back to Vienna, this time as Director of the State Opera, where until 1935 he worked to achieve a high standard in production and ensemble.

Then came two years at the Berlin State Opera, and from 1937 until 1943 a glorious period in Munich, where many great performances of Strauss' works were given. Krauss' leading singers were faithful to him, and they followed him from Vienna to Berlin, and Berlin to Munich.

As a close friend of Strauss, Krauss conducted the first performances of a number of his works: *Arabella* at Dresden in 1933, *Friedenstag* in Munich in 1938, *Capriccio* (for which he collaborated in writing the libretto) in Munich, 1942, and *Die Liebe der Danae* in Salzburg ten years later.

Krauss first appeared in London at Covent Garden in 1934, conducting *Arabella* and *Schwanda*; then he returned in 1947 with the Vienna State Opera, and conducted a memorable performance of *Salome* with Welitsch. He returned to Covent Garden on a number of occasions in recent years to conduct the regular company in performances of *Fidelio*, *Tristan*, and *Meistersinger*; and was also heard at the Stoll Theatre in 1949, when he conducted *Falstaff* and *Tosca*.

Krauss conducted all over Europe, at Salzburg and Bayreuth, and in South America. His untimely death in 1954 came as a heavy blow to the world of opera.

From the Decca Book of Opera

Auber

Fra Diavolo, Overture

Vienna   VPO   78: HMV C 1785
1930

Beethoven

Symphony No 2

Vienna   VPO   78: HMV C 2030-3
1930   78: Victor M 131

Piano Concerto No 1

Vienna   VPO   Decca unpublished
April 1951   Backhaus

Piano Concerto No 2

Vienna   VPO   LP: Decca LX 3083
April 1951   Backhaus   LP: Decca ACL 148
                                    LP: Decca ECM 524/ECS 524
                                    LP: Telefunken 648.057

Piano Concerto No 4

Vienna   VPO   78: Decca AKX 28542-5
May 1951   Backhaus   LP: Decca LXT 2629
                                    LP: Decca ACL 36
                                    LP: Turnabout THS 65004-6
                                    LP: Telefunken 648.057/641.745
                                    CD: Decca 425 9622

Piano Concerto No 5 "Emperor"

Vienna   VPO   LP: Decca LXT 2839/LXT 5355
May 1953   Backhaus   LP: Decca ACL 98
                                    LP: Turnabout THS 65004-6
                                    LP: Telefunken 648.057
                                    CD: Decca 425 9622

Choral Fantasy

Vienna	VSO	LP: Vox PL 6480
1950	Akademiechor	CD: Tuxedo TUXCD 9001
	Wührer	

Cantata on the Death of Joseph II

Vienna	VSO	LP: Vox PL 6820
1950	Kammerchor	LP: Turnabout TV 34399
	Steingruber	LP: Lyrichord LL 107
	Poell	

Missa Solemnis

Vienna	VPO	CD: Melodram CDM 28036
November 1940	Vienna Opera	CD: DG 435 3292/435 3212
	Concert Choir	
	Eipperle, Willer,	
	Patzak, Hann	

Fidelio, Overture

London	LPO	Decca unpublished
January 1949		

Vienna	VPO	LP: Decca LW 5165
March 1954		LP: Decca ECM 558/ECS 558
		LP: Telefunken ND 602

Leonore No 1, Overture

Vienna	VPO	LP: Decca LW 5164
March 1954		LP: Decca ECM 558/ECS 558
		LP: Telefunken ND 602

Leonore No 2, Overture

Vienna	VPO	LP: Decca LW 5164
March 1954		LP: Decca ACL 116
		LP: Decca ECM 558/ECS 558
		LP: Telefunken ND 602

Leonore No 3, Overture

Vienna	VPO	LP: Decca LW 5165
March 1954		

Another version of Leonore 3 (also VPO March 1954) exists in the Clemens-Krauss-Archiv, Vienna

Brahms

Symphony No 3

Vienna 1930	VPO	78: HMV C 2026-9/7129-32 suto

Haydn Variations (St Antoni Chorale)

London October 1947	LSO	78: Decca K 2107-8

Academic Festival Overture

London October 1947	LSO	78: Decca K 1726

Alto Rhapsody

London December 1947	LPO Chorus Ferrier	78: Decca K 1847-8 LP: Decca LXT 2850 LP: Decca ACL 306 45: Decca CEP 569 LP: Telefunken 648.048 LP: Decca AKF 1-7 CD: Decca 421 2992/433 4772/433 8022 CD: Gala GL 307

Zigeunerlieder

Vienna June 1940	Krauss, piano Ursuleac	LP: Acanta DE 23122-3

Hungarian Dances Nos 1 in G minor and 3 in F

Vienna Date uncertain	VPO	78: HMV B 3145
London January 1949	LPO	78: Decca F 9301 LP: Decca LK 4007

Bruckner

Scherzo (Symphony No 4 "Romantic")

Vienna 1930	VPO	78: HMV C 1789 78: Electrola EH 392

Dukas

L'apprenti sorcier

Vienna   VPO   CD: DG 435 3292/435 3212
January 1953

Another version of this work (with Bamberg SO 1953) exists in the Clemens-Krauss-Archiv, Vienna

Dvorak

Slavonic Dances op 46, nos 3, 5 and 8

London   LPO   78: Decca K 2233 (Nos 5 and 8)
January 1949   78: Decca K 2822 (No 3)
                                   LP: Decca LK 4007

Enescu

Rumanian Rhapsody No 1

Vienna   VPO   78: Telefunken E 3836-7
1949

Another version of this work (VPO March 1952) exists in the Clemens-Krauss-Archiv, Vienna

Falla

El sombrero de 3 picos: 3 Dances (Los vecinos; Danza del molinero; Danza finale)

Vienna   VPO   78: Telefunken SK 3329-30
1942   LP: Telefunken LGM 65022
                                   LP: Capitol L 8096

PROGRAMM-BUCH

SAISON 1922/23

Außerordentliches Konzert

VEREIN WIENER TONKÜNSTLER-ORCHESTER

Donnerstag, den 19. April 1923, abends 7 Uhr
im Großen Musikvereins-Saale

AUSSERORDENTLICHES KONZERT

Dirigent:

CLEMENS KRAUSS
(Staatsoper)

Mitwirkend:

Das Wiener Sinfonie-Orchester.

PROGRAMM:

BEETHOVEN .... Ouverture „Leonore III."
BRUCKNER ..... VIII. Sinfonie C-moll.

Voranzeige:

Donnerstag, den 10. Mai 1923, abends 7 Uhr
im Großen Musikvereins-Saale

Außerordentliches Konzert
Dirigent: **Prof. Hans Knappertsbusch**
Bayr. Generalmusikdirektor, Staatsoper München.

PROGRAMM:

WAGNER................Vorspiel zu „Die Meistersinger von Nürnberg"
BRAHMS.................Variationen über ein Thema von Haydn.
TSCHAIKOWSKY ....VI. Sinfonie, H-moll (Pathétique).

Karten von K 30.000 bis K 4.000 in der Vereinskanzlei I., Canovagasse 4 (Halbstock) von 10—1 Uhr und von ¼5—¼7 Uhr (Samstag Nachmittag geschlossen) u. zw. für die Mitglieder der Gesellschaft der Musikfreunde am 20. und 21. April, für die Mitglieder des Vereines Wiener Tonkünstler-Orchester vom 23. bis inkl. 25. April. — Ab 26. April allgemeiner Verkauf.

Goldmark

Im Frühling (Rustic Wedding Symphony)

Vienna	VPO	78: HMV C 1802
1930		78: HMV (Austria) AN 438

Sakuntala, Overture

Vienna	VPO	78: HMV C 1820-1
1930		78: HMV (Austria) AN 439-40
		LP: Past Masters PM 36

Das Heimchen am Herd, Act 3 Prelude

Vienna	VPO	78: HMV (Austria) AN 451
1930		LP: Past Masters PM 36

Haydn

Symphony No 31 "Horn Signal"

Vienna	VSO	78: Supraphon 1400-2
1949		78: Ultraphon H 23265-7

Symphony No 88

Vienna	VPO	78: Electrola E 539-41/EW 71-3
June and		78: HMV (Austria) AM 2280-2
July 1929		CD: Preiser 90112
		CD: Koch Legacy 3-7011-2
Munich	Bavarian RO	LP: Amadeo AVRS 5035
June 1953		CD: Orfeo C 196.891 A

Another version of this Symphony (VPO in Klagenfurt November 1952) exists in the Clemens-Krauss-Archiv, Vienna

Symphony No 93

Munich	Bavarian RO	LP: Amadeo AVRS 5035
July 1952		

Another version of this Symphony (VPO October 1952) exists in the Clemens-Krauss-Archiv, Vienna

Symphony No 104 "London"

Vienna	VSO	78: Ultraphon H 23407-10
1949		Also issued on 78 on Supraphon label

Cello Concerto in D (arr. Gevaert)

Berlin	BPO	LP: Urania RS 731
November 1944	Hölscher	

Another version of the Concerto (same soloist and orchestra but recorded in 1941 in Vienna) exists in the Clemens-Krauss-Archiv, Vienna

Theresienmesse

Vienna	VPO	LP: Vox PL 6740
1950	Vienna Opera Chorus	
	Felbermayer,	
	Hermann, Patzak,	
	Poell	

Die Jahreszeiten

Vienna	VPO	LP: Haydn Society HSLP 2027
June 1942	Vienna Opera Chorus	LP: Parlophone PMA 1018-20 np
	Eipperle, Riegler,	LP: Odeon ODX 111-3
	Patzak, Hann,	CD: Preiser 93053
	Pernerstorfer	

Die Schöpfung

Vienna	VPO	LP: Haydn Society HSLP 2005
1944	Vienna Opera Chorus	LP: Nixa HLP 2005
	Eipperle,	LP: Saga 6213-4
	Patzak, Hann	LP: Erato LDE 3005-6/ERH 160062
		Excerpts
		LP: Erato LDE 1003

Hérold

Zampa, Overture

Vienna	VPO	78: HMV C 1803
1930		78: HMV (Austria) AN 441

Lanner

Waltzes: Die Romantiker; Die Kosenden

Vienna	VPO	78: HMV C 2337
Date uncertain		

Mendelssohn

A Midsummer Night's Dream, Incidental Music

Vienna	VSO	LP: Vox PL 8630
1950	Vienna Opera Chorus	LP: Vox STPL 513050
	Steingruber,	CD: Tuxedo TUXCD 1070
	Hermann	Overture
		45: Vox VIP 45380
		Nocturne
		45: Vox VIP 45350
		Scherzo
		45: Vox VIP 55350

Mozart

Symphony No 41 "Jupiter"

Milan 1949	La Scala Orchestra	Decca unpublished

Serenade No 7 "Haffner"

Vienna 1950	VSO	LP: Vox PL 6850

Così fan tutte, Overture

Vienna 1931	VPO	78: HMV C 2233 78: HMV (Austria) AN 724 CD: EMI CHS 764 2942/CDH 764 2952

Don Giovanni: Excerpt (La ci darem la mano)

Berlin 1936	Berlin Staatskapelle Berger, Schlusnus Sung in German	78: Polydor 62755 78: Decca DE 7070 45: DG NL 32153 CD: Preiser 89035 Also issued on LP by Preiser

Don Giovanni: Excerpts (1. Deh vieni alla finestra; 2. Madamina)

London September- October 1947	National SO Schöffler	78: Decca M 613 (1) Decca unpublished (2)

Die Entführung aus dem Serail, Overture

Vienna January 1931	VPO	78: HMV C 2194 78: HMV (Austria) AN 666 78: Victor M 584

Idomeneo: Excerpts (1. Non temer, amato bene; Se il padre perdei)

Vienna May 1952	VPO Güden	78: Decca K 28570 78: Decca K 23292 (2) LP: Decca LX 3067 LP: Decca LXT 5242 (2) LP: Decca ECM 557/ECS 557

SALZBURGER FESTSPIELE
1932

Im Festspielhaus

Die Frau ohne Schatten

Oper in 3 Akten von Hugo v. Hofmannsthal
Musik von Richard Strauß

Dirigent: Clemens Krauss
Inszenierung: Lothar Wallerstein
Bühnenentwürfe: Alfred Roller

Der Kaiser . . . . Franz Völker
Die Kaiserin . . . . Viorica Ursuleac
Die Amme . . . . Gertrud Rünger
Der Geisterbote . . . . . . Karl Ettl
Ein Hüter des Tempels . . . . Eva Hadrabova
Erscheinung des Jünglings . . Helge Roswaenge
Barak, der Färber . . . . . . Josef v. Manowarda
Sein Weib . . . . Lotte Lehmann
Der Einäugige ⎫   Viktor Madin
Der Einarmige ⎬ des Färbers Brüder   Alfred Muzzarelli
Der Bucklige ⎭   William Wernigk
Die Ungeborenen . . . . . . Adele Kern, Aenne Michalsky, Marie Neudorfer, Mitzi Mathias, Polly Batic und Rosa Brunnbauer
Die Stimme des Falken . . . . Eva Hadrabova
Drei Sklavinnen . . . . Kern, Michalsky, Batic
Drei Wächter der Stadt . . . Gallos, Madin, Ettl
Eine Stimme von oben . . . . Polly Batic

Kaiserliche Diener, fremde Kinder, dienende Geister, Geisterstimmen

Ort der Handlung: 1. Aufzug auf einer Terrasse über den kaiserlichen Gärten, Färberhaus; 2. Aufzug Färberhaus, Wald vor dem Pavillon der Falkner, Schlafgemach der Kaiserin, Färberhaus; 3. Aufzug unterirdischer Kerker, Geistertempel, Eingang Geistertempel, Inneres, Landschaft im Geisterreich.

Orchester: Wiener Philharmoniker
Chor: Wiener Staatsoper

Opernteater

Sonntag den 30. März 1930
Besondere Preise
Zum 1. Male:

WOZZECK

Oper in drei Akten (15 Szenen) nach Georg Büchners Drama von Alban Berg

Spielleitung: Hr. Dr. Wallerstein   Musikalische Leitung: Hr. Cremens Krauß

Wozzeck	Hr. Manowarda
Tambourmajor	Hr. Graarud
Andres	Hr. Gallos
Hauptmann	Hr. Maikl
Doktor	Hr. Wiedemann
Erster } Handwerksbursch	Hr. Norbert
Zweiter }	Hr. Madin
Der Narr	Hr. Wernigk
Marie	Fr. Pauly
Margret	Fr. Witt
Mariens Knabe	A. Keh
Ein Soldat	Hr. Maiwald

Soldaten und Burschen, Mägde und Dirnen, Kinder

Ort der Handlung:

1. Akt: I. Zimmer des Hauptmannes   2. Akt: I. Mariens Stube
II. Freies Feld, die Stadt in der Ferne   II. Straße in der Stadt
III. Mariens Stube   III. Toreinfahrt bei Mariens Wohnung
IV. Studierstube des Doktors   IV. Wirtshausgarten
V. Toreinfahrt bei Mariens Wohnung   V. Wachstube der Kaserne

3. Akt: I. Mariens Stube
II. Waldweg am Teich
III. Schenke
IV. Waldweg am Teich
V. Toreinfahrt bei Mariens Wohnung

In Szene gesetzt von Dr. Lothar Wallerstein
Entwürfe der Dekorationen und Kostüme: Prof. Oskar Strnad
Das offizielle Programm nur bei den Billetteuren erhältlich. Preis 50 Groschen

Nach dem zweiten Akt (zehnten Bild) eine größere Pause

Der Beginn der Vorstellung sowie jedes Aktes wird durch ein Glockenzeichen bekanntgegeben

Kassen-Eröffnung nach 6½ Uhr   Anfang 7½ Uhr   Ende nach 10 Uhr

Während der Vorspiele und der Akte bleiben die Saaltüren zum Parkett, Parterre und den Galerien geschlossen. Zuspätkommende können daher nur während der Pausen Einlaß finden.

Der Kartenverkauf findet heute statt für obige Vorstellung und für

Montag den 31. Der Evangelimann. Theatergemeinde Serie E, gelbe Mitgliedskarten. Beschränkter Kartenverkauf (Anfang 7 Uhr)
Dienstag den 1. April. Ariadne auf Naxos. Dirigent: Hr. Dr. Richard Strauß. Im Abonnement. Erhöhte Preise (Anfang 7½ Uhr)

Weiterer Spielplan:

Mittwoch den 2. Die Bohème. Im Abonnement (Anfang 7½ Uhr)
Donnerstag den 3. Carmen. Zu besonderen Preisen (Anfang 7 Uhr)

Le Nozze di Figaro, Overture

Vienna January 1931	VPO	78: HMV C 2194 78: HMV (Austria) AN 666 78: Electrola EW 1229 LP: Electrola 1C 187 29225-6M

Le Nozze di Figaro: Excerpt (Che soave zeffiretti)

Berlin 1936	Berlin Staatskapelle Berger, Ursuleac Sung in German	78: Polydor 62755 78: Decca DE 7070 45: DG NL 32153 LP: DG 2700 708 LP: Preiser LV 1384 LP: Discophilia KG-U 1 CD: Preiser 89035

Le Nozze di Figaro: Excerpts (1. Se vuol ballare; 2. Non più andrai)

London September- October 1947	National SO Schöffler	78: Decca M 613 (1) Decca unpublished (2)

Le Nozze di Figaro: Excerpts (1. Voi che sapete; 2. Deh vieni, non tardar)

Vienna May 1952	VPO Güden	78: Decca K 28575 (1) LP: Decca LX 3067 LP: Decca LXT 5242 LP: Decca ECM 557/ECS 557

Palestrina

O süsser Schlummer

Salzburg August 1942	Vienna Opera Chorus	LP: Melodiya M10 4698 001

Puccini

La Bohème

Munich December 1951	Bavarian Radio Chorus & Orchestra Eipperle, Lipp, Terkal, Nissen, Poell Sung in German	LP: Past Masters AM 3 Incorrectly dated 1954

Il Tabarro

Stuttgart January 1938	Stuttgart Radio Orchestra Ranczak, Waldenau Welter, Ahlersmeyer Sung in German	LP: BASF 10.223655 LP: Acanta BB 22365 Excerpts LP: BASF KBF 21491

Tosca: Excerpt (Vissi d'arte)

Berlin 1936	Berlin Staatskapelle Ursuleac Sung in German	78: Polydor 35033 LP: Preiser LV 1384 LP: Discophilia KG-U 1 LP: Acanta 98.221776

Turandot: Excerpt (In questa reggia)

Berlin 1936	Berlin Staatskapelle Ursuleac Sung in German	78: Polydor 35033 LP: Preiser LV 1384 LP: Discophilia KG-U 1

Ravel

Rapsodie espagnole

Vienna 1944	VPO	LP: Melodiya M10 46981 001
Munich June 1953	Bavarian RO	CD: Orfeo C 196.891 A

Respighi

I pini di Roma

Salzburg   VPO   LP: Melodiya M10 46981 001
August 1942   Recording incomplete

Another version of this work (VPO March 1952) exists in the Clemens-Krauss-Archiv, Vienna

Schubert

Symphony No 8 "Unfinished"

Bamberg   Bamberg SO   LP: Amadeo AVRS 5035
April 1951

Symphony No 9 "Great"

Vienna   VSO   LP: Supraphon 14250-6
1949   LP: Ultraphon H 23259-64
                                      LP: Telefunken E 1030-5

Ballet Music No 1 in G (Rosamunde)

Vienna   VPO   78: HMV C 2233
1930   78: HMV (Austria) AN 724
                                      78: Electrola EH 494

Previous rearchers have mentioned a 1930 recording of Rosamunde Overture, but this cannot be traced

Gesang der Geister über den Wassern

Vienna   VSO   LP: Vox PL 6480
1950   Vienna Opera Chorus   LP: Lyrichord LL 93

Smetana

The Bartered Bride, Overture

Vienna   VPO   LP: Melodiya M10 46981 001
1944

Another version of this work (Bamberg SO April 1951) exists in the Clemens-Krauss-Archiv, Vienna

Johann Strauss

An der schönen blauen Donau, Waltz

Vienna 1942	VPO	78: Telefunken SK 3150 LP: Capitol P 8061
Vienna Date uncertain	VPO	LP: Eurochord (France) TGV 111
Vienna December 1953	VPO	LP: Decca LXT 2913 LP: Decca ACL 99 LP: Telefunken 635.003/641.940 LP: Preiser PR 135033/PR 135040 CD: London (Japan) K35Y-1017

Another version of this work (VPO January 1952) exists in the Clemens-Krauss-Archiv, Vienna

Annen Polka

Vienna July 1929	VPO	78: HMV B 3149 78: HMV (Austria) AM 2283 78: Electrola EG 1626 LP: Electrola 1C 053 01534M CD: DG 435 3352 CD: Preiser 90112
Vienna December 1953	VPO	LP: Decca LXT 2913 LP: Decca ACL 99 LP: Telefunken 641.940 LP: Preiser PR 135033/PR 135040 CD: London (Japan) K35Y-1015

Auf der Jagd, Galop

Vienna September 1952	VPO	LP: Decca LXT 2755 LP: Decca LW 5025 LP: Decca ACL 80 LP: Telefunken 635.003 LP: Preiser PR 135032/PR 135040 CD: London (Japan) K35Y-1016

ROYAL
ALBERT
HALL

Manager: C. S. Taylor

Tuesday Evening
November 18th, 1952
at 8 p.m.

VICTOR HOCHHAUSER and the ANGLO-AUSTRIAN MUSIC SOCIETY

present the

VIENNA PHILHARMONIC ORCHESTRA

Conductor: **CLEMENS KRAUSS**

Souvenir Programme

Programme

GOD SAVE THE QUEEN
THE AUSTRIAN NATIONAL ANTHEM

Symphony No. 1, in C - - - - **Beethoven**
1770-1827

1. Adagio molto — allegro con brio   2. Andante cantabile con moto; Menuetto e trio
3. Finale: Adagio — allegro molto e vivace

Symphonic Poem: Don Juan - - - - **Richard Strauss**
1864-1949

Fragments and Interlude from *Die Liebe der Danaë* ("The love of Danaë")
(First performance in England)   **Richard Strauss**

INTERVAL

Symphony No. 1, in C minor - - - - **Brahms**
1833-1897

1. Un poco sostenuto — Allegro   2. Andante Sostenuto
3. Un poco allegretto e grazioso   4. Adagio — più andante — allegro non troppo ma con brio

Bei uns z' Haus, Waltz

Vienna	VSO	78: Supraphon 53913
1949		78: Ultraphon H 23257
		78: Telefunken E 3824
		LP: Supraphon VE 9004
		LP: Remington 149-26

Vienna	VPO	LP: Decca LXT 2913/LXT 2991
December 1953		LP: Decca ACL 99
		LP: Telefunken 635,003/641.090
		LP: Preiser PR 135033/PR 135040
		CD: London (Japan) K35Y-1016

Egyptian March

Vienna	VPO	78: Telefunken SK 3241
1942		

Vienna	VPO	78: Decca K 23210/K 28584
May 1952		LP: Decca LXT 2645
		LP: Decca ACL 49
		LP: Decca ECS 2058
		LP: Telefunken 635.003
		LP: Preiser PR 135031
		CD: London (Japan) K35Y-1015
		CD: Decca 425 9902

Eljen a Magyar, Polka

Vienna	VPO	LP: Vox VL 3140
1950		45: Vox VIP 30040

Vienna	VPO	78: Decca (Switzerland) M 38127
May 1952		LP: Decca LXT 2645
		LP: Decca ACL 49
		LP: Decca ECS 2058
		LP: Telefunken 635.003
		LP: Preiser PR 135031
		CD: London (Japan) K35Y-1015
		CD: Decca 425 9902

Die Fledermaus

Vienna September 1950	VPO Vienna Opera Chorus Güden, Lipp, Wagner, Patzak, Dermota, Poell, Preger	78: Decca AX 470-81 78: Decca K 23112-22 LP: Decca LXT 2550-1 LP: Decca ACL 145-6 LP: Decca DPA 585-6 LP: Telefunken KD 11011 LP: Preiser PR 135035-6 CD: Decca 425 9902 Excerpts LP: Decca LXT 2576 LP: Decca LW 5020/LW 5138 LP: Decca BR 3062 45: Decca CEP 552 LP: Decca ACL 73 Overture LP: Decca LXT 2634/LXT 2695 LP: Decca LW 5005 LP: Decca ACL 24 LP: Decca ECS 2058 LP: Telefunken 635.003 LP: Preiser PR 135031 CD: London (Japan) K35Y-1015

Die Fledermaus, Overture

Vienna July 1929	VPO	78: HMV C 1755 78: HMV (Austria) AN 377 LP: Electrola 1C 053 01534M CD: Preiser 90112 CD: EMI CHS 764 2942/CDH 764 2992
Vienna 1942	VPO	78: Telefunken SK 3241

Frühlingsstimmen, Waltz

Vienna 1942	VPO	78: Telefunken E 1075 LP: Capitol P 8061
Vienna June 1950	VPO	78: Decca K 23226/K 28374 78: Telefunken E 3861 LP: Decca LXT 2634/LXT 2695 LP: Decca ACL 24 LP: Decca ECS 2058 LP: Telefunken 635.003 LP: Preiser PR 135032/PR 135040 CD: London (Japan) K35Y-1016 CD: DG 435 3352 Also included in the complete recording of Die Fledermaus (see above)

Im Krapfenwaldl, Polka française

Vienna   VPO   78: Decca K 23310/K 28584
May 1952   45: Decca 45-71079
                                       LP: Decca LXT 2645
                                       LP: Decca ACL 49
                                       LP: Telefunken 635.003
                                       LP: Preiser PR 135031
                                       CD: London (Japan) K35Y-1016
                                       CD: Decca 425 9902

Indigo und die 40 Räuber, Overture

Vienna   VPO   45: Vox VIP 30100
1950

Another version of this work (VPO 1941) exists in the Clemens-Krauss-Archiv, Vienna

Klangfiguren, Waltz

Vienna   VPO   LP: Vox VL 3140
1950

Another version of this work (VPO 1941) exists in the Clemens-Krauss-Archiv, Vienna

Künstlerleben, Waltz

Vienna   VPO   78: Decca K 23037/K 28373
June 1950   LP: Decca LXT 2634/LXT 2965
                                       LP: Decca ACL 24
                                       LP: Decca ECS 2058
                                       LP: Telefunken 635.003
                                       LP: Preiser PR 135033/PR 135040
                                       CD: London (Japan) K35Y-1015

Leichtes Blut, Polka

Vienna   VPO   78: HMV B 3221
October 1929   78: HMV (Austria) AM 2496
                                       78: Electrola EG 1780
                                       LP: Electrola 1C 053 01534M
                                       CD: Preiser 90112

Liebeslieder, Waltz

Vienna   VPO   78: HMV C 2339
January and   78: Electrola EH 829
September 1931   78: Victor M 907
                                       LP: Electrola 1C 053 01534M
                                       CD: Preiser 90112

Morgenblätter, Waltz

Vienna   VPO
July 1929

78: HMV C 1756
78: Electrola EH 416
78: Victor M 907
LP: Electrola 1C 053 01534M
CD: Preiser 90112/90090

Vienna   VPO
May 1952

LP: Decca LXT 2755/LXT 2991
LP: Decca LW 5020
LP: Decca ACL 80
LP: Preiser PR 135032
CD: London (Japan) K35Y-1015

O schöner Mai, Waltz

Vienna   VSO
1949

78: Ultraphon H 23406
78: Telefunken E 3874/VE 9004
Also issued on 78 by Supraphon

Perpetuum mobile

Vienna   VPO
July 1929

78: HMV B 3149
78: Electrola EG 1626
LP: Electrola 1C 053 01534M
LP: Electrola 1C 147 30226-7M
CD: Preiser 90112
CD: EMI CHS 764 2942/CDH 764 2992

Vienna   VPO
September 1952

LP: Decca LXT 2755
LP: Decca ACL 80
LP: Preiser PR 135032
CD: London (Japan) K35Y-1016

Ritter Pasman, Csardas

Vienna   VPO
May 1952

LP: Decca LXT 2755
LP: Decca ACL 80
LP: Preiser PR 135032
CD: London (USA) K35Y-1015

Rosen aus dem Süden, Waltz

Vienna   VPO
1942

78: Telefunken SK 3187
LP: Capitol P 8061

Seid umschlungen, Waltz

Vienna   VSO
1949

78: Supraphon 53914
78: Ultraphon H 23256
78: Telefunken E 3823
78: Eurochord (France) TSV 142
LP: Supraphon LPV 130
LP: Remington 149-26

Bayerische Staatsoper
National-Theater

Mittwoch den 28. Oktober 1942

Uraufführung
Capriccio
Ein Konversationsstück für Musik in einem Aufzug
von
Clemens Krauß
und
Richard Strauß

Musikalische Leitung: Clemens Krauß

Inszenierung: Rudolf Hartmann Bühnenbild und Kostüme: Rochus Gliese

Die Gräfin	Viorica Ursuleac
Der Graf, ihr Bruder	Walter Höfermayer
Flamand, ein Musiker	Horst Taubmann
Olivier, ein Dichter	Hans Hotter
La Roche, der Theaterdirektor	Georg Hann
Die Schauspielerin Clairon	Hildegarde Ranczak
Monsieur Taupe	Carl Seydel
Eine italienische Sängerin	Irma Beilke a. G.
Ein italienischer Tenor	Franz Klarwein
Eine junge Tänzerin	Liselotte Schwarz
Der Haushofmeister	Georg Wieter
Acht Diener	Josef Trojan-Regar
	Franz Theo Reuter
	Walther Carnuth
	Karl Schmidt
	Arno Lehner-Schwed
	Karl Mücke
	Willi Günther
	Walter Bracht

Ort der Handlung: Ein Schloß in der Nähe von Paris, zur Zeit als Gluck dort sein Reformwerk der Oper begann.
Etwa um 1775.

Einstudierung der Tanz-Szene: Pino Mlakar
Kostümgestaltung und Maske: Alexander C Stenz-Hentze

Anfang 19 Uhr Ende gegen 21½ Uhr

Programm zu RM 1.—; Textbuch zu RM 1.— an der Kasse, zu RM 1.10 bei den Einlaßdienern zu haben

Sächsische Staatstheater
Opernhaus

Sonnabend, am 1. Juli 1933

Anfang 7 Uhr

Außer Anrecht

Uraufführung

Arabella

Lyrische Komödie in drei Aufzügen von Hugo v. Hofmannsthal

Musik von Richard Strauß

Musikalische Leitung: **Clemens Krauss** a. G.   Inszenierung: **Josef Gielen**

Künstlerischer Beirat für Regie und Vortrag: Eva Plaschke-von der Osten

Personen:

Graf Waldner, Rittmeister a. D.	Friedrich Plaschke
Adelaide, seine Frau	Camilla Kallab
Arabella } ihre Töchter	Viorica Ursuleac
Zdenka }	Margit Bokor
Mandryka	Alfred Jerger a. G.
Matteo, Jäger-Offizier	Martin Kremer
Graf Elemer }	Karl Albrecht Streib
Graf Dominik } Verehrer der Arabella	Kurt Böhme
Graf Lamoral }	Arno Schellenberg
Die Fiakermilli	Ellice Illiard
Eine Kartenschlägerin	Jessyka Koettrik
Welko, Leibhusar des Mandryka	Robert Büssel
Djura } Diener des Mandryka	Rudolf Schmalnauer
Jankel }	Horst Falke
Ein Zimmerkellner	Ludwig Eybisch

Begleiterin der Arabella. Drei Spieler. Ein Arzt. Groom. Fiaker. Hotelgäste. Kellner.
Ballgäste: Hilde Schlieben, Gino Neppach, Peter Pawlinin, Damen und Herren der Tanzgruppe

Ort: Wien — Zeit: 1869

I. Akt: Salon in einem Wiener Stadthotel
II. Akt: Ein öffentlicher Ballsaal
III. Akt: Offener Raum mit Stiegenhaus im Hotel

Chöre: Karl Maria Pembaur

Dekorative Ausstattung: Leonhard Fanto und Johannes Rothenberger

Trachten: Leonhard Fanto. — Technische Einrichtung: Georg Brandt

Längere Pause nach dem zweiten Aufzug

Sämtliche Plätze müssen vor Beginn der Vorstellung eingenommen werden

Textbücher sind für 1,00 R.M. vormittags an der Kasse und abends bei den Türschließern zu haben

Gekaufte Karten werden nur bei Änderung der Vorstellung zurückgenommen

Kassenöffnung 6 Uhr   Einlaß 6¼ Uhr   Anfang 7 Uhr   Ende geg. 10¼ Uhr

Stadt und Land, Polka

Vienna	VPO	LP: Vox VL 3140
1950		45: Vox VIP 30040

Vienna	VPO	LP: Decca LXT 2755
September 1952		LP: Decca LW 5052
		LP: Decca ACL 80
		LP: Preiser PR 135032
		CD: London (Japan) K35Y-1015

Tales from the Vienna Woods, Waltz

Vienna	VPO	78: Decca K 28581-2
May 1952		LP: Decca LXT 2645/LXT 2695
		LP: Decca LW 5020
		LP: Decca ACL 49
		LP: Decca ECS 2058
		LP: Telefunken 635.003
		LP: Preiser PR 135031/PR 135040
		CD: London (Japan) K35Y-1016
		CD: Decca 425 9902

1001 Nacht, Waltz

Vienna	VPO	78: HMV C 2093
October 1930		78: HMV (Austria) AN 630
		78: Electrola EH 484
		LP: Electrola 1C 053 01534M
		CD: Preiser 90112

Vergnügungszug, Polka

Vienna	VPO	CD: DG 435 3352
December 1944		

Vienna	VPO	LP: Vox VP 3140
1950		45: Vox VIP 30040

Vienna	VPO	78: Decca (Switzerland) M 38128
May 1952		LP: Decca LXT 2645
		LP: Decca LW 5052
		LP: Decca ACL 49
		LP: Decca ECS 2058
		LP: Telefunken 635.003
		LP: Preiser PR 135031
		CD: London (Japan) K35Y-1016
		CD: Decca 425 9902

Der Zigeunerbaron

Vienna April 1951	VPO Vienna Opera Chorus Loose, Zadek, Anday, Patzak, Dönch, Poell	78: Decca K 28526-37 LP: Decca LXT 2612-3 LP: Decca ACL 166-7 LP: Decca ECM 2148-9 LP: Telefunken 648.056 Excerpts LP: Decca BR 3033/BR 3062 45: Decca CEP 585 Overture LP: Decca LXT 2634/LXT 2991 LP: Decca LW 5005 LP: Decca ACL 24 LP: Decca ECS 2058 LP: Telefunken 635.003 LP: Preiser PR 135032 CD: London (Japan) K35Y-1016

Einzugsmarsch (Der Zigeunerbaron)

Vienna October 1929	VPO	78: HMV B 3149/B 3221 78: HMV (Austria) AM 2496 78: Electrola EG 1780 LP: Electrola 1C 053 01534M CD: Preiser 90112

Johann Strauss father

Donaulieder, Waltz

Vienna 1930	VPO	78: HMV C 2338

Radetzky March

Vienna December 1953	VPO	LP: Decca LXT 2913 LP: Decca ACL 99 LP: Telefunken 641.940 LP: Preiser PR 135033 CD: London (Japan) K35Y-1017 CD: DG 435 3352

Johann & Josef Strauss

Pizzicato Polka

Vienna May 1952	VPO	78: Decca (Switzerland) M 38128 LP: Decca LXT 2645 LP: Decca LW 5052 LP: Decca ACL 49 LP: Decca ECS 2058 LP: Telefunken 635.003 LP: Preiser PR 135031 CD: London (Japan) K35Y-1016 CD: DG 435 3352 CD: Decca 425 9902

Another version of this work (Mainz August 1932/orchestra unspecified) exists in the Clemens-Krauss-Archiv, Vienna

Josef Strauss

Dorfschwalben aus Oesterreich, Waltz

Vienna May 1952	VPO	LP: Decca LXT 2755/LXT 2991 LP: Decca LW 5019 LP: Decca ACL 80 LP: Telefunken 635.003 LP: Preiser PR 135032 CD: London (Japan) K35Y-1017 CD: DG 435 3352

Dynamiden, Waltz

Vienna 1949	VSO	78: Supraphon 53950 78: Ultraphon H 23258 78: Eurochord (France) TSV 143

Auf Ferienreisen, Polka

Vienna December 1953	VPO	LP: Decca LXT 2913 LP: Decca ACL 99 LP: Telefunken 635.003/641.940 LP: Preiser PR 135031 CD: London (Japan) K35Y-1017

Feuerfest, Polka

Vienna 1942	VPO	78: Telefunken SK 3241
Vienna May 1952	VPO	LP: Decca LXT 2755 LP: Decca LW 5053 LP: Decca ACL 80 LP: Telefunken 635.003 LP: Preiser PR 135032 CD: London (Japan) K35Y-1017

Jockey Polka

Vienna May 1952	VPO	78: Decca (Switzerland) M 38127 LP: Decca LXT 2645 LP: Decca LW 5053 LP: Decca ACL 49 LP: Telefunken 635.003 LP: Preiser PR 135031 CD: London (Japan) K35Y-1017 CD: Decca 425 9902

Die Libelle, Polka-Mazurka

Vienna 1950	VPO	LP: Vox VL 3140
Vienna May 1952	VPO	78: Decca K 28582 LP: Decca LXT 2645 LP: Decca LW 5053 45: Decca 45-71079 LP: Decca ACL 49 LP: Telefunken 635.003 LP: Preiser PR 135031 CD: London (Japan) K35Y-1017 CD: Decca 425 9902

Mein Lebenslauf ist Lieb' und Lust, Waltz

Vienna 1950	VPO	LP: Vox VL 3140
Vienna May 1952	VPO	78: Decca K 28583 LP: Decca LXT 2645/LXT 2991 LP: Decca LW 5019 LP: Telefunken 635.003 LP: Preiser PR 135031 CD: London (Japan) K35Y-1017 CD: Decca 425 9902

VICTOR HOCHHAUSER and the ANGLO-AUSTRIAN MUSIC SOCIETY present

VIENNA PHILHARMONIC ORCHESTRA

Conductor: **CLEMENS KRAUSS**

Remaining Concerts

Wednesday Next, at 8 p.m.

BEETHOVEN CONCERT

Overture: Egmont	BEETHOVEN
Symphony No. 7	BEETHOVEN
Symphony No. 6 (Pastoral)	BEETHOVEN
Overture: "Leonora" No. 3	BEETHOVEN

Thursday Next, at 8 p.m.

Grand Farewell Concert

JOHANN STRAUSS EVENING

Programme will include

Overture: "Die Fledermaus"	JOHANN STRAUSS
Tales from the Vienna Woods	JOHANN STRAUSS
Pizzicato Polka	JOHANN STRAUSS
Emperor Waltz	JOHANN STRAUSS
Perpetuum Mobile	JOHANN STRAUSS
Libellen Polka	JOHANN STRAUSS
Egyptian March	JOHANN STRAUSS

Tickets can be obtained during the Interval at the Box Office

CLEMENS KRAUSS

conducts

THE VIENNA PHILHARMONIC ORCHESTRA

on

DECCA LONG PLAYING

(33⅓ r.p.m.) RECORDS

gives you THE WORLD'S FINEST RECORD

JOHANN STRAUSS

Music of Johann Strauss No. 2
Die Fledermaus & Der Zigeunerbaron
Overtures; Künstlerleben;
Frühlingsstimmen LXT 2634

Die Fledermaus (*Complete recording*)
Gueden, Patzak, Dermota, Lipp, with
The Vienna State Opera Chorus
LXT 2550-1

Der Zigeunerbaron (*Complete recording*)
Loose, Patzak, Poell, with
The Vienna State Opera Chorus
LXT 2612-3

Vienna Philharmonic "New Year" Concert
A selection of works by Johann
and Josef Strauss
LXT 2615

RICHARD STRAUSS

Don Juan;
Till Eulenspiegels lustige Streiche
LXT 2540

Also sprach Zarathustra
LXT 2546

Symphonia Domestica
LXT 2643

Ein Heldenleben
LXT 2720
(*available shortly*)

BEETHOVEN

Piano Concerto No. 4 in G major, Op. 58
Wilhelm Backhaus Piano
LXT 2529

THE DECCA RECORD COMPANY LTD. 1-3 BRIXTON ROAD, LONDON, S.W.9

Moulinet Polka

Vienna	VPO	LP: Decca LXT 2775
May 1952		LP: Decca LW 5053
		LP: Decca ACL 80
		LP: Preiser PR 135032
		CD: London (Japan) K35Y-1017

Ohne Sorgen, Polka

Vienna	VPO	LP: Vox VL 3140
1950		45: Vox VIP 30040

Vienna	VPO	LP: Decca LXT 2744/LXT 2913
September 1952		LP: Decca LW 5053
		LP: Decca ACL 80
		LP: Telefunken 635.003
		LP: Preiser PR 135032
		CD: London (Japan) K35Y-1017

Plappermäulchen, Polka

Vienna	VPO	LP: Decca LXT 2913
December 1953		LP: Decca ACL 80/ACL 99
		LP: Telefunken 635.003/641.940
		LP: Preiser PR 135033
		CD: London (Japan) K35Y-1017

Sphärenklänge, Waltz

Vienna	VPO	78: HMV C 2195
January 1931		78: HMV (Austria) AN 667
		78: Electrola EH 491
		LP: Electrola 1C 053 01534M
		CD: Preiser 90112

Vienna	VPO	LP: Decca LXT 2913/LXT 2991
December 1953		LP: Decca ACL 99
		LP: Telefunken 635.003/641.940
		LP: Preiser PR 135033
		CD: London (Japan) K35Y-1017

Richard Strauss

Also sprach Zarathustra

Vienna June 1950	VPO	78: Decca K 23097-23100 LP: Decca LXT 2548 LP: Decca ECM 572/ECS 572 LP: Telefunken 635.246 CD: Decca 425 9742

Aus Italien

Vienna December 1953	VPO	LP: Decca LXT 2917 LP: Decca ACL 249 LP: Decca ECM 610/ECS 610 LP: London (USA) R 23210 LP: Telefunken 635.246

Der Bürger als Edelmann, Suite

Vienna 1930	VPO	78: HMV C 2034-7 78: HMV (Austria) AN 585-8 78: Victor M 101
Vienna September 1952	VPO	LP: Decca LXT 2756 LP: Decca ECM 608/ECS 608 LP: London (USA) STS 15504 LP: Telefunken 635.246

Divertimento after Couperin

Bamberg April 1954	Bamberg SO	LP: Amadeo AVRS 5033/AVRS 19063 LP: Philips G 04861 L/GL 5843 LP: World Records CM 74

Another version of this work (also Bamberg December 1953) exists in the Clemens-Krauss-Archiv, Vienna

Don Juan

Vienna June 1950	VPO	78: Decca K 28364-7 LP: Decca LXT 2549 LP: Decca ACL 16 LP: Decca ECM 608/ECS 608 LP: London (USA) STS 15504 LP: Telefunken 635.246 CD: Decca 425 9932/433 3402

Four other versions of this work (Havana 1948/Bamberg April 1951/Salzburg August 1952/Vienna September 1952) exist in the Clemens-Krauss-Archiv, Vienna

Ein Heldenleben

Vienna September 1952	VPO	LP: Decca LXT 2729 LP: Decca ACL 241 LP: Decca ECM 584/ECS 584 LP: London (USA) R 23209 LP: Telefunken 635.246 CD: Decca 425 9932

Don Quixote

Vienna June 1953	VPO Fournier	LP: Decca LXT 2842 LP: Decca ECM 609/ECS 609 LP: London (USA) R 23241 LP: Telefunken 635.246 CD: Decca 425 9742

Sinfonia Domestica

Vienna May 1952	VPO	78: Decca AKX 28576-80 LP: Decca LXT 2643 LP: Decca ECM 506/ECS 506 LP: London (USA) R 23239 LP: Telefunken 635.246
Munich June 1953	Bavarian RO	CD: Orfeo C 196.891 A

Another version of this work (Vienna April 1954) exists in the Clemens-Krauss-Archiv, Vienna

Till Eulenspiegels lustige Streiche

Vienna 1942	VPO	78: Telefunken SK 3139-40 LP: Capitol P 8100 LP: Telefunken LGX 66032
Milan 1949	La Scala Orchestra	78: Decca K 1681-2
Vienna June 1950	VPO	78: Decca K 28364-5 LP: Decca LXT 2549 LP: Decca ACL 16 LP: Decca ECM 572/ECS 572

Five other versions of this work (Bremen February 1952/Bremen March 1952/Klagenfurt November 1952/Vienna March 1953/Graz June 1953) exist in the Clemens-Krauss-Archiv, Vienna

Tod und Verklärung

London   LPO   78: Decca AK 1892-4
December 1947

Two other versions of this work (Vienna November 1951/Bamberg December 1953) exist in the Clemens-Krauss-Archiv, Vienna

Metamorphosen

Bamberg   Bamberg SO   LP: Amadeo AVRS 5034
January 1953   LP: Philips G 04862 L/GL 5844

Orchestral Songs: Cäcilie; Frühlingsfeier

Berlin   Berlin   78: Polydor 30017
1942   Staatskapelle   78: Decca DE 7063
                 Ursuleac   LP: Discophilia KG-U 1
                                       LP: Preiser LV 1384

Orchestral Songs: Ich trage meine Minne; Freundliche Vision

Vienna   VPO   LP: BASF 10.220559/40.22055
November 1944   Patzak

Songs: Einkehr; Wie sollten wir geheim sie halten?

Vienna   Krauss, piano   LP: Acanta 40.23546
June 1940   Ursuleac

Songs: Madrigal; Lob des Leidens; Muttertändelei; Für 15 Pfennige; Aus den Liedern der Trauer; Seitdem dein Aug' in meines schaute; Blindenklage; O wärst du mein

Munich   Krauss, piano   LP: Amadeo AVRS 19064
August 1952   Ursuleac   LP: Philips G 04862 L/GL 5844

Die Aegyptische Helena: Excerpt (Eilig zusammengeraffte Gaben)

Vienna
September 1933

VPO
Völker, Jerger,
Rosvaenge

LP: Teletheater 120.747

Arabella

Salzburg
August 1942

VPO
Vienna Opera Chorus
Ursuleac, Willer,
Eipperle, Taubmann,
Reinmar, T.Herrmann

CD: Myto MCD 92154

Arabella: Excerpts (1. Aber der Richtige; 2. Und du wirst mein Gebieter sein; 3. Das war sehr gut, Mandryka)

Berlin
1933

Berlin
Staatskapelle
Ursuleac, Bokor,
Jerger

78: Polydor 62711 (3)
78: Polydor 62712 (1 and 2)
78: Decca DE 7024 (3)
78: Decca DE 7025 (1 and 3)
LP: DG 88017 (1)
LP: Discophilia KG-U 1
LP: Preiser LV 1384
LP: BASF 72.221792 (1)

Arabella: Excerpts (Aber der Richtige; So fliesst die helle stille Donau; Fand ein Mädchen)

Vienna
October 1933

VPO
Ursuleac, Bokor,
Kern, Rünger,
Jerger, Mayr

LP: Teletheater 120.841

Ariadne auf Naxos (Opera, without prologue)

Stuttgart
June 1935

Stuttgart RO
Ursuleac, Berger,
Korjus, Rünger,
Rosvaenge

LP: BASF 22.218066
LP: Acanta DE 21806
Excerpts
LP: BASF 98.221776/72.221792
LP: Acanta DE 23122-3
LP: Preiser LV 1384
Some issues incorrectly labelled Berlin 1935

Capriccio: Excerpts

Munich October 1944	Bavarian State Orchestra Ursuleac, Klarwein, Hann, Hotter, Wieter	LP: Rococo 1021 LP: BASF 10.213633 LP: BASF KBF 21363 Ihr Streiter in Apoll LP: BASF KBF 21486 Ein schönes Gedicht; Closing scene LP: Acanta DE 23122-3 Some issues incorrectly attribute the role of Olivier to Kronenburg instead of Hotter

Capriccio, Closing scene

Munich June 1943	Bavarian State Orchestra Ursuleac	78: Polydor 68125 LP: Amadeo AVRS 5035/AVRS 19063 LP: Discophilia KG-U 1 LP: World Records CM 74

Capriccio, Orchestral Interlude

Munich November 1953	Bavarian RO	LP: Philips G 04861 L/GL 5843

Friedenstag: Excerpt (Nur einer hier in diesem wilden Turm)

Vienna June 1939	VPO Ursuleac	LP: Acanta DE 23122-3

Die Frau ohne Schatten: Excerpts

Vienna June 1933	VPO Ursuleac, Völker	LP: Ed Smith UORC 345 Wenn das Herz aus Kristall LP: Teletheater 120.747

Die Liebe der Danae

Salzburg August 1952	VPO Vienna Opera Chorus Kupper, Gostic, Traxel, Szemere, Schöffler	LP: Ed Smith SP 4 LP: Discocorp IGI 464 LP: Melodram MEL 111 CD: Melodram MEL 37061

SALZBURGER FESTSPIELE 1952

DIE LIEBE DER DANAE

Heitere Mythologie in drei Akten
mit Benützung eines Entwurfes von Hugo von Hofmannsthal
von Joseph Gregor

Musik von
RICHARD STRAUSS
OP. 83

Dirigent:
CLEMENS KRAUSS

Inszenierung:
RUDOLF HARTMANN

Bühnenbild und Kostüme:
EMIL PREETORIUS

Orchester:
DIE WIENER PHILHARMONIKER
CHOR DER WIENER STAATSOPER

DIE LIEBE DER DANAE

Heitere Mythologie in drei Akten
mit Benützung eines Entwurfes von Hugo von Hofmannsthal
von Joseph Gregor
Musik von Richard Strauß, op. 83

Jupiter	Paul Schöffler
Merkur	Josef Traxel
Pollux, König von Eos	Laszlo Szemere
Danae, dessen Tochter	Annelies Kupper
Xanthe, Danaes Dienerin	Anny Felbermayer
Midas	Josef Gostic
Vier Könige, Neffen des Pollux	August Jaresch Erich Majkut Harald Pröglhöf Franz Bierbach
Semele	Dorothea Siebert
Europa } vier Königinnen	Esther Rethy
Alkmene	Georgine Milinkovic
Leda	Sieglinde Wagner

Vier Wächter, Chor der Gläubiger, Gefolge und Diener des
Pollux, Gefolge und Dienerinnen der Danae, Volk

ERSTER AKT
Thronsaal des Königs Pollux — Schlafgemach der Danae —
ein Säulenhof am Palaste — Hafen

ZWEITER AKT
Saal im Palast des Königs

DRITTER AKT
Landstraße im Orient — südliche Berglandschaft —
Hütte des Midas

Der Rosenkavalier

Munich April 1944	Bavarian State Chorus & Orchestra Ursuleac, Kern, Milinkovic, Hann, Weber	LP: Vox PL 7774 LP: Vox OPBX 140 LP: Melodiya M10 41788-93 Excerpts LP: Vox PL 8200 45: Vox VIP 45330 LP: BASF 10.223221 LP: Eurodisc 70548 KR LP: Acanta DE 23122-3

Another complete recording of the opera (Salzburg July 1953) exists in the Clemens-Krauss-Archiv, Vienna

Der Rosenkavalier: Excerpts

Vienna January 1933	VPO Ursuleac, Kern, Hadrabova, Mayr, Pataky	LP: Ed Smith UORC 346

Der Rosenkavalier: Excerpts (1. Hab mir's gelobt; 2. Ist ein Traum, kann nicht wirklich sein)

Berlin 1936	Berlin Staatskapelle Ursuleac, Berger, Lemnitz	78: Polydor 67075 78: Decca CA 8328 LP: Preiser LV 1384 (1) CD: Preiser 89035

Der Rosenkavalier, Waltz sequence

Bamberg January 1953	Bamberg SO	LP: Amadeo AVRS 5033/AVRS 19063 LP: Philips G 04861 L/GL 5843 LP: World Records CM 74

Salome

Vienna March 1954	VPO Vienna Opera Chorus Goltz, Kenney, Dermota, Patzak, Braun, Weber, Berry	LP: Decca LXT 2863-4 LP: Decca GOM 549-550 LP: Telefunken 648.041 Excerpts LP: Decca BR 3021 LP: Telefunken 635.246

Salome, Dance of the 7 Veils

Vienna 1942	VPO	78: Telefunken SK 3199 LP: Capitol L 8036

Stravinsky

Pulcinella, Suite

Vienna March 1952	VPO	CD: DG 435 3292/435 3212

Verdi

Don Carlo: Excerpt (Sì, vi feci chiamar, mio padre!)

Vienna February 1933	VPO Manowarda, Jerger Sung in German	LP: Teletheater 120.747

Otello: Excerpt (Ora e per sempre addio)

Vienna December 1933	VPO Völker, Manowarda Sung in German	LP: Teletheater 120.841

Rigoletto: Excerpts (Caro nome; Tutte le feste)

Vienna May 1952	VPO Güden	78: Decca K 23277/K 28571 LP: Decca LX 3067

Il Trovatore: Excerpt (Mira, d'acerbe lagrime)

Berlin 1936	Berlin Ursuleac, Sved Sung in German	78: Polydor 67173 LP: DG 88017 LP: Discophilia KG-U 1 LP: Preiser LV 1384

Wagner

Der fliegende Holländer

Munich 1944	Bavarian State Chorus & Orchestra Ursuleac, Willer, Ostertag, Hann, Hotter	LP: Mercury (USA) MGL 2 LP: Discocorp IGI 381 LP: Acanta HA 23135-7 LP: Rodolphe RP 12388-90 CD: Rodolphe RPC 32515 CD: Laudis LCD 24007 Excerpts LP: BASF 10.215385 LP: Top Classic H 702-3 LP: Acanta 40.23502 LP: Acanta DE 22017 LP: Acanta DE 23122-3

Götterdämmerung

Bayreuth August 1953	Bayreuth Festival Chorus & Orchestra Varnay, Malaniuk, Hinsch-Gröndahl, Windgassen, Uhde, Neidlinger, Greindl	LP: Foyer FO 1011 LP: Melodram MEL 539 LP: Foyer 4CF-2010/15CF-2011 CD: Rodolphe RPC 32503-9

Parsifal

Bayreuth August 1953	Bayreuth Festival Chorus & Orchestra Mödl, Vinay, Uhde, London, Greindl, Weber	LP: Documents OR 305 LP: Melodram MEL 533 LP: Rodolphe RP 12378-81 CD: Rodolphe RPC 32516-7 CD: Laudis LCD 44006 Excerpts LP: Melodram MEL 650

Parsifal: Excerpt (Enthülle den Gral! Nein! Nicht mehr)

Vienna April 1933	VPO Vienna Opera Chorus Graarud, Schipper	LP: Teletheater 120.747

Parsifal, Good Friday Music

London January 1949	LPO	LP: Decca LXT 2527

Das Rheingold

Bayreuth August 1953	Bayreuth Festival Orchestra Malaniuk, Falcon, Ilosvay, Stolze, Witte, Neidlinger, Uhde, Greindl, Weber	LP: Foyer FO 1008 LP: Melodram MEL 536 CD: Foyer 3CF-2007/15CF-2011 CD: Rodolphe RPC 32503-9

Das Rheingold: Excerpt (Rheingold! Rheingold!)

Vienna February 1933	VPO Helletsgruber, With, Szantho, Wiedemann	LP: Teletheater 120.747

Other excerpts from this performance exist in the Clemens-Krauss-Archiv, Vienna

Siegfried

Bayreuth August 1953	Bayreuth Festival Orchestra Varnay, Streich Ilosvay, Kuen, Windgassen, Hotter, Neidlinger, Greindl	LP: Foyer FO 1010 CD: Foyer 4CF-2009/15CF-2011 CD: Rodolphe RPC 32503-9

Tristan und Isolde, Prelude and Liebestod

London January 1949	LPO	78: Decca AK 2245-6 LP: Decca LXT 2527

Die Walküre

Bayreuth August 1953	Bayreuth Festival Orchestra Varnay, Resnik, Malaniuk, Vinay Hotter, Greindl	LP: Foyer FO 1009 LP: Melodram MEL 537 CD: Foyer 4CF-2008/15CF-2011 CD: Rodolphe RPC 32503-9

Die Walküre: Excerpts

Vienna March 1933	VPO Ursuleac, Ohms, Szantho, Völker, Mayr, Manowarda	LP: Ed Smith UORC 437 <u>Winterstürme; Heilig ist mein Herd</u> LP: Teletheater 120.747

Die Walküre: Excerpts (Heiligste Minne, höchste Not; Nun zäume dein Ross)

Vienna June 1933	VPO Hüni-Mihacsek, Jeritza, Völker, Schorr	LP: Teletheater 120.747

Weber

Jubel, Overture

Vienna   VPO   78: HMV C 2193
1931   78: HMV (Austria) AN 665

Peter Schmoll, Overture

Vienna   VPO   78: HMV C 2344
1931   78: HMV (Austria) AN 739

Ziehrer

Weaner Mad'ln, Waltz

Vienna   VPO   78: HMV C 2195
January 1931   78: Electrola EH 491
                                           LP: Electrola 1C 053 01534M
                                           CD: Preiser 90112
                                           CD: EMI CHS 764 2942/CDH 764 2992

Clemens Krauss:
Unpublished recordings

In the discography of published recordings indication is made where other unpublished versions of a work exist. However, the Clemens-Krauss-Archiv in Vienna contains many other taped performances of works where no published version exists. With the help of Johann Gratz and Simon Clark I have listed these below, as they would form the basis for future Krauss issues.

Bach	Brandenburg 3 (Berlin November 1938)
Beethoven	Symphony 6 (Vienna March 1952)
	Symphony 6 (Klagenfurt November 1952)
	Coriolan Overture (Havana 1948)
	Egmont Overture (Vienna March 1952)
	Fidelio/complete (London September 1947)
Brahms	Symphony 1 (Bremen February-March 1952)
	Symphony 1 (Vienna November 1952)
	Symphony 2 (Graz June 1953)
	Piano Concerto 2 (Backhaus/Vienna Jan.53)
	Serenade 1 (Vienna March 1952)
Bruckner	Te Deum (Vienna November 1944)
Debussy	Childrens Corner (Vienna September 1952)
	Childrens Corner (Bamberg January 1953)
	La Mer (Vienna March 1953)
	Clarinet Rhapsody (Wlach/Vienna March 45)
	Epigraphes antiques (Vienna November 1951)
Granados	3 Spanish Dances (Vienna October 1941)
Haydn	Symphony 94 (Vienna 1941-Berlin 1944)
	Symphony 100 (Vienna September 1952)
Honegger	Joan of Arc Closing scene (Vienna 1950)
Mancinelli	Scene veneziane 3 (Vienna March 1945)
Martucci	Notturno (Vienna March 1945)

Marx	2 Songs (Ursuleac/Berlin November 1944)
	3 Songs (Ursuleac/Graz June 1953)
Mozart	Symphony 40 (Vienna October 1941)
	Symphony 41 (Vienna 1941)
	Symphony 41 (Bremen March 1952)
	Symphony 41 (Salzburg August 1952)
	Violin Cto 4 (Boskovsky/Klagenfurt 52)
	Zauberflöte Overture (Klagenfurt 1952)
	Figaro Closing scene (Salzburg 1942)
Mussorgsky	Pictures (Vienna date uncertain)
Paganini	Moto perpetuo (Vienna March 1945)
Pfitzner	Von deutscher Seele (Vienna Jan.1945)
Ravel	Bolero (Vienna October 1952)
	Daphnis 2nd Suite (Vienna March 1945)
	Alborada del gracioso (Vienna March.45)
	Barque sur l'océan (Vienna March 1945)
	Pavane (Vienna March 1945-Graz June 1953)
Respighi	Fontane di Roma (Vienna 1945-1950)
	Gli uccelli (Vienna March 1953)
Reznicek	Donna Diana Ov.(Klagenfurt Nov.1952)
Rimsky-Korsakov	Flight of bumble bee (Vienna 1941)
Rossini	Semiramide Ov. (Vienna March 1953)
Schubert	5 German Dances D90 (Vienna Feb.1944)
	Grand Duo D812 (Munich July 1952)
	Mass D960 (Vienna March-December 1944)
	Ständchen (Vienna 1941)
Smetana	Moldau (Berlin November 1944)
	Libussa Overture (Vienna October 1951)
Johann Strauss	New Year's Concert (Vienna January 1941)
	New Year's Concert (Vienna January 1954)
	Cagliostro Overture (Vienna date uncertain)
Richard Strauss	Burleske (Schilhawsky/Salzburg 1949)
	Duet-Concertino (Vienna April 1954)
	Festive Prelude (Berlin May 1935)
	Festive Prelude (Berlin November 1938)
	Friedenstag/complete (Vienna June 1939)
	Danae Symphonic Fragments (Vienna 1954)
	Salome/complete (London 1947)
	Hymne (Vienna October 1941)
	4 Letzte Lieder (Ursuleac/Vienna Apr.51)
	3 Letzte Lieder (Ursuleac/Graz June 53)
	Lied der Frauen (Ursuleac/Berlin Nov.44)
	Morgen (Patzak/Berlin November 1949)
	Zueignung (Ursuleac/Vienna April 1940)
Uhl	Sinfonia concertante (Wlach/Vienna Nov.44)

Verdi	Aida/complete (Munich September 1953) Eri tu (Ballo)(Ahlersmayer/Stuttgart ?) Falstaff excerpts (Vienna 1942) 4 pezzi sacri (Vienna March 1952)
Wagner	Senta's Ballad (Flagstad/Havana 1948) Götterdämmerung excpts (Vienna Nov.1934) Meistersinger excpts (Vienna Jan.1933) Meistersinger Overture (Vienna Jan.1933) Meistersinger Overture (Klagenfurt Mar.52) Die Walküre (Vienna June 1933
Weber	Abu Hassan Overture (Vienna March 1941) Oberon Overture (Vienna October 1952) Oberon Overture (Bamberg January 1953)

Salzburger Festspiele 1933

Im Festspielhaus
Uraufführung der neuen Wiener Fassung

Die ägyptische Helena

Oper in 2 Aufzügen von Hugo v. Hofmannsthal
Musik von Richard Strauß

Dirigent: Clemens Krauss
Inszenierung: Lothar Wallerstein
Bühnenbild: Alfred Roller und Robert Kautsky

Helena . . . . Viorica Ursuleac
Menelas . . . . Franz Völker
Hermione, beider Kind . . . . Irene Eisinger
Aithra, eine ägyptische Königstochter und
    Zauberin . . . . Margit Angerer
Altair . . . . Alfred Jerger
Da-Ud, sein Sohn . . . . Helge Roswaenge
Erste Dienerin der Aithra . . . . Luise Helletsgruber
Zweite Dienerin der Aithra . . . . Polly Batic
Erster Elf . . . . Aenne Michalsky
Zweiter Elf . . . . Margit Szathmary
Dritter Elf . . . . Fanny Salinger
Vierter Elf . . . . Frieda Stroinigg
Die alles wissende Muschel . . . . Gertrud Rünger

Elfen, männliche und weibliche Krieger, Sklaven, Eunuchen

Der erste Aufzug spielt auf der kleinen Insel der Aithra, unweit von Ägypten; der zweite in einem einsamen Palmenhain zu Füßen des Atlas

Krauss: a postscript

Some people are fated to be the subject of controversy and legend. One such was Austria's greatest conductor. Born on Good Friday, March 31, 1893 to dancer Clementine Krauss (then hardly 17 years old), who was not allowed to marry a father 30 years her senior, Clemens Krauss arrived with a golden spoon in his mouth. Never to meet cavalier Hector Baltazzi, Krauss was to be bothered all his life with tales of more aristocratic parentage, to the point that he would later have to declare publicly the circumstances of his birth.

His was the happiest and easiest of childhoods. His paths were made straight and rough places plain. The maternal great aunt, celebrated <u>diva</u> Gabrielle Krauss, would take the little boy regularly to a box at the State Opera. By the age of ten his beautiful voice has assured success as a leading boy soprano in the St. Stephen's Cathedral Imperial Choir. The world was his oyster and as Krauss grew he swept through the musical scene dispensing his unique brand of arrogance and charm. It is easy to see him, leaving the artists entrance of the Vienna State Opera clad in blue silk-lined hussars cape and smoking the inevitable Havana cigar, stepping into his magnificent Hispano-Suiza--the monarch of all he surveys. One hardly needed to see those Franz Josef sideburns to realize he was someone intimately connected with highest Court circles.

Many these days deplore the excessive haste with which young <u>wunderkind</u> conductors are brought forward without time to properly mature, and protest that this could not have happened in the old days. Krauss proves them wrong. By the age of 19 he was conducting opera in Brno. Appointed a full <u>Kappelmeister</u> in Riga, he must have been very nearly the youngest musican to hold so presitgious a post. Pushed to the "big time" too soon, the effects could have been disasterous. Fortunately--unlike some of the young lions today--Krauss' training and talent were equal to the challenge.

Soon after the Great War, as he was conducting opera at Graz, he was heard by Franz Schalk and brought to Vienna. At the age of 29 he became a conductor at the State Opera and on Schalk's retirement in 1929, its Director. This was a golden age for that august ensemble, particularly for singers, who adored Krauss--even if they did take exception to his habit, even at performances, of ostentatiously waving a large white handkerchief if they strayed from his beat. A fine singer himself, Krauss well understood their problems, supporting their voices on a cushion of sound rather than drowning them as some conductors did. They could rely on him to expose their voices when they were in top form and to cleverly cover them with the orchestra when they were not. Managers were not always as enamoured with him, for with them he could be autocratic and high-handed. But the Viennese Musical Establishment was never really sympathetic to so flamboyant a figure as Krauss. The official history of the State Opera has this to say of him:

> Schalk retired in 1929 to be followed by Clemens Krauss, who had been junior conductor in the early twenties, when by virtue of a carefully cultivated "glamour image" and affected mannerisms he had a bobby-soxer following worthy of a film star.

But his singers always doted on him, to such an extent that as Krauss moved about Europe, from one prestigious post to the next (The Berlin State Opera in 1934, Munich in 1937 and Salzburg in 1939) a galaxy of international stars would follow him like the Pied Piper.

In fact, just about the only fault they had to find with their maestro was that he would push his adored wife, soprano Viorica Ursuleac, into lead roles not always suited to her light coloratura voice.

The thirties and forties were the period of his great friendship with Richard Strauss. Krauss was always the composer's favorite conductor, and if you play those famous recordings of the tone poems issued by Decca in the early days of LP--still (amazingly) available today--you can see why. Karajan's discs may be superior from the standpoint of stereophonic richness, but musically speaking there is no contest. For sweetness without sentimentality and, at opposite ends of the orchestral palette for surging power and light-footed panache, they are unapproached. Strauss recognized this and was careful to arrange for his friend to conduct the world premieres of his new works.

Although some maintain that, like Herbert von Karajan, Krauss joined the Nazi party for reasons of advancement, those close to him state that this is not so. His life in Hitler's Germany shows a strong ambivalence: abhorrence of oppression and injustice impelled him to aid the escape of Jews, yet in things musical Krauss served the regime enthusiastically. Hitler, who thought Krauss the best conductor in Europe after Furtwangler, rewarded him with plum engagements, presents, decorations (including the Goethe Medal and the much-prized Order of the German Eagle) and gifts of money. This latter must have been especially welcome, since in spite of his and Viorica's large salaries there never seemed quite enough for them to live on in the princely style to which they were accustomed. Goering was an especial friend. After conducting the jovial Reich Marshall's birthday concert in January 1941 Krauss was presented with a magnificent sapphire ring, and his wife with a mink coat.

Throughout the war years Krauss guest-conducted throughout Hitler's Europe, frequently visiting France and conducting not only in Paris but also in provincial cities like Lyon, Marseilles and Bordeaux. Boulez has said that it was a golden age of music-making in the French capital, with a continued round of superb concerts by such masters as Gieseking, Mengelberg and Krauss.

After the war this did not sit well with the Allied authorities, who singled out Krauss for small-minded and spiteful harassment. He ended the war in Vienna, still conducting opera with Russian shells almost literally crashing around his ears. Indeed, he was engaged to lead the first post-war concert in the battered Musikverein with a multitude of Russian generals sitting in the front row of the stalls. The concert was a great success, the said generals inviting Krauss to a champagne supper afterward, and he was engaged to conduct several more. Then the Russian authorities found out that not only had Krauss frequently conducted at Nazi offical functions, but that he had been a personal friend of Hitler and Goering.

He was forbidden to perform or earn a living in any way connected with music. Retiring to his villa near Salzburg, Krauss lived in semi-retirement. He managed, illegally, to coach singers privately in his own home, and Viorica still managed to obtain a few engagements. From the summer of 1945 until the spring of 1947 they eked out this miserable existence.

In the autumn of 1947 he was invited to England to conduct concerts at the Albert Hall and opera at Covent Garden. It is interesting to note that Britian, which had suffered more in the war than any other country except the Soviet Union, was the first to extend the hand of reconciliation and friendship to such artists as Richard Strauss, Furtwangler, and Krauss.

But when these London engagements were over there was still no place for Krauss in the musical life of Europe. He managed to get to Lisbon, and from there sailed to South America. He had good contacts in Argentina especially, where he had conducted opera annually at the Teatro Colon beginning in 1927. Twice in the early thirties he had travelled there on the fabulous Graf Zeppelin, on one occasion sharing a cabin with his pianist friend Wilhelm Kempff.

In Buenos Aires he was able to renew his career in a sympathetic milieu--to conduct a series of concerts and some opera, including Honegger's Jeanne d'Arc. He stayed in South America for the whole of 1948, only returning to appear before the customary denazification Tribunal.

Soon the authorities began to relent. It is difficult, after all, to hand over your best posts to politically impeccable musical nomenties while artists of the calibre of Furtwangler, Knappertsbusch and Krauss languish in idleness. Krauss again began conducting regularly in West Berlin and Vienna and taking the Vienna Philharmonic on tours to countries as widely spaced as Greece, Portugal and Egypt.

In 1949 he took a flat in Rome, making it his base. That year he guest conducted in Vienna, Milan, London (recording with the London Symphony and London Philharmonic orchestras) and at the Bergen Festival.

In 1950 he finally returned to live in his beloved Vienna. Among the many triumphs of the year were four memorable performances of Tristan und Isolde at Covent Garden. He also began reappearing annually at the Salzburg Festival. In 1952 Krauss broke new ground, as far as his own career was concerned, by conducting the German repertory at La Scala. In 1953, with his heart already giving warnings, he became busier than ever, appearing at Covent Garden for a still-remembered production of Die Meistersinger, the Paris Opera with Strauss' Danae and Salzburg with Rosenkavalier. For the first time he conducted at Bayreuth and was responsible for both the Ring and Parsifal.

1953 brought the blow which many said killed Krauss. The Vienna City Council decided to appoint again a Chief Conductor of the State Opera, perhaps--with the conductorship of the Berlin Philharmonic--one of the two most sought-after posts in Europe. The position belonged to Krauss almost by divine right, or so went gossip in the Vienna coffeehouses. Certainly, Krauss expected to be appointed. When everybody had made up their minds that the actual announcement would be a mere formality--at the very last moment--the decision went to Karl Bohm instead.

It could only have been a political decision. Many felt this blow aggravated the heart condition which was within a year to kill him. However, it must be said that it probably would have happened anyway. Krauss had grown first stout and, by now, positively corpulent. He always lived like a Rajah and his energetic and flamboyant style of conducting must have imposed a considerable strain. John L. Holmes states in his Conductors on Record that Krauss gestures "were economical"--a statement not born out by a film clip I saw some years ago in which he wielded the baton like a duellist his rapier! And that excellent critic, George R. Marek, speaks of his flamboyant, actor-like gestures on the podium. Certainly he seems to have enjoyed "hamming it up." His musical taste was, however, always impeccable and his musicianship superb. His style was compounded of steely springing rhythms and what I can only describe as a unique kind of swagger. Listen to the grand opening pages of his recording of the "Emperor" Concerto with Backhaus and you will see what I mean.

In the end he ignored his doctors and declined to slow down. The last few months of his life found him conducting in cities as far apart as London and Caracas, Sofia and Cairo, Barcelona and Rio.

In May of 1954 he was in Mexico City to conduct a series of concerts in connection with the German Trade Fair being held in that city. The effort of performing in that thin atmosphere brought on a heart attack and he died at his hotel on the night of May 16, 1954. He was but 61 years of age. He lay in state in the Opera House: the flags of the Trade Fair flew at half mast. A Lufthansa airliner brought his body back to Vienna and a few days later he was buried high on a mountain side in the Austrian Tyrol. At the time of his death he was fully booked for the next two years: tours of South America, Australia and Japan; three cycles of the Ring for that Summer's Bayreuth Festival; Mozart and Wagner at Covent Garden and a film of Die Fledermaus to be made by the same company that had produced Beecham's superb Tales of Hoffman. But these plans were not for this lifetime. Fortunately, he left a wonderful legacy of recordings, including a live Ring from Bayreuth. His reputation is safe, lovingly fostered to this day by Docktor Klauss Kende, head of the Clemens Krauss Archiv in Vienna, his glorious music-making ever ready to soar again at the touch of a switch.

The memory of Clemens Krauss, as one of the most colorful and romantic interpreters from the golden age of great conducting, is still with those of us who had the good fortune to see and hear him "live." Those who came too late can at least obtain his recordings as they appear--and will be well advised to do so. Nothing comparable is being produced today.

Bill Flowers kindly contributed this article, which he originally wrote for the Si Thomas Beecham Society

Anton Dermota
Discography

compiled by John Hunt

ANTON DERMOTA

THE LEADING lyric tenor of the Vienna State Opera and one of the finest of present-day Mozart singers, Anton Dermota was born in Yugoslavia. He was one of seven children, all of whom sang in the local church choir.

Dermota had no intention of taking up singing as a career; his musical studies in Laibach were the organ and composition. In 1934 he went to Vienna to further his studies, and his vocal qualities were discovered. He continued at the Academy for a further two years and then was engaged for the Vienna State Opera by Bruno Walter. His first big role was that of Lensky in *Eugene Onegin*, which he sang during the 1937-8 season; and in the summer of 1938 he made a sensational Salzburg début as Don Ottavio, a role he has sung there many times since.

Dermota's roles in Vienna include most of the lyric parts in the Italian repertory—Ernesto, Alfredo, the Duke of Mantua, Rodolfo, etc.; the Mozart parts of Tamino, Ottavio, Belmonte, Ferrando; the title role in *Les Contes d'Hoffmann*, des Grieux in *Manon*, David in *Meistersinger*, Jacquino in *Fidelio*, Flamand in Strauss' *Capriccio*, and Eisenstein in *Die Fledermaus*.

Dermota sang at Covent Garden with the Vienna Company in 1947 and has appeared with success in Paris, Milan, Rome, Naples, and South America.

Dermota is also a fine *Lieder* singer and is often accompanied at his recitals by his wife, herself an accomplished musician.

Dermota possesses a remarkably beautiful tenor voice, and is certainly one of the most accomplished Mozart stylists since Richard Tauber.

From the Decca Book of Opera

THE ROYAL PHILHARMONIC SOCIETY

Founded 24th January, 1813

Under the immediate patronage of
HER MAJESTY THE QUEEN

150th ANNIVERSARY SEASON
1962 — 1963

ROYAL FESTIVAL HALL
(General Manager: T. E. Bean, c.b.e.)

LAST CONCERT OF SERIES

Wednesday April 24, at 8 p.m.
HERBERT VON KARAJAN

Symphony No. 1 in C	*Beethoven*
Symphony No. 9 in D Minor (Choral)	*Beethoven*
(Composed for and dedicated to the Society)	

VIENNA PHILHARMONIC ORCHESTRA
(*Leader:* WILLI BOSKOVSKY)

PHILHARMONIA CHORUS
(*Chorus Master:* WILHELM PITZ)

Soloists

ANTON DERMOTA	HILDE RÖSSEL-MAJDAN
GUNDULA JANOWITZ	OTTO WIENER

STALLS 63/- 42/- 30/-   TERRACE 63/- 42/- 30/- 21/- 15/-   BOXES 63/- 42/- per seat
GRAND TIER 42/- 30/- 21/- 15/-   ANNEXE 30/- 15/-

Tickets on sale March 23rd from usual agencies, ROYAL FESTIVAL HALL (WATerloo 3191) and CHAPPELL & CO. LTD., 50 New Bond Street, W.1 (MAYfair 7600).

For particulars of membership, apply Hon. Sec., 4 St. James's Square, S.W.1 (TRAfalgar 2585)

Bach

Cantata No 12 "Weinen, Klagen, Sorgen, Zagen"; Cantata No 29 "Wir danken dir, Gott"

Vienna May 1960	Tenor soloist Davrath, Berry, Rössl-Majdan Kammerchor VPO Wöldike	LP: Bach Guild BG 610/BG 5035 LP: Amadeo AVRS 6212 LP: Philips SAL 3514

Cantata No 78 "Jesu, der du meine Seele"; Cantata No 106 "Gottes Zeit ist die allerbeste Zeit"

Vienna 1954	Tenor soloist Stich-Randall, Hermann, Braun Orchestra Prohaska	LP: Bach Guild BG 537 LP: Amadeo AVRS 6003 LP: Vanguard HM 21

Magnificat

Vienna 1957	Tenor soloist Coertse, Rössl-Majdan, Guthrie ORF Chorus VPO Prohaska	LP: Bach Guild BG 555/BG 5005 LP: Amadeo AVRS 6076 LP: Vanguard HM 22 LP: Top Rank XRK 507

Mass in B minor

Vienna 1950	Tenor soloist Loose, Ceska, Burgsthaler-Schuster, Poell Akademiechor VSO Scherchen	LP: Westminster WL 5037-9/3WEST 3305 LP: Nixa WLP 6301

Saint Matthew Passion

Vienna April 1954	Evangelist and tenor arias Grümmer, Höffgen, Fischer-Dieskau, Edelmann Singakademie VPO Furtwängler	LP: Fonit Cetra LO 50 LP: Movimento Musica 03.008 LP: Fonit Cetra FE 34 CD: Movimento Musica 013.005
Buenos Aires May 1950	Evangelist and tenor arias N.Hoffmann, Klose, Mattiello, Greindl Teatro Colon Chorus & Orchestra Furtwängler	LP: Japan AT 115-6 Abridged version

Beethoven

Fidelio

Salzburg
August 1950

Role of Jacquino
Flagstad,
Schwarzkopf,
Patzak, Greindl,
Schöffler, Braun
Vienna Opera Chorus
VPO
Furtwängler

LP: Morgan MOR 5001
LP: MRF Records MRF 50
LP: BJR REcords BJR 112
LP: Discocorp IGI 328
LP: Fonit Cetra FE 44
CD: Hunt CDWFE 304/CDWFE 354

Vienna
November 1955

Role of Florestan
Mödl, Seefried,
Kmennt, Weber,
Schöffler, Kamann
Vienna Opera Chorus
VPO
Böhm

LP: Melodram MEL 008
CD: Frequenz CMM 2
CD: Movimento Musica 051.024
Gott, welch Dunkel hier
CD: Melodram CDM 26522

Fidelio: Excerpt (Gott, welch Dunkel hier)

Ljublyana
1970

Role of Florestan
Llubjana RO
Hubad

LP: Preiser SPR 3310
CD: Preiser 90022

Leonore

Bregenz
July 1960

Role of Florestan
Zadek, Scheyrer,
Pfeifle, Schöffler,
Von Rohr, Braun
Vienna Opera Chorus
VSO
Leitner

LP: Melodiya M10 47907 009
CD: Melodram CDM 27085
CD: Memories HR 4251-2

Missa Solemnis

Berlin
1955

Tenor soloist
Stader, Radev,
Greindl
St Hedwig's Choir
BPO
Böhm

LP: DG LPM 18 224-5/auto LPM 18 232-3
LP: DG 89 679-80
LP: Discocorp IGI 384
Discocorp incorrectly labelled as
wartime performance

Choral Fantasy

Vienna
June 1957

Tenor soloist
Stich-Randall,
Hellwig, Majkut,
Rössl-Majdan,
Schöffler,
Richter-Haaser, piano
Vienna Opera Chorus
VSO
Böhm

LP: Philips 663 000 ER
LP: Philips 6833 188
This appears to be the only recorded
version employing solo voices in
addition to a chorus

Symphony No 9 "Choral"

Vienna June 1952	Tenor soloist Güden, Wagner, Weber Singverein VPO Kleiber	LP: Decca LXT 2725-6/LXT 5362-3 LP: Decca LXT 5645 LP: Decca LXT 6277-80/SXL 6277-80 LP: Decca ECM 501/ECS 501 CD: Decca 425 9552
Vienna May 1953	Tenor soloist Seefried, Anday, Schöffler Singakademie VPO Furtwängler	LP: Discocorp RR 460 LP: German Furtwängler Society F669.056-7 CD: Rodolphe RPC 32465 CD: Hunt CD 532 CD: Nuova Era 6301/6300 CD: Virtuoso 269.7202 CD: DG 435 3252/435 3212
Vienna June 1957	Tenor soloist Stich-Randall, Rössl-Majdan, Schöffler Vienna Opera Chorus VSO Böhm	LP: Philips 698 000 CL LP: Philips GL 5810 LP: Philips 6833 080 Last movement LP: Philips 6833 188
Geneva April 1959	Tenor soloist Sutherland, Procter, Van Mill Suisse Romande Chorus & Orchestra Ansermet	LP: Decca SXL 2274 LP: Decca ACL 77 LP: Decca SDD 108 CD: Pickwick PWK 1150

An die ferne Geliebte, song-cycle

Vienna October 1974	H.Dermota, piano	LP: Preiser SPR 3292 CD: Preiser 93256

Brahms

Wiegenlied

London April 1948	Newton, piano	78: Decca M 620

Wir wandelten; Ständchen

Vienna January 1975	H.Dermota, piano	LP: Preiser SPR 3256 CD: Preiser 93256

Cornelius

Der Barbier von Bagdad: Excerpt (Vor deinem Fenster die Blumen)

Berlin 1944	Role of Nureddin Berlin RO Rother	LP: Acanta DE 23.120-1

Der Barbier von Bagdad: Excerpt (So leb' ich noch)

Hamburg 1950	Role of Nureddin NDR Orchestra Schüchter	LP: Melodram MEL 090

Donizetti

L'Elisir d'amore: Excerpt (Una furtiva lagrima)

Berlin 1943	Role of Nemorino Berlin RO Heger	78: Telefunken E 3755/E 1046 LP: Acanta DE 23.120-1
Berlin May 1954	Role of Nemorino Städtische Oper Orchestra Rother	78: Telefunken A 11599 LP: Telefunken LGX 66048/TM 68037 LP: Telefunken NT 382/BLE 14503 LP: Preiser PR 135003 CD: Preiser 90022

Flotow

Alessandro Stradella: Excerpt (Wie freundlich strahlt der Tag - Jungfrau Maria)

Berlin 1944	Role of Stradella Berlin RO Rother	LP: Acanta DE 23.120-1

Martha: Excerpt (Ach so fromm)

Berlin 1944	Role of Lyonel Berlin RO Rother	LP: Acanta DE 23.120-1

Gluck

Paride ed Elena: Excerpt (O del mio dolce ardor)

Berlin November 1956	Role of Paride Städtische Oper Orchestra Rother	LP: Telefunken BLE 14503

Grieg

Ich liebe dich

London April 1948	Newton, piano	78: Decca M 620

Haydn

Nelson Mass (Missa Solemnis)

Vienna 1955	Tenor soloist Stich-Randall, Höngen, Guthrie Akademiechor VPO Rossi	LP: Vanguard VRS 470 LP: Amadeo AVRS 6021/AVRS 19023

Paukenmesse (Missa in tempore belli)

Vienna May 1960	Tenor soloist Davrath, Berry, Rössl-Majdan Kammerchor VPO Wöldike	LP: Vanguard VRS 1061/VRS 2075 LP: Amadeo AVRS 6193 LP: Vanguard VSL 11030

Die Schöpfung

Vienna January 1955	Tenor soloist Stich-Randall, Felbermayer, Guthrie, Schöffler Vienna Opera Chorus VPO Wöldike	LP: Vanguard VRS 471-2 LP: Amadeo AVRS 6024-5 LP: Philips G 04203-4 L LP: Philips GL 5726-7

Ipavec

Songs: Ce na poljane rosa pade; Pozabil sem mnogokaj, dekle; Iz gozda so ptice odplule; Ciganka Marija; V spominsko knjigo; Oblaku; Mak zari; Na poljani; Menih; V mrak in vihar

Vienna 1972	H.Dermota, piano	LP: Gallus LP 54

Janacek

Jenufa: Excerpt (Gehen sie, geh' auch du)

Place and date uncertain	Lienbach Orchestra Sung in German	LP: Melodram MEL 090

Jez

Na gori

Vienna Date uncertain	H.Dermota, piano	LP: Gallus LP 44

Kienzl

Der Evangelimann: Excerpt (Selig sind, die Verfolgung leiden)

Hamburg 1950	Role of Mathias NDR Orchestra Schüchter	LP: Melodram MEL 090

Kogoj

Otoznost

Vienna Date uncertain	H.Dermota, piano	LP: Gallus LP 44

Korngold

Die tote Stadt: Excerpt (Glück, das mir verblieb)

Vienna 1949	Role of Paul Steingruber Austrian RO Korngold	CD: Cambria 1032
Vienna Date uncertain	Role of Paul Zadek Tonkünstler- orchester Loibner	78: Harmonia 14004/15012 LP: Remington R 199.123 LP: Varèse Sarabande 81040

Die Kathrin: Excerpts (Szene im Nachtlokal; Wanderlied)

Vienna 1949	Role of Francois Schwaiger Austrian RO Kassowitz/ Korngold (Wanderlied)	CD: Cambria 1032

Kozina

Songs: V dno srca; Veseli gosti

Vienna Date uncertain	H.Dermota, piano	LP: Gallus LP 44

Lajovic

Songs: Cveti, cveti rozica; Mesec v izbi; Vecer

Vienna Date uncertain	H.Dermota, piano	LP: Gallus LP 44

Lehar

Giuditta: Excerpt (Du bist meine Sonne)

Berlin   Role of Octavio   78: Telefunken A 10455
1939   Orchestra and
           conductor uncertain

Das Land des Lächelns: Excerpt (Dein ist mein ganzes Herz)

Berlin   Role of Sou-Chong   78: Telefunken A 10455
1939   Orchestra and
           conductor uncertain

Leoncavallo

I Pagliacci: Excerpts (1. Ah! Colombina, il tenero fido Arlecchin; 2. Vesti la giubba

Berlin   Roles of Beppe (1)   LP: Acanta DE 23.120-1
1944   and Canio (2)
           Berlin RO
           Rother
           Sung in German

I Pagliacci: Excerpt (Un tal gioco, credetemi)

Hamburg   Role of Canio   LP: Melodram MEL 090
1950   NDR Orchestra
            Schüchter
            Sung in German

Lipovsek

Ti si zacarala me

Vienna   H.Dermota, piano   LP: Gallus LP 44
Date uncertain

Lotti

Pur dicesti

Berlin   Städtische Oper   LP: Telefunken BLE 14503
November 1956   Orchestra
                 Rother

Mahler

Das Lied von der Erde

Vienna	Tenor soloist	LP: Vox PL 7000
May 1951	Cavelti	LP: Vox VBX 115
	VSO	LP: Vox GBY 11890
	Klemperer	LP: Pickwick MPD 901
		CD: Tuxedo TUXCD 1036

Maillart

Das Glöckchen des Eremiten: Excerpt (O schweige still)

Berlin	Role of Sylvain	LP: Acanta DE 23.120-1
1944	Berlin RO	
	Rother	

Marx

Lieder: Japanisches Wiegenlied; Marienlied; Selige Nacht; Waldseligkeit; Venezianische Wiegenlied; Hat dich die Liebe berührt; other Lieder sung by Wilma Lipp)

Vienna	Marx, piano	LP: Amadeo AVRS 3006
1957		

Mascagni

Cavalleria Rusticana: Excerpt (Mamma, quel vino è generoso)

Berlin	Role of Turiddu	78: Telefunken E 3871
1943	Berlin RO	
	Heger	
	Sung in German	

Cavalleria Rusticana: Excerpt (O Lola ch' hai di latti la cammisa sì bianca)

Berlin	Role of Turiddu	LP: Acanta DE 23.120-1
1944	Berlin RO	
	Rother	
	Sung in German	

Massenet

Manon: Excerpts (En fermant les yeux; Ah fuyez, douce image)

Berlin 1939-1944 Precise date uncertain	Role of Des Grieux Berlin RO Heger Sung in German	78: Telefunken E 2910 LP: Acanta DE 23.120-1

Manon: Extracts

Hamburg 1950	Role of Des Grieux Jurinac, Roth NDR Orchestra Schüchter Sung in German	LP: Melodram MEL 089/MEL 090

Mendelssohn

Die erste Walpurgisnacht

Vienna April 1952	Tenor soloist Wagner, Edelmann, Singakademie VSO Markevitch	CD: Memories HR 4193-4

Meyerbeer

L'Africaine: Excerpt (O paradis!)

Stuttgart 1953	Role of Vasco SDR Orchestra Müller-Kray Sung in German	LP: Melodram MEL 090

Mozart

Così fan tutte

Vienna May 1955	<u>Role of Ferrando</u> Della Casa, C.Ludwig, Loose Kunz, Schöffler Vienna Opera Chorus VPO Böhm	LP: Decca LXT 5107-9 LP: Decca GOM 543-5/GOS 543-5 <u>Excerpts</u> LP: Decca LXT 5111/SXL 2058 LP: Decca BR 3085 45: Decca CEP 572

Così fan tutte: Excerpt (Un aura amorosa)

Berlin 1943	<u>Role of Ferrando</u> Berlin RO Heger <u>Sung in German</u>	78: Telefunken E 3871 LP: Acanta DE 23.120-1
Berlin April 1955	<u>Role of Ferrando</u> Städtische Oper Orchestra Rother <u>Sung in German</u>	LP: Telefunken LGX 66048/TM 68047 LP: Telefunken NT 382 LP: Preiser PR 135003 CD: Preiser 90022
Hamburg Date uncertain	<u>Role of Ferrando</u> NDR Orchestra Brückner-Rüggeberg	LP: World Records TP 77 LP: Joker SM 1143

Don Giovanni

Salzburg July and August 1950	Role of Ottavio Schwarzkopf, Welitsch, Seefried, Gobbi, Greindl, Kunz, Poell Vienna Opera Chorus VPO Furtwängler	LP: Ed Smith EJS 419 LP: Olympic 9109 LP: Discocorp RR 407 LP: Turnabout THS 65154-6 LP: Melodram MEL 713 CD: RCA (Japan) R30C 1014-6 CD: Priceless D 16581 CD: Laudis LCD 34001 Excerpts CD: Melodram MEL 26511
Hamburg 1951	Role of Ottavio Martinis, Danco, Lore Hoffmann, Kunz, Schöffler, Neidlinger, Ludwig Hoffmann NDR Chorus and Orchestra L.Ludwig	LP: Melodram MEL 015
Salzburg July 1953	Role of Ottavio Schwarzkopf, Grümmer, Berger, Siepi, Edelmann, Arié, Berry Vienna Opera Chorus VPO Furtwängler	CD: Rodolphe RPC 32527-30 CD: Virtuoso 269.9052
Salzburg August 1954	Role of Ottavio Schwarzkopf Grümmer, Berger, Siepi, Edelmann, Ernster, Berry Vienna Opera Chorus VPO Furtwängler	LP: Morgan MOR 5302 LP: Discocorp MORG 003 LP: Fonit Cetra LO 7 LP: Foyer FO 1017 LP: Fonit Cetra FE 23 LP: EMI EX 29 06673 CD: Music and Arts CD 003 CD: Hunt CD 509 CD: EMI CMS 763 8602 Excerpts LP: Gioielli della lirica GML 05 Final scene taken from the 1953 performance
Vienna June 1955	Role of Ottavio Della Casa, Danco, Güden, Siepi, Corena, Böhme, Poell Vienna Opera Chorus VPO Krips	LP: Decca LXT 5103-6/SXL 2117-20 LP: Decca GOS 604-6 CD: Decca 411 4262 Excerpts LP: Decca LXT 5443 LP: Decca BR 3025/SWL 8003 45: Decca CEP 613/SEC 5032 LP: Decca SDD 460

ROYAL OPERA HOUSE

COVENT GARDEN

VIENNA STATE OPERA

1947

Saturday, September 20th, 1947

DON GIOVANNI

An Opera Bouffe in Two Acts by Da Ponte after
a Spanish Tale by Tirso de Molina

Music by Mozart

Conductor : Josef Krips

Producer : Oscar Fritz Schuh

Costumes and Decor : Robert Kautsky

Don Giovanni, a Castilian Dandy	PAUL SCHOEFFLER
The Commandant	LUDWIG WEBER
Donna Anna, his daughter	LJUBA WELITSCH
Don Octavio, Donna Anna's fiancé	ANTON DERMOTA
Donna Elvira, A lady of Burgos, and wife of Don Giovanni	ELISABETH SCHWARZKOPF
Leporello, servant of Don Giovanni	GEORG HANN
Zerlina, a peasant	EMMY LOOSE
Masetto, betrothed to Zerlina	ALFRED POELL

Don Giovanni: Excerpt (Dalla sua pace)

Berlin 1943	<u>Role of Ottavio</u> Berlin RO Heger <u>Sung in German</u>	78: Telefunken E 3162 LP: Acanta DE 23.120-1
London April 1948	<u>Role of Ottavio</u> New SO Krips	78: Decca K 2125
Vienna September 1950	<u>Role of Ottavio</u> VPO Böhm	78: Decca K 28393 LP: Decca LXT 2592/LXT 2685 LP: Everest 3202 LP: Telefunken 642.233
Vienna November 1955	<u>Role of Ottavio</u> VPO Böhm <u>Sung in German</u>	CD: Melodram CDM 26522
Hamburg Date uncertain	<u>Role of Ottavio</u> NDR Orchestra Brückner-Rüggeberg	LP: World Records TP 77/Saga 5362 LP: Joker SM 1142 CD: Tuxedo TUXCD 1018

Don Giovanni: Excerpt (Il mio tesoro)

Berlin 1943	Role of Ottavio Berlin RO Heger Sung in German	LP: Acanta DE 23.120-1
Vienna September 1950	Role of Ottavio VPO Böhm	78: Decca K 28393 LP: Decca LXT 2592/LXT 2685 LP: Everest 3202 LP: Telefunken 642.233
Vienna November 1955	Role of Ottavio VPO Böhm Sung in German	CD: Melodram CDM 26522
Hamburg Date uncertain	Role of Ottavio NDR Orchestra Brückner-Rüggeberg	LP: World Records TP 77/Saga 5362 LP: Joker SM 1142 CD: Tuxedo TUXCD 1018

Don Giovanni: Excerpt (Fuggi, crudele, fuggi....Or sai che l'onore)

Vienna November 1955	Role of Ottavio Della Casa VPO Böhm Sung in German	CD: Melodram CDM 26522

Don Giovanni: Excerpt (Final scene)

Salzburg August 1954	Role of Ottavio Della Casa, Berger, Grümmer, Siepi, Edelmann, Berry VPO Furtwängler	LP: Furtwängler Series (Japan) W 28-29 Taken from the film soundtrack (Connoisseur Films/Beta Films)

Die Entführung aus dem Serail

Vienna 1945	Role of Belmonte Schwarzkopf, Loose, Klein, Alsen Austrian Radio Chorus & Orchestra Moralt	LP: Melodram MEL 047 Excerpt LP: BASF 05215490 BASF incorrectly labelled as conducted by Böhm 1944
Berlin December 1949	Role of Belmonte Barabas, Streich, Krebs, Greindl Berlin Radio Chorus & Orchestra Fricsay	LP: Movimento Musica 02.001

Die Entführung aus dem Serail: Excerpts (Hier soll ich dich denn sehen?; Konstanze! Dich wiederzusehen?)

Berlin April 1955	Role of Belmonte Städtische Oper Orchester Rother	LP: Telefunken LGX 66048/TM 68047 LP: Telefunken NT 382 LP: Preiser 135 003 CD: Preiser 90022
Vienna 1969	Role of Belmonte VPO Wallberg	CD: Melodram CDM 26522

Die Entführung aus dem Serail: Excerpt (Wenn der Freude Tränen fliessen)

Berlin 1944	Role of Belmonte Berlin RO Heger	LP: Acanta DE 23.120-1
Berlin April 1955	Role of Belmonte Städtische Oper Orchester Rother	LP: Telefunken LGX 66048/TM 68047 LP: Telefunken NT 382 LP: Preiser 135 003 CD: Preiser 90022
Vienna 1969	Role of Belmonte VPO Wallberg	CD: Melodram CDM 26522

Die Entführung aus dem Serail: Excerpt (Ich baue ganz)

Berlin November 1956	Role of Belmonte Städtische Oper Orchester Rother	LP: Telefunken BLE 14503

Die Entführung aus dem Serail: Excerpt (Welch ein Geschick!)

Vienna 1969	Role of Belmonte Coertse VPO Wallberg	CD: Melodram CDM 26522

Die Zauberflöte

Salzburg July 1937	Role of First Armed Man Novotna, Osvath, Komarek, Rosvaenge, Domgraf-Fassbänder, Kipnis, Jerger Vienna Opera Chorus VPO Toscanini	LP: Toscanini Society ATS 1025-7 LP: MRF Records MRF 71 LP: Estro Armonico EA 056 LP: Fonit Cetra LO 44 CD: Melodram MEL 37040
Vienna November 1950	Role of Tamino Seefried, Lipp, Loose, Kunz, Weber, London Singverein VPO Karajan	78: Columbia (Austria) LWX 426-444 LP: Columbia 33CX 1013-5 LP: EMI SLS 5052 LP: Electrola 1C 197 54200-8M CD: EMI CHS 769 6312 Excerpts LP: Columbia 33CX 1572 LP: Electrola 1C 187 29235-6M LP: EMI RLS 764
Salzburg August 1951	Role of Tamino Seefried, Lipp, Oravez, Kunz, Greindl, Schöffler Vienna Opera Chorus VPO Furtwängler	LP: Fonit Cetra LO 9 LP: Foyer FO 1028 LP: Fonit Cetra FE 19 CD: Foyer 3CF-2008 CD: Priceless D 16603 CD: Rodolphe RPC 32527-30 CD: Hunt CDWFE 361 Excerpts LP: Gioielli della lirica GML 14
Buenos Aires September 1958	Role of Tamino Lorengar, Streich, Chelavine, Berry, Van Mill, Schöffler Teatro Colon Chorus & Orchestra Beecham	LP: Melodram MEL 462

Die Zauberflöte: Excerpt (Dies Bildnis ist bezaubernd schön)

Berlin 1943	Role of Tamino Berlin RO Heger	78: Telefunken E 3162 LP: Acanta DE 23.120-1
London April 1948	Role of Tamino New SO Krips	78: Decca K 2125
Vienna September 1950	Role of Tamino VPO Böhm	45: Decca 45-71116 LP: Decca LXT 2592/LXT 2685 LP: Everest 3202 LP: Telefunken 642.233
Hamburg Date uncertain	Role of Tamino NDR Orchestra Brückner-Ruggeberg	LP: World Records TP 77
Vienna 1970	Role of Tamino VPO Krips	CD: Melodram CDM 26522

Die Zauberflöte: Excerpt (Wie stark ist nicht dein Zauberton)

Stuttgart 1953	Role of Tamino SDR Orchestra Müller-Kray	LP: Melodram MEL 090
Berlin April 1955	Role of Tamino Städtische Oper Orchestra Rother	LP: Telefunken LGX 66048 LP: Telefunken NT 382 LP: Preiser PR 135003 CD: Preiser 90022

Die Zauberflöte: Excerpts (Wo willst du, kühner Fremdling, hin?; Der, welcher wandert diese Strassen)

Vienna 1970	Role of Tamino Janowitz, Wächter, Beirer, Pernerstorfer VPO Krips	CD: Melodram CDM 26522

Die ihr des unermesslichen Weltalls

Berlin November 1956	Städtische Oper Orchestra Rother	LP: Telefunken BLE 14503

Per pietà, non ricercate, concert aria K420

Berlin November 1956	Städtische Oper Orchestra Rother	LP: Preiser PR 135003 CD: Preiser 90022

Lieder: An Chloe; Abendempfindung

Vienna January 1975	H.Dermota, piano	LP: Preiser SPR 3256 CD: Preiser 93256

Mass in C minor

Vienna 1976	Tenor soloist Gruberova, Winkelmayer, Holl Austrian Radio Chorus & Orchestra Heiller	ORF private issue

Requiem

Paris June 1937	Tenor soloist Schumann, Thorborg, Kipnis Vienna Opera Chorus VPO Walter	LP: EMI EG 29 07811 CD: EMI CHS 763 9122
Vienna June 1956	Tenor soloist Lipp, Rössl-Majdan, Edelmann Singverein VPO Walter	LP: Sony (Japan) SOCO 111
Salzburg July 1956	Tenor soloist Della Casa, Malaniuk, Siepi Vienna Opera Chorus VPO Walter	LP: Fonit Cetra LO 516 CD: Nuova Era 2209
Berlin October 1961	Tenor soloist Lipp, Rössl-Majdan, Berry Singverein VPO Karajan	LP: DG LPM 18 767/SLPM 138 767 LP: DG 2535 257 CD: DG 423 2132/429 1602

Offenbach

Les Contes d'Hoffmann: Excerpt (Il était une fois)

Stuttgart 1953	Role of Hoffmann SDR Orchestra Müller-Kray Sung in German	LP: Melodram MEL 090

Osterc

Sonce v zaresah

Vienna Date uncertain	H.Dermota, piano	LP: Gallus LP 44

Pavcik

Pred durmi; Mlada pesem

Vienna Date uncertain	H.Dermota, piano	LP: Gallus LP 44

Pergolesi

Nina

Berlin November 1956	Städtische Oper Orchestra Rother	LP: Telefunken BLE 14503

Puccini

La Bohème: Excerpt (O Mimì, tu più non torni)

Berlin	Role of Rodolfo	78: Telefunken E 3880
1943	Berlin RO	
	Heger	
	Sung in German	

La Fanciulla del West: Excerpt (Ch' ella mi creda)

Berlin	Role of Johnson	LP: Acanta DE 23.120-1
1944	Berlin RO	
	Rother	

Madama Butterfly: Excerpts (Io so che alle sue pene....; Addio, fiorito asil)

Berlin	Role of Pinkerton	78: Telefunken A 11054
1943	Demmer, Oeggl	
	Orchestra and	
	conductor uncertain	
	Sung in German	

Manon Lescaut: Excerpt (Donna non vidi mai)

Berlin	Role of Des Grieux	LP: Acanta DE 23.120-1
1944	Berlin RO	
	Heger	
	Sung in German	

La Rondine: Excerpts

Vienna	Role of Ruggiero	LP: Melodram MEL 090/MEL 095
1955	Welitsch	
	Austrian RO	
	Zallinger	
	Sung in German	

Tosca: Excerpt (Recondita armonia)

Berlin 1939	Role of Cavaradossi Berlin RO Rother	78: Telefunken A 10000 LP: Acanta DE 23.120-1
Berlin May 1954	Role of Cavaradossi Städtische Oper Orchestra Rother	78: Telefunken A 11599 LP: Telefunken TM 68037 LP: Telefunken NT 382/BLE 14503 LP: Preiser PR 135003 CD: Preiser 90022

Tosca: Excerpt (E lucevan le stelle)

Berlin 1939	Role of Cavaradossi Berlin RO Rother	78: Telefunken A 10000 LP: Acanta DE 23.120-1
Saarbrücken 1951	Role of Cavaradossi Saarland RO Michl	LP: Melodram MEL 090 CD: Melodram CDM 26522
Berlin May 1954	Role of Cavaradossi Städtische Oper Orchestra Rother	78: Telefunken A 11599 LP: Telefunken TM 68037 LP: Telefunken NT 382/BLE 14503 LP: Preiser PR 135003 CD: Preiser 90022

Turandot: Excerpt (Non piangere, Liù)

Berlin 1940	Role of Calaf Berlin RO Rother Sung in German	78: Telefunken A 10087 LP: Acanta DE 23.120-1

Turandot: Excerpt (Nessun dorma)

Berlin 1940	Role of Calaf Berlin RO Rother Sung in German	78: Telefunken A 10087
Berlin 1948	Role of Calaf Berlin RO Hundertmark Sung in German	LP: Melodram MEL 090

Ravnik

Songs: Vasovalec; Temna, lepa noc; V razkusni sreci

Vienna   H.Dermota, piano   LP: Gallus LP 44
Date uncertain

Rossini

Stabat mater

Vienna	Tenor soloist	LP: Oceanic OCS 24
1952	Steingruber,	LP: Quadrofoglio VDS 379
	Herrmann, Schöffler	LP: Saga XID 5216
	Akademiechor	Also issued on Classics Club label
	VPO	
	Sternberg	

Schmidt

Das Buch mit sieben Siegeln

Salzburg	Role of Johannes	LP: Melodram MEL 705
August 1959	Güden, Malaniuk,	CD: Melodram MEL 27078
	Wunderlich, Berry	
	Vienna Opera Chorus	
	VPO	
	Mitropoulos	
Vienna	Role of Johannes	LP: Preiser SPR 3263-4
December 1975	Kyriaki, Töpper,	
	Moser, Holl	
	Graz Choir	
	Tonkünstlerorchester	
	Hochstrasser	

Schubert

Winterreise

Vienna September 1962	H.Dermota, piano	LP: Telefunken BLE 43072-3/SLT 43072-3 Selection LP: Telefunken NT 538
Vienna December 1976	H.Dermota, piano	LP: Preiser SPR 3287

Die schöne Müllerin

Vienna 1952	H.Dermota, piano	LP: London (USA) LL 971
Vienna December 1976	H.Dermota, piano	LP: Preiser SPR 3274

Auf dem Strome

Vienna February 1977	H.Dermota, piano Freund, horn	LP: Preiser SPR 3292

Nacht und Träume; Der Musensohn

Vienna January 1975	H.Dermota, piano	LP: Preiser SPR 3256 CD: Preiser 93256

Schumann

Dichterliebe

Berlin May 1954	H.Dermota, piano	LP: Telefunken LE 6522/LGX 66023
Vienna January 1975	H.Dermota, piano	LP: Preiser SPR 3256 CD: Preiser 93256

Liederkreis op 39

Vienna October 1974	H.Dermota, piano	LP: Preiser SPR 3292

Mondnacht (Liederkreis op 39)

London September 1947	H.Dermota, piano	78: Decca M 619
Berlin May 1954	H.Dermota, piano	LP: Telefunken LE 6522/LGX 66023 LP: Melodram MEL 090

Schöne Fremde (Liederkreis op 39)

Berlin May 1954	H.Dermota, piano	LP: Telefunken LE 6522/LGX 66023 LP: Telefunken BLE 14503

Die Lotosblume

Vienna September 1950	H.Dermota, piano	78: Decca M 38124 LP: Decca LXT 2592 LP: Telefunken BLE 14503 LP: Everest 3202 LP: Telefunken 642.233
Berlin May 1954	H.Dermota, piano	LP: Telefunken LE 6522/LGX 66023

Der Nussbaum

London September 1947	H.Dermota, piano	78: Decca M 619
Vienna September 1950	H.Dermota, piano	78: Decca M 38123 LP: Decca LXT 2592 LP: Everest 3202 LP: Telefunken 642.233
Berlin May 1954	H.Dermota, piano	LP: Telefunken LE 6522/LGX 66023 LP: Telefunken BLE 14503 LP: Melodram MEL 090

Widmung

Berlin May 1954	H.Dermota, piano	LP: Telefunken LE 6522/LGX 66023 LP: Telefunken BLE 14503

Sivic

O saj ni smirti

Vienna Date uncertain	H.Dermota, piano	LP: Gallus LP 44

Skerjanc

Songs: Pocitek pod goro; Vecerna impresija; Vizija

Vienna Date uncertain	H.Dermota, piano	LP: Gallus LP 44

Skorzeny

Lieder: Frühlingsregen; Leise Lieder; Der Abend; Ich wünsch' es mir; Die Widmung

Vienna   H.Dermota, piano   LP: Amadeo AVRS 3010
Date uncertain

Smetana

Dalibor: Excerpts (Dalibor's Dream; Kde meskas zdenku)

Vienna	Role of Dalibor	CD: Melodram CDM 26522
1970	Rysanek	
	VPO	
	Klobucar	
	Sung in German	

The Bartered Bride: Excerpt (Verne milovani)

Vienna	Role of Jenik	LP: Melodiya M10 46955 001
1942	Rethy	CD: Melodram CDM 26522
	VPO	
	Moralt	
	Sung in German	

The Bartered Bride: Excerpt (Jak mozna verit)

Berlin	Role of Jenik	LP: Acanta DE 23.120-1
1944	Berlin RO	
	Rother	
	Sung in German	

The Bartered Bride: Excerpt (Nuze, mily chasniku)

Munich	Role of Jenik	LP: Melodram MEL 090
1950	Kamann	CD: Melodram CDM 26522
	Bavarian RO	
	Zallinger	
	Sung in German	

Operntheater

Im Abonnement   **Dienstag den 1. Juni 1937**   I. Gruppe

Anfang 6½ Uhr

Tristan und Isolde
von Richard Wagner
Handlung in drei Aufzügen

Spielleitung: Hans Duhan   Dirigent: •°•

Tristan	Josef Kalenberg
König Marke	Alexander Kipnis
Isolde	Anny Konetzni
Kurwenal	Fred Destal
Melot	Hans Duhan
Brangäne	Enid Szantho
Ein Hirt	Hermann Gallos
Ein Steuermann	Karl Ettl
Stimme des Seemannes	Anton Dermota

Schiffsvolk, Ritter und Knappen

Schauplatz der Handlung: Erster Aufzug: Auf dem Verdeck von Tristans Schiff, während der Überfahrt von Irland nach Kornwall — Zweiter Aufzug: In der königlichen Burg Markes in Kornwall — Dritter Aufzug: Tristans Burg in Bretagne

•°• Dirigent: Generalmusikdirektor **Herbert von Karajan**, Stadttheater Aachen, a. G.

Nach jedem Aufzuge eine größere Pause

Das offizielle Programm nur bei den Billetteuren erhältlich. Preis 50 Groschen — Garderobe frei

Kassen-Eröffnung vor 6 Uhr   Anfang 6½ Uhr   Ende nach 11 Uhr

Während der Vorspiele und der Akte bleiben die Saaltüren zum Parkett, Parterre und den Galerien geschlossen. Zuspätkommende können daher nur während der Pausen Einlaß finden.

Telephonische Bestellungen von Sitzen, R-28-329 (ausgenommen Säulensitze) zum Preise von S 4.— aufwärts werden für folgende Vorstellungen entgegengenommen.

Der Kartenverkauf findet heute statt für obige Vorstellung und für

Mittwoch den 2. Tosca. Im Abonnement I. Gruppe (Anfang 7½ Uhr)
Donnerstag den 3. Oberon. Dirigent: Bruno Walter a. G. (Anfang 7 Uhr)

Weiterer Spielplan:

Freitag den 4. Der Barbier von Sevilla. Bei aufgehobenem Abonnement. Kein Kartenverkauf (Anfang 7½ Uhr)
Samstag den 5. Der fliegende Holländer. Im Abonnement I. Gruppe (Anfang 7½ Uhr)
Sonntag den 6. Der Schmuck der Madonna. Dirigent: Generalmusikdirektor **Hans Knappertsbusch** a. G. Im Abonnement (Anfang 7½ Uhr)
Montag den 7. Elektra. Dirigent: Generalmusikdirektor **Hans Knappertsbusch** a. G. Theatergemeinde Serie C, rote Mitgliedskarten (Anfang 8 Uhr)

Kartenverkauf für alle Bundestheater (Burg-, Opern- und Akademie-Theater) an den Tageskassen: I. Bräunerstraße 14, an Werktagen von 9—18 Uhr, an Sonn- und Feiertagen von 9—17 Uhr und an der Abendkassa am Vorstellungstage. Telephonische Bestellungen von Sitzen (ausgenommen Säulensitze) zum Preise von S 4.— aufwärts ausschließlich unter der Telephonnummer R-28-3-29 von 8—18 Uhr.

STAATSOPER

Mittwoch, 26. Oktober 1977

Beschränkter Kartenverkauf – Preise B

Anläßlich der 40jährigen Zugehörigkeit zur Wiener Staatsoper
von Kammersänger Anton Dermota

PALESTRINA

Musikalische Legende in drei Akten von Hans Pfitzner

Dirigent: Horst Stein   Inszenierung: Hans Hotter   Spielleitung: Richard Bletschacher
Bühnenbild: Günther Schneider-Siemssen   Kostüme: Renny Reiter

Kassenöffnung 17 Uhr   Anfang 18 Uhr   Ende nach 22 Uhr

Donnerstag, 27. Oktober: Richard Strauss Tage: Die Frau ohne Schatten. Bei aufgehobenem Abonnement. Beschränkter Kartenverkauf. Preise V (Anfang 18 Uhr)
Freitag, 28. Oktober: Richard Strauss Tage: Capriccio. Im Abonnement 5. Gruppe. Beschränkter Kartenverkauf. Preise IV (Anfang 19.30 Uhr)
Samstag, 29. Oktober: In russischer Sprache: Boris Godunow. Beschränkter Kartenverkauf. Preise V (Anfang 19.30 Uhr)
Samstag, 30. Oktober: Ballettabend: Adagio Hammerklavier – Nomos Alpha – Apollo – Lieder eines fahrenden Gesellen.
Bei aufgehobenem Abonnement. Preise IV (Anfang 19 Uhr)

Johann Strauss

Cagliostro in Wien: Excerpt (Könnt' ich mit ihnen fliegen)

Vienna 1975	Role of Cagliostro Gruberova Austrian RO Rudel	ORF private issue

Die Fledermaus

Vienna
September 1950
Role of Alfred
Güden, Lipp,
Wagner, Patzak,
Poell, Preger
Vienna Opera Chorus
VPO
Krauss

78: Decca AX 470-481/K 23112-22/K 28405-16
LP: Decca LXT 2550-1
LP: Decca ACL 145-6
LP: Decca DPA 595-6
LP: Telefunken KD 11011
LP: Preiser 135 035-6
CD: Decca 425 9902
Excerpts
LP: Decca LXT 2576
LP: Decca LW 5138/LW 5020
45: Decca CEP 552
LP: Decca ACL 73

London
June and
July 1959
Role of Alfred
Scheyrer, Lipp,
C. Ludwig, Terkal,
Berry, Wächter,
Kunz
Philharmonia
Chorus & Orchestra
Ackermann

LP: Columbia 33CX 1688-9/SAX 2336-7
LP: Electrola 1C 147 01652-3
LP: EMI CFPD 4702
CD: EMI CDCFPD 4702
Excerpts
LP: EMI XLP 20091/SXLP 20091

Eine Nacht in Venedig: Excerpt (Komm' in die Gondel)

Berlin
1940
Role of Caramello
Orchestra and
conductor uncertain

78: Telefunken A 10501

1001 Nacht: Excerpt (Ich hab' auf meiner Fahrt gar viel geseh'n)

Bregenz
1959
Role of Prince
VSO
Hollreiser

LP: Amadeo AVRS 1064

Das Spitzentuch der Königin: Excerpt (Du Märchenstadt im Donautal)

Berlin
1940
Role of Cervantes
Orchestra and
conductor uncertain

78: Telefunken A 10501

Das Spitzentuch der Königin: Excerpt (Wo die wilde Rose erblüht)

Vienna
1975
Role of Cervantes
Austrian RO
Rudel

ORF private issue

Richard Strauss

Arabella

Vienna May and June 1957	Role of Matteo Della Casa, Güden, Malaniuk, London, Edelmann VPO Solti	LP: Decca LXT 5403-6/SXL 2050-3 LP: Decca GOS 571-3 CD: Decca 430 3872

Capriccio: Excerpt (Kein andres, das mir so im Herzen loht)

Vienna September 1950	Role of Flamand VPO Böhm	45: Decca 45-71116 LP: Decca LXT 2592 LP: Everest 3202 LP: Telefunken 642.233 LP: EMI EX 769 7411 CD: EMI CMS 769 7412

Daphne

Buenos Aires 1948	Role of Leukippos Bampton, Svanholm, Weber Teatro Colon Orchestra E.Kleiber	LP: Discocorp IGI 295

Der Rosenkavalier

Vienna May and June 1954	Role of Singer Reining, Güden, Jurinac, Weber, Poell Vienna Opera Chorus VPO E.Kleiber	LP: Decca LXT 2954-7 LP: Decca 4BB 115-8 CD: Decca 425 9502 Excerpts LP: Decca LW 5336
Vienna November 1968	Role of Landlord Crespin, Donath, Minton, Jungwirth, Wiener Vienna Opera Chorus VPO Solti	LP: Decca SET 418-21 CD: Decca 417 4932

Der Rosenkavalier: Excerpt (Di rigori armato)

Berlin 1944	Role of Singer Berlin RO Heger	LP: Acanta DE 23.120-1

Salome

Vienna March 1954	Role of Narraboth Goltz, Kenney, Patzak, Braun, Weber, Berry VPO Krauss	LP: Decca LXT 2863-4 LP: Decca GOM 549-50 LP: Telefunken 648.041

Ach weh mir unglückhaftem Mann

Vienna January 1975	H.Dermota, piano	LP: Preiser SPR 3256 LP: Melodram MEL 090 CD: Preiser 93256

All mein Gedanken

Vienna 1943	Strauss, piano	LP: Preiser PR 3261 CD: Preiser 93261

Breit über mein Haupt

Vienna April 1942	Strauss, piano	LP: Rococo 5350 LP: Preiser PR 3262 CD: Preiser 93262

Die Nacht

Vienna April 1942	Strauss, piano	LP: Rococo 5350 LP: Preiser PR 3262 CD: Preiser 93262

Du meines Herzens Krönelein

Vienna April 1942	Strauss, piano	LP: Rococo 5350 LP: Preiser PR 3262 CD: Preiser 93262
Vienna January 1975	H.Dermota, piano	LP: Preiser SPR 3256 CD: Preiser 93256

Glückes genug

Vienna 1943	Strauss, piano	LP: Preiser PR 3261 CD: Preiser 93261

Heimkehr

Vienna 1943	Strauss, piano	LP: BASF 22.21807 LP: Preiser PR 3261 CD: Preiser 93261

Heimliche Aufforderung

Vienna April 1942	Strauss, piano	LP: Rococo 5350 LP: Preiser PR 3262 CD: Preiser 93262
London April 1948	Newton, piano	78: Decca F 9355

Ich liebe dich

Vienna April 1942	Strauss, piano	LP: Rococo 5350 LP: Preiser PR 3262 CD: Preiser 93262

Ich trage meine Minne

Vienna April 1942	Strauss, piano	LP: Rococo 5350 LP: Preiser PR 3262 CD: Preiser 93262

In goldener Fülle

Vienna 1943	Strauss, piano	LP: Preiser PR 3261 CD: Preiser 93261

Morgen

London April 1948	Newton, piano	78: Decca F 9355

Sehnsucht

Vienna 1943	Strauss, piano	LP: Preiser PR 3261 CD: Preiser 93261

Seitdem dein Aug' in meines schaute

Vienna April 1942	Strauss, piano	LP: Rococo 5350 LP: Preiser PR 3262 CD: Preiser 93262
Vienna 1943	Strauss, piano	LP: Preiser PR 3261 CD: Preiser 93261

Ständchen

Vienna September 1950	H.Dermota, piano	78: Decca M 38123 LP: Decca LXT 2592 LP: Everest 3202 LP: Telefunken 642.233 LP: Melodram MEL 090
Vienna January 1975	H.Dermota, piano	LP: Preiser SPR 3256 CD: Preiser 93256

Zueignung

Vienna April 1942	Strauss, piano	LP: Rococo 5350 LP: Preiser PR 3262 CD: Preiser 93262
Vienna September 1950	H.Dermota, piano	78: Decca M 38124 LP: Decca LXT 2592 LP: Everest 3202 LP: Telefunken 642.233

Tchaikovsky

Eugene Onegin

Vienna January 1961	Role of Lensky Jurinac, Cvejic, Rössl-Majdan, Fischer-Dieskau, Kreppel Vienna Opera Chorus VPO Matacic Sung in German	LP: Melodram MEL 046

Eugene Onegin: Excerpt (Kuda, kuda)

Berlin 1944	Role of Lensky Berlin RO Rother Sung in German	LP: Acanta DE 23.120-1
Berlin May 1954	Role of Lensky Städtische Oper Orchestra Rother Sung in German	45: Telefunken UV 110 LP: Telefunken TM 68037/LGX 66048 LP: Telefunken NT 382/BLE 14503 LP: Preiser PR 135003 CD: Preiser 90022

Toselli

Celebre serenata

Berlin 1940	Orchestra and conductor uncertain	78: Telefunken A 10413

Tosti

La serenata

Berlin 1940	Orchestra and conductor uncertain	78: Telefunken A 10413

Ukmar

Vse je tiho

Vienna Date uncertain	H.Dermota, piano	LP: Gallus LP 44

Verdi

La Forza del destino: Excerpt (Solenne in quest' ora)

Berlin   Role of Alvaro   78: Telefunken E 3880
1943   Oeggl
                Orchestra and
                conductor uncertain
                Sung in German

Luisa Miller: Excerpt (Quando le sere)

Berlin   Role of Rodolfo   LP: Acanta DE 23.120-1
1944   Berlin RO
                Rother
                Sung in German

Macbeth: Excerpt (Ah, la paterno mano)

Berlin   Role of Macduff   LP: Melodram MEL 090
1948   Berlin RO
                Hundertmark
                Sung in German

Otello

Salzburg   Role of Cassio   LP: MRF Records MRF 45
August 1951   Martinis, Wagner,   LP: Discocorp IGI 342
                Vinay, Schöffler   LP: Fonit Cetra LO 6
                Vienna Opera Chorus   LP: Turnabout THS 65120-2
                VPO   LP: Foyer FO 1018
                Furtwängler   LP: Fonit Cetra FE 28
                                           CD: Foyer 2CF-2002
                                           CD: Hunt CDWFE 303

Rigoletto: Excerpt (Ella mi fu rapita)

Berlin   Role of Duke   78: Telefunken E 3356
1944   Berlin RO   LP: Telefunken LGX 66048
                Rother
                Sung in German

Il Trovatore: Excerpt (Ah sì, ben mio)

Berlin   Role of Manrico   78: Telefunken E 3356
1944   Berlin RO   LP: Telefunken LGX 66048
                Rother   LP: Acanta DE 23.120-1
                Sung in German

Wagner

Das Liebesverbot

Vienna 1962	Role of Claudio Zadek, Steffek, Imdahl Austrian RO Heger	LP: Penzance Records 42 LP: Melodram MEL 224

Lohengrin: Excerpt (Das süsse Lied verhallt)

Ljubljana 1970	Role of Lohengrin Bukovec Ljubljana RO Basic	LP: Preiser SPR 3310

Lohengrin: Excerpt (In fernem Land)

Ljubljana 1970	Role of Lohengrin Ljubljana RO Hubad	LP: Preiser SPR 3310

Die Meistersinger von Nürnberg

Salzburg August 1937	Role of Zorn Reining, Thorborg, Noort, Sallaba, Nissen, Alsen, Wiedemann Vienna Opera Chorus VPO Toscanini	LP: Toscanini Society ATS 1062-6 np LP: MRF Records MRF 16 LP: Accent ACC 150040 LP: Melodram MEL 012 CD: Melodram MEL 47041
Vienna September 1950 (Act 2) and September 1951 (Acts 1 & 3)	Role of David Güden, Schürhoff, Treptow, Schöffler, Edelmann, Dönch Vienna Opera Chorus VPO Knappertsbusch	78: Decca K 53046-53/28385-92 (Act 2) LP: Decca LXT 2560-1 (Act 2) LP: Decca LXT 2646-7 (Act 1) LP: Decca LXT 2648-50 (Act 3) LP: Decca LXT 2659-64 LP: Decca GOM 535-9 Excerpts LP: Decca LXT 5544 LP: Decca BR 3089

Die Meistersinger von Nürnberg: Excerpts (Am stillen Herd; Morgenlich leuchtend)

Ljubljana 1970	Role of Stolzing Ljubljana RO Hubad	LP: Preiser SPR 3310

Tristan und Isolde

Dresden   Role of Shepherd   LP: DG 413 3151
                        M.Price, Kollo,   CD: DG 413 3152
                        Fassbänder,
                        Fischer-Dieskau,
                        Moll
                        Leipzig Radio Chorus
                        Dresden Staatskapelle
                        C.Kleiber

Weber

Euryanthe: Excerpt (Unter blühenden Mandelbäumen)

Berlin   Role of Adolar   LP: Acanta DE 23.120-1
1944   Berlin RO
                        Rother

Der Freischütz: Excerpt (Nein, länger trag' ich nicht die Qualen)

Ljubljana   Role of Max   LP: Preiser SPR 3310
1970   Ljubljana RO   CD: Preiser 90022
                        Hubad

Wolf

Auf ein altes Bild

Vienna September 1950	H.Dermota, piano	78: Decca K 28400 LP: Decca LXT 2592 LP: Everest 3202 LP: Telefunken 642.233

Der Gärtner

Vienna September 1950	H.Dermota, piano	78: Decca K 28400 LP: Decca LXT 2592 LP: Everest 3202 LP: Telefunken 642.233
Vienna January 1975	H.Dermota, piano	LP: Preiser SPR 3256 CD: Preiser 93256

Der Musikant

Vienna September 1950	H.Dermota, piano	78: Decca K 28400 LP: Decca LXT 2592 LP: Everest 3202 LP: Telefunken 642.233 LP: Melodram MEL 090

Nimmersatte Liebe

Vienna September 1950	H.Dermota, piano	78: Decca K 28400 LP: Decca LXT 2592 LP: Everest 3202 LP: Telefunken 642.233 LP: Melodram MEL 090
Vienna January 1975	H.Dermota, piano	LP: Preiser SPR 3256 CD: Preiser 93256

Dermota:
roles performed with the Vienna State Opera

Includes performances with the Vienna company on tour
Figure against each role indicates number of times the part was performed
Some roles performed only before 1945 may be missing

16	Admetos (Alceste)
4	Adorno (Simone Boccanegra)
41	Alfred (Die Fledermaus)
41	Alfredo (La Traviata)
88	Almaviva (Il Barbiere di Siviglia)
2	Altoum (Turandot)
17	Beichtvater (Dialogue des Carmélites)
164	Belmonte (Die Entführung aus dem Serail)
9	Beppe (I Pagliacci)
41	Cassio (Otello)
10	Dalibor (Dalibor)
32	David (Die Meistersinger von Nürnberg)
21	Des Grieux (Manon)
131	Don Ottavio (Don Giovanni)
17	Duke (Eine Nacht in Venedig)
39	Duke (Rigoletto)
4	Elemer (Arabella)
19	Ernesto (Don Pasquale)
7	Fenton (Falstaff)
2	Fenton (The Merry Wives of Windsor)
4	Ferdinand (The Tempest)*
111	Ferrando (Così fan tutte)
1	First Armed Man (Die Zauberflöte)
2	First Prisoner (Fidelio)
30	Flamand (Capriccio)
46	Florestan (Fidelio)

6	Froh (Das Rheingold)
33	Hans (The Bartered Bride)
5	Herald (Murder in the Cathedral)**
72	Hoffmann (Les contes d'Hoffmann)
115	Italian Singer (Der Rosenkavalier)
36	Jacquino (Fidelio)
27	Lensky (Eugene Onegin)
16	Leukippos (Daphne)
20	Lionel (Martha)
17	Matteo (Arabella)
7	1st Meister (Palestrina)
93	Narraboth (Salome)
4	Nemorino (L'Elisir d'amore)
8	Nureddin (Der Barbier von Bagdad)
19	Palestrina (Palestrina)
26	Rodolfo (La Bohème)
7	Schwalb (Mathis der Maler)
8	Sextus (Giulio Cesare)
57	Seemann (Tristan und Isolde)
4	Shepherd (Die toten Augen)
6	Sinovi (Katerina Ismailova)
79	Steuermann (Tristan und Isolde)
176	Tamino (Die Zauberflöte)
10	Titorelli (Der Prozess)***
19	Triquet (Eugene Onegin)
24	Vladimir (Prince Igor)
1	Vogelgesang (Die Meistersinger v.Nürnberg)
49	Walther von der Vogelweide (Tannhäuser)

```
  *    Frank Martin
 **    Pizzetti
***    Von Einem
```

Dermota: a postscript

With Tauber before him and Wunderlich and Schreier in the generation that followed him, Anton Dermota (1910-1989) stands in the middle of an eminent tradition of German-speaking lyric tenors who added particular lustre to the Viennese stage. Of all of them, Dermota was by far the most loyal and omnipresent over 4 decades, an ensemble member with an immense repertoire but with a first love for the Mozart tenor roles of which he became the very embodiment in Vienna, Salzburg and elsewhere.

Anton Dermota's singing was described by one English critic as displaying "smooth line and gleaming tone", to which I would add a slight and appealing nasal quality, which perhaps betrayed his Yugoslav origins and which certainly brought a distinctly personal emission of tone and treatment of words. For my taste, these qualities amounted to a style of utterly winning and irresistible beauty. For me, in fact, Dermota's was the only male voice to place alongside those female representatives of Viennese style, Schwarzkopf, Seefried, Güden and Jurinac.

A typical part for Dermota, displaying his qualities to the full, was the role of Lensky in "Eugene Onegin", which was in fact one of his very first successes in pre-war Vienna under the baton of Bruno Walter. The singer tells in his autobiography how his own particular idol and role model for that part and many others was not Tauber but Koloman von Pataky, a Mozart stylist well-known to early Glyndebourne audiences.

He also recalled, with moving involvement, his first-hand experience as the Vienna Staatsoper burnt down before his very eyes after an incendiary attack in 1944, and how he joined those colleagues trying to salvage valuable library material and works of art from the blazing building. In contrast, Dermota humorously recalled his first encounter with Herbert von Karajan, arriving late for a recording session of "Die Zauberflöte" after a hazardous tram journey across Vienna and having to plunge straight into a (perfect) take of one of Tamino's arias.

During the 1980s the enterprising German record label Acanta presented a series of double albums devoted to singers of the past, much of the material being drawn from the wartime archives of the Reichsrundfunk. The sound on the Dermota album of arias recorded between 1939 and 1944 is so good as to suggest that these are Telefunken studio takes, many of them never published in 78 format. Embracing his Mozart roles as well as French, Italian and Slav repertoire, the collection presents my dream tenor at his finest.

Leonie Rysanek
Discography

compiled by John Hunt

Introduction

It is difficult to be objective in assessing a voice which has the immediate thrill and physical impact of a Maria Callas or a Leonie Rysanek (born 1926). If I had never seen them on stage, I might have found it easier to get into perspective the fact that their approach was based on the most careful study and hard concentration and that it was not merely based on their being gifted actresses.

There is one parallel between these two sopranos which needs to be demolished. Leonie Rysanek did not make her New York debut as a substitute for Maria Callas - she was already singing in America and contracted at the Metropolitan when the chance came, at several months' notice, to take over the new production of "Macbeth" originally planned for Callas.

This was a voice of unbelievable range, mysteriously smoky in its middle but with an extended top which seemed to know no upper limit and to exhilarate in that knowledge. And those screams! Sieglinde's ecstasy, the calls of Chrysothemis to Orestes and, more recently and unfortunately not yet preserved on published recordings, the imprecations of Ortrud or the death-throes of Klytemnestra.

Rysanek's rise in Europe as a new star in the Wagner-Strauss repertoire and, in the USA, in a quartet of Verdi roles did not automatically make her into a regular recording star with the big companies: 1 opera for Decca, 3 for RCA and 1 for DG is the sum total of officially recorded complete operas.

And her Covent Garden appearances in the 1950s - Danae, Tosca, Sieglinde - lead on only to Elsa and the Marschallin, nothing more after 1963. But that was our loss, for most of the rest of the operatic world has enjoyed another 30 years of the Rysanek phenomenon. I have travelled to Vienna for her Leonore, Medea and Kundry, to Salzburg for her Empress, to Stuttgart for her Kostelnicka and to Bayreuth for her Elsa, bringing back with me on each occasion the impact of those ultra-vivid impersonations.

Her Wagner role above all others was Sieglinde - she remembers with the deepest gratitude the advice given to her by Karl Böhm not to undertake the mountain peaks of Isolde or Brünnhilde (she did sing one Brünnhilde as a beginner) - and it is her Sieglinde which we have preserved in official versions under both Böhm and Furtwängler. Let us still hope for the publication of her 1951 Bayreuth debut in the same part, recorded yet never published by both Decca and EMI (except for Act 3 under Karajan).

One always longs for traditions to be continued, and closer to home there have been some fine sopranos with dramatic flair comparable to Rysanek's. They are not necessarily evenly produced voices of the kind to go down well with recording producers, but viscerally thrilling and worth catching when they perform with our British opera companies. Their names are Pauline Tinsley, Josephine Barstow and Suzanne Murphey.

Essential reading for the Rysanek fan, and still worth it for the pictures even if you cannot read the German text, is "Leonie Rysanek: 40 Jahre Operngeschichte" by Dusek & Schmidt, published Hamburg 1990 by Hoffmann & Campe.

Postscript
Rysanek's voice was also heard briefly, in fragments from "Der fliegende Holländer", "Die Walküre" and "Götterdämmerung" in the film "Magic Fire" (1954, adapted and supervised by Walter Korngold). The soundtrack was issued on LP Varèse Sarabande STD 81179.

STAATSOPER

Mittwoch, den 29. März 1967
Bei aufgehobenem Abonnement
Sehr beschränkter Kartenverkauf — Preise IV

FESTAUFFÜHRUNG
anläßlich der 125-Jahr-Feier der Wiener Philharmoniker

Fidelio

Oper in zwei Akten von L. van Beethoven
Text nach Bouilly von Sonnleithner und Treitschke

Dirigent: Karl Böhm
Nach einer Inszenierung von Herbert v. Karajan
Bühnenbilder: Günther Schneider-Siemssen
Kostüme: Charlotte Flemming
Einstudierung der Chöre: Richard Roßmayer

Florestan, ein Gefangener . .	James King
Leonore, seine Gemahlin, unter dem Namen Fidelio . .	Leonie Rysanek-Großmann
Don Fernando, Minister . . .	Paul Schöffler
Don Pizarro, Kommandeur eines Staatsgefängnisses	Otto Wiener
Rocco, Kerkermeister	Walter Kreppel
Marzelline, seine Tochter . .	Anneliese Rothenberger
Jacquino, Pförtner	Murray Dickie
Erster Gefangener	Karl Terkal
Zweiter Gefangener	Ljubo Pantscheff

Staatsgefangene, Wachen, Volk

Technische Einrichtung: Hans Felkel
Beleuchtung: Albin Rotter

Nach dem zweiten Bild eine größere Pause

Anfang 20 Uhr   Ende vor 23 Uhr

D'Albert

Tiefland: Excerpt (Ich weiss nicht, wer mein Vater war)

London April 1952	Role of Marta Philharmonia Schüchter	78: Columbia LX 1559 LP: Electrola 1C 147 29150-1M

Beethoven

Fidelio

Munich June 1957	Role of Leonore Seefried, Lenz, Häfliger, Frick, Fischer-Dieskau, Engen Bavarian State Chorus & Orchestra Fricsay	LP: DG LPM 18 350-1/SLPM 138 390-1 LP: DG 2726 088 LP: DG 2727 006 Excerpts LP: DG LPEM 19 215/SLPEM 136 215 45: DG EPL 30408/SEPL 30408 LP: DG 2535 298/2548 118 CD: IMP IMPX 9021
San Francisco November 1968	Role of Leonore Blegen, Dickie, Vickers, Tozzi, Berry, Macurdy San Francisco Chorus & Orchestra Böhm	CD: Melodram CDM 27086

Fidelio: Excerpt (Abscheulicher! Wo eilst du hin?)

Saarbrücken 1950	Role of Leonore Saarland RO Michl	LP: Melodram MEL 085 LP: Rodolphe RP 12433-4

Giordano

Andrea Chenier: Excerpt (La mamma morta)

Rome June-July 1958	<u>Role of Maddalena</u> Rome Orchestra Basile	LP: RCA Victor LM 2262 LP: RCA RB 16148 LP: RCA AGL1-1282 LP: RCA VICS 1752 LP: RCA (Germany) 26.41004

Janacek

<u>Jenufa</u>

New York March 1988	<u>Role of Kostelnicka</u> Benackova, Ochman, Kazaras, Johnson Opera Orchestra of New York Queler	CD: BIS CD 449-450

Mascagni

Cavalleria Rusticana: Excerpts (1. Innegiamo, il Signor non è morto; 2. Oh! Il Signore vi manda, compar Alfio!; 3. Avete altro da dirmi?...to end; other excerpts without Rysanek)

Berlin
October 1955

Role of Santuzza
Schock, Metternich
St Hedwig's Choir
Deutsche Oper
Orchestra
Schüchter
Sung in German

LP: Electrola E 80617/E 60076
LP: Electrola 1C 063 28999
LP: Electrola 1C 147 29150-1M (2)

Cavalleria Rusticana: Excerpt (Voi lo sapete)

Rome
June-July
1958

Role of Santuzza
Rome Orchestra
Basile

LP: RCA Victor LM 2262
LP: RCA RB 16148
LP: RCA AGL1-1282
LP: RCA VICS 1752
LP: RCA (Germany) 26.41004

Cavalleria Rusticana: Excerpt (Tu qui, Santuzza?)

Munich
1978

Role of Santuzza
Domingo
Bavarian State
Orchestra
Santi

LP: Legendary LR 101

Ponchielli

La Gioconda: Excerpts (Che fai! vaneggi?; E un anatema!...to end Act 2; Suicidio!)

Berlin
1976

Role of Gioconda
Tagliavini, Kerns,
Mattiucci
Deutsche Oper
Orchestra
Gomez-Martinez

LP: Legendary LR 101

Puccini

Tosca

Munich　　　　　Role of Tosca　　　　　　　LP: Melodram MEL 436
1953　　　　　　Hopf, Metternich　　　　　Lo dici male
　　　　　　　　Bavarian Radio　　　　　　　LP: Melodram MEL 085
　　　　　　　　Chorus & Orchestra
　　　　　　　　Kraus
　　　　　　　　Sung in German

Vienna　　　　　Role of Tosca　　　　　　　LP: HRE Records HRE 433
1964　　　　　　Labo, Bacquier
　　　　　　　　Vienna Opera Chorus
　　　　　　　　VPO
　　　　　　　　Quadri

San Francisco　 Role of Tosca　　　　　　　CD: Melodram CDM 27508
November 1969　 Tucker, Macneil
　　　　　　　　San Francisco
　　　　　　　　Chorus & Orchestra
　　　　　　　　Molinari-Pradelli

Tosca: Act 2 (from "Ed or fra noi parliam da buoni amici" to end)

Munich　　　　　Role of Tosca　　　　　　　LP: Legendary LR 101
1977　　　　　　Lamberti, Diaz　　　　　　 Vissi d'arte
　　　　　　　　Bavarian State　　　　　　 LP: Rodolphe RP 12433-4
　　　　　　　　Orchestra
　　　　　　　　Santi

Tosca: Excerpt (Vissi d'arte)

Rome　　　　　　Role of Tosca　　　　　　　LP: RCA Victor LM 2262
June-July　　　 Rome Orchestra　　　　　　 LP: RCA RB 16148
1958　　　　　　Basile　　　　　　　　　　 45: RCA Victor ERA 9731
　　　　　　　　　　　　　　　　　　　　　　LP: RCA AGL1-1282
　　　　　　　　　　　　　　　　　　　　　　LP: RCA VICS 1752
　　　　　　　　　　　　　　　　　　　　　　LP: RCA (Germany) 26.41004

Turandot: Excerpt (In questa reggia)

Munich　　　　　Role of Turandot　　　　　 LP: Melodram MEL 085
1953　　　　　　Bavarian RO　　　　　　　　LP: Rodolphe RP 12433-4
　　　　　　　　Sawallisch
　　　　　　　　Sung in German

Rome　　　　　　Role of Turandot　　　　　 LP: RCA Victor LM 2262
June-July　　　 Rome Orchestra　　　　　　 LP: RCA RB 16148
1958　　　　　　Basile　　　　　　　　　　 LP: RCA AGL1-1282
　　　　　　　　　　　　　　　　　　　　　　LP: RCA VICS 1752
　　　　　　　　　　　　　　　　　　　　　　LP: RCA (Germany) 26.41004

Smetana

Dalibor: Excerpt (Kde meskas zdenku)

Vienna 1970	Role of Milada Dermota VPO Klobucar Sung in German	CD: Melodram CDM 26522

Richard Strauss

Die Aegyptische Helena

Munich August 1956	Role of Helena Kupper, Aldenhoff, Uhde, Holm Bavarian State Chorus & Orchestra Keilberth	LP: Melodram MEL 109 CD: Melodram MEL 27066 Zweite Brautnacht LP: Melodram MEL 085 LP: Rodolphe RP 12433-4 CD: HRE Records HRE 1005 CD: Hunt CDKAR 207

Arabella: Excerpt (Das war sehr gut, Mandryka)

London April 1952	Role of Arabella Philharmonia Schüchter	78: Columbia LX 1559 LP: Electrola 1C 147 29150-1M LP: EMI EX 769 7411 CD: EMI CHS 769 7412

Ariadne auf Naxos

Vienna 1960	Role of Ariadne Jurinac, Peters, Peerce, Berry VPO Leinsdorf	LP: RCA RE 25023-5/SER 4253-5 LP: Decca 2BB 112-4 Excerpts LP: Decca 414 1771

Ariadne auf Naxos: Excerpt (Ein Schönes war's...Es gibt ein Reich)

Vienna November 1967	Role of Ariadne Holm, Holecek, Equiluz, Lackner VPO Böhm	CD: HRE Records HRE 1005 CD: Hunt CDKAR 207

Elektra

Vienna 1981	Role of Elektra Ligendza, Varnay, Fischer-Dieskau, Beirer, Greindl VPO Böhm	VHS Video: Fecca 071.4003 Laserdisc: Decca 071.4001 Scene Elektra-Klytemnestra LP: Legendary LR 204
Cologne 1953	Role of Chrysothemis Varnay, Fischer, Hotter, Melchert WDR Orchestra Kraus	LP: Melodram MEL 112
Vienna December 1965	Role of Chrysothemis Nilsson, Resnik, Windgassen, Wächter VPO Böhm	LP: HRE Records HRE 314 CD: Legato SRO 833 Ich kann nicht sitzen CD: HRE Records HRE 1005 CD: Hunt CDKAR 207
Paris January 1984	Role of Chrysothemis Vintzing, Forrester, Hiestermann, Norup Orchestre National Prick	LP: Rodolphe RP 12420-1 CD: Rodolphe RPC 32420-1 Closing scene LP: Rodolphe RP 12433-4

Elektra: Excerpts (1. Ich kann nicht sitzen; 2. Closing scene)

Munich August 1955	Role of Chrysothemis Goltz Bavarian State Orchestra Böhm	LP: Melodram MEL 085 (1) LP: Orfeo S120.8421 (2)

Elektra: Excerpts (Ah! Das Gesicht!..Ich kann nicht sitzen; Closing scene)

Vienna September 1975	Role of Chrysothemis Nilsson VPO Böhm	LP: Legendary LR 101

Die Frau ohne Schatten

Munich August 1954	Role of Empress Schech, Hopf, Benningsen, Metternich, Köth, Böhme Bavarian State Chorus & Orchestra Kempe	LP: Melodram MEL 108
Vienna November and December 1955	Role of Empress Goltz, Höngen, Hopf, Loose, Schöffler, Böhme Vienna Opera Chorus VPO Böhm	LP: Decca LXT 5180-4 LP: Decca GOM 554-7/GOS 554-7 CD: Decca 425 9812 Excerpts LP: Decca 414 1771
Vienna June 1964	Role of Empress C.Ludwig, G.Hoffman Thomas, Popp, Berry, Kreppel Vienna Opera Chorus VPO Karajan	CD: Nuova Era 2288-90 CD: Hunt CDKAR 207
Vienna October 1977	Role of Empress Nilsson, Hesse, Lotte Rysanek, King, Berry, Wimberger Vienna Opera Chorus VPO Böhm	LP: HRE Records HRE 322 LP: DG 415 4721 CD: DG 415 4722

Die Frau ohne Schatten: Excerpt (Aus unseren Taten)

Munich 1956	Role of Empress Bavarian State Orchestra Zallinger	LP: Melodram MEL 085

Die Liebe der Danae: Excerpts

Munich 1953	Role of Danae Frantz Bavarian State Orchestra Kempe	CD: Melodram MEL 37061 Wie umgibst du mich mit Frieden LP: Melodram MEL 085 CD: Hunt CDKAR 207

Donnerstag, 11. April 1974　*Staatsoper*

In italienischer Sprache

MEDEA

Tragödie in drei Akten von　François Benoît Hoffman
Italienisches Libretto von　Carlo Zangarini

Musik　Luigi Cherubini

Dirigent　Alexander Sander
Inszenierung　August Everding
Bühnenbild und Kostüme　Erich Brauer

Kreon　Nicola Ghiuselev
Glauce, Tochter Kreons　Edita Gruberova
Jason　Juan Oncina
Medea　Leonie Rysanek-Gausmann
Neris, Begleiterin Medeas　Margarita Lilowa
Hauptmann der Wache　Hans Braun
1. Magd　Sona Ghazarian
2. Magd　Olga Busina
Ein Argonaute　Ewald Aichberger

Die zwei Söhne Medeas und Jasons,
Dienerinnen Glauces, Argonauten,
Priester, Krieger, Volk von Korinth

Musikalische Studienleitung　Arnold Hartl
Chorleitung　Norbert Balatsch
Technik　Hans Langer
　Robert Stangl

Größere Pause　nach dem zweiten Akt

Beginn　19 Uhr
Ende　nach 21.30 Uhr

Programmdienst der Bundestheater　Telefon 15 18

Preis des Programms　S 8,—

MÜNCHNER OPERNFESTSPIELE

München, Freitag, 19. August 1955

Die Frau ohne Schatten

Oper in 3 Akten von Hugo von Hofmannsthal

Musik von RICHARD STRAUSS

Musikalische Leitung: George Sébastian   Inszenierung: Rudolf Hartmann
Bühnenbild und Kostüme: Emil Preetorius

Der Kaiser	Hans Hopf
Die Kaiserin	Leonie Rysanek
Die Amme	Ursula Boettcher
Der Geisterbote	Kurt Böhme
Hüter der Schwelle	Erika Köth
Erscheinung eines Jünglings	Howard Vandenburg
Stimme des Falken	Gerda Sommerschuh
Stimme von oben	Lilo Gebhart
Barak, der Färber	Josef Metternich
Sein Weib	Christel Goltz
Der Einäugige	Karl Hoppe
Der Einarmige	Rudolf Wünzer
Der Bucklige	Karl Ostertag

Stimmen der Ungeborenen:
Anny von Krupoyck
Antonie Fahberg
Lisbeth Lindermeier
Rosl Michaelis
Eva Gerken

Kaiserliche Diener, Fremde Kinder, Geisterstimmen:
Max Proebstl
Lotti Hoppe
Hans Bernard Nissen
Erika Köth
Rosl Fahrner
Ruth Michaelis

Ort der Handlung:
1. Akt: Auf einer Terrasse über dem kaiserlichen Garten, Falkenhaus
2. Akt: Färberhaus, Wald v. d. Pavillon des Falkners, Färberhaus, Schatten und Katarakt im Färberhaus
3. Akt: Unterirdischer Kerker, Geistertempel, Landschaft im Geisterreich

Solo-Violine: Herbert Becker — Solo-Cello: Oswald Uhl

Technische Oberleitung: Emil Buchsenberger – Chefe Michael Hartenwehr
Anfertigung der Kostüme: Alexander Schatzkovsky – Maskenbild: Georg Rauth,
Anfertigung der Dekorationen: Oswald Schwarzberger – Technische Einrichtung: Anton Ott
Beleuchtung: Josef Buchsenberger und Ludwig Baumhörer
Inspizient: Anton Hackel und Martin Prucksammer – Souffleur: Hans Nerl

---

Sohngers OPTIK
München 2, Brennerstr. 3
gegenüb. d. Wittelsbacherplatz

Formschöne, hervorragend angepaßte Brillen, - auch Sonnenschutz-,
und unsichtbare Augengläser,
Den Augen zuliebe:

Wäschehaus Weinhold
München   Dienerstr. 22

Feine Wäsche - Ausstattungen
Bade- und Strickmoden - Blusen
Kleinkinderbekleidung

Theaterkasse Marienplatz,
direkt am Alten Rathaus
Straßenbahnen 1, 2, 6, 19, 29

Alle Eintrittskarten für sämtliche
Münchener Veranstaltungen

Sie erhalten die praktische Gelegenheit...

Theaterkasse Marienplatz 16,
im Kaufhausviertel Beamten
täglich 8.30 bis 18.30 Uhr, Samstag 8.30 bis 15 Uhr

Wer an
Bademode
denkt — denkt an

LUDWIG BECK
AM RATHAUS ECK

Nach der Vorstellung
in die
REGINA-BAR
Münchens größte Tanzbar mit
Gastspielen berühmter Kapellen

Wäschehaus Rosner & Seidl
gegenüber dem Ratskeller
Erstklassige Popeline
in einzigartiger Auswahl

Schirme aller Art

LINDBERG
FERNSEHGERÄTE
Augenblickliche Teilzahlung
MÜNCHEN 2
GARMISCH

Der Rosenkavalier

Moscow October 1971	Role of Marschallin C.Ludwig, De Groote, Jungwirth, Kunz, Blankenship Vienna Opera Chorus VPO Krips	LP: Melodiya C10 28033 007

Der Rosenkavalier: Excerpt (Da geht er hin)

Berlin October 1955	Role of Marschallin BPO Schüchter	LP: HMV CLP 1139 LP: Electrola E 60066 LP: Electrola 1C 047 38566M LP: EMI MFP 2058 LP: Electrola 1C 147 29150-1M
Frankfurt 1976	Role of Marschallin Frankfurt Opera Orchestra Dohnanyi	LP: Legendary LR 101
Vienna 1978	Role of Marschallin H.Schwarz VPO Heger	CD: HRE Records HRE 1005

Der Rosenkavalier: Excerpt (Marie Theres')

Berlin October 1955	Role of Marschallin Grümmer, Köth BPO Schüchter	LP: HMV CLP 1139 LP: Electrola E 60066 LP: Electrola 1C 047 38566M LP: EMI MFP 2058 LP: Electrola 1C 147 29150-1M
Vienna 1978	Role of Marschallin H.Schwarz, Malone VPO Heger	CD: HRE Records HRE 1005
Vienna 1979	Role of Marschallin Baltsa, Popp VPO R.Schwarz	LP: Legendary LR 101

Der Rosenkavalier: Excerpt (Heut' oder morgen)

Vienna 1978	Role of Marschallin H.Schwarz, Malone VPO Heger	CD: HRE Records HRE 1005

Salome

Munich July 1971	Role of Salome Varnay, Stolze, Fischer-Dieskau, Ochman Bavarian State Orchestra Leitner	LP: Legendary LR 204 Closing scene CD: HRE Records HRE 1005
Orange July 1974	Role of Salome Hesse, Vickers, Stewart, Laubenthal Orchestre National Kempe	LP: HRE Records HRE 396
Berlin September 1990	Role of Herodias Malfitano, Estes, Hiestermann Deutsche Oper Orchestra Sinopoli	VHS Video: Teldec 9031 738273 Laserdisc: Teldec 9031 738276
Berlin September and October 1990	Role of Herodias Studer, Terfel, Hiestermann Deutsche Oper Orchestra Sinopoli	CD: DG 431 8102

Salome: Excerpt (Closing scene)

Vienna December 1972	Role of Salome G.Hoffman, Hopf VPO Böhm	LP: Legendary LR 101

Monday, 23rd December, 1963

The 142nd performance at the Royal Opera House of

DER ROSENKAVALIER

COMEDY FOR MUSIC

Words by Hugo von Hofmannsthal

Music by RICHARD STRAUSS

Conductor ANTAL DORATI

Production rehearsed by JOHN COPLEY

Scenery by ROBIN IRONSIDE

THE FELDMARSCHALLIN PRINCESS VON WERDENBERG	LEONIE RYSANEK
OCTAVIAN, called Quinquin, a young gentleman of noble family	JOSEPHINE VEASEY
BLACK PAGE TO THE PRINCESS	RAYMOND HATCH
THE PRINCESS'S FOOTMEN	AFAN DAVIES WILFRED JONES CLIFFORD STARR STANLEY COOPER
BARON OCHS VON LERCHENAU	MICHAEL LANGDON
MAJOR DOMO TO THE PRINCESS	JOSEPH WARD
A NOBLE WIDOW	MOYNA COPE
THREE NOBLE ORPHANS	JEAN CROSS JEANNE BOWDEN MARYBELLE OAKES
A MILLINER	ANNE FINLEY
AN ANIMAL SELLER	ARTHUR COBBIN
A HAIRDRESSER	PETER CLEGG
AN ATTORNEY	DENNIS WICKS
VALZACCHI, an Intriguer	ROBERT BOWMAN
ANNINA, his accomplice	MONICA SINCLAIR
A TENOR	KENNETH MACDONALD
A FLUTE PLAYER	ERNEST ROSSER
LEOPOLD	LEONARD LAW
HERR VON FANINAL, a rich merchant, newly ennobled	RONALD LEWIS
SOPHIE, his daughter	BARBARA HOLT
MARIANNE LEITMETZERIN, Sophie's Duenna	JUDITH PIERCE
MAJOR DOMO TO FANINAL	JOHN DOBSON
BARON OCHS' RETINUE	KEITH RAGGETT (Almoner) CHARLES MORRIS GEORGE REIBBITT ANDREW SELLARS GLYNNE THOMAS
A DOCTOR	IGNATIUS McFADYEN
A LANDLORD	JOHN DOBSON
WAITERS	KEITH RAGGETT AFAN DAVIES ARTHUR COBBIN GEORGE REIBBITT
A COMMISSIONER OF POLICE	ERIC GARRETT

Saturday, 28th September, 1963

The 237th performance at the Royal Opera House of

LOHENGRIN

ROMANTIC OPERA IN THREE ACTS

Words and music by RICHARD WAGNER

Conductor NORMAN DEL MAR

Producer JOSEF GIELEN

Production rehearsed by JOHN COPLEY

Scenery and costumes by HAINER HILL

HERALD	VICTOR GODFREY
KING HENRY I OF SAXONY	DAVID WARD
FRIEDRICH, Count of Telramund	GUSTAV NEIDLINGER
ORTRUD	RITA GORR
ELSA	LEONIE RYSANEK
LOHENGRIN	HANS HOPF
NOBLES OF BRABANT	JOHN DOBSON ARTHUR COBBIN ERIC GARRETT DENNIS WICKS
PAGES	MORAG NOBLE ANNE PASHLEY MARGARET PRICE SALLY LANGFORD
DUKE GOTTFRIED	PETER MILLS

Verdi

Aida

Vienna November 1955	Role of Aida Madeira, Hopf, London, Frick Vienna Opera Chorus VPO Kubelik Sung in German	LP: Legendary LR 145

Aida: Excerpt (Ritorna vincitor)

Rome June-July 1958	Role of Aida Rome Orchestra Basile	LP: RCA Victor LM 2262 LP: RCA RB 16148 LP: RCA AGL1-1282 LP: RCA VICS 1752 LP: RCA (Germany) 26.41004

Aida: Excerpt (O patria mia)

Berlin May 1955	Role of Aida Berlin SO Schüchter Sung in German	78: Electrola DB 11584 LP: Electrola E 80588 LP: Electrola 1C 047 28581 LP: Electrola 1C 147 29150-1M
Munich 1953	Role of Aida Bavarian State Orchestra Heger Sung in German	LP: Melodram MEL 085 LP: Rodolphe RP 12433-4
Rome June-July 1958	Role of Aida Rome Orchestra Basile	LP: RCA Victor LM 2262 LP: RCA RB 16148 LP: RCA AGL1-1282 LP: RCA VICS 1752 LP: RCA (Germany) 26.41004

Aida: Excerpts (Ciel! mio padre!; La fatal pietra sovra me si chiuse..O terra addio)

Berlin May 1955	Role of Aida Wagner, Schock, Metternich Deutsche Oper Chorus Berlin SO Schüchter Sung in German	LP: Electrola E 80588 LP: Electrola 1C 047 28581 LP: Electrola 1C 147 29150-1M

Un Ballo in Maschera

New York
March 1962

Role of Amelia
Madeira, Bergonzi,
Rothenberger,
Merrill
Metropolitan Opera
Chorus & Orchestra
Santi

CD: Nuova Era 6710

Don Carlo

New York
April 1959

Role of Elisabetta
Thebom, Gari,
Merrill, Hines,
Uhde
Metropolitan Opera
Chorus & Orchestra
Cleva

LP: Melodram MEL 001
Tu che la vanita
LP: Rodolphe RP 12433-4

Don Carlo: Abridged

New York
March 1964

Role of Elisabetta
Dalis, Corelli,
Herlea, Tozzi,
Diaz
Metropolitan Opera
Chorus & Orchestra
Adler

LP: GOP Records GFC 021

Don Carlo: Excerpt (Giustizia, Sire!)

Vienna
1962

Role of Elisabetta
G.Hoffman, Kreppel,
Bastianini
VPO
Verchi

LP: Melodram MEL 665

La Forza del destino: Excerpt (Pace, pace)

Berlin
May 1955

Role of Leonora
Berlin SO
Schüchter
Sung in German

78: Electrola DB 11584
LP: Electrola 1C 147 29150-1M

Rome
June-July
1958

Role of Leonora
Rome Orchestra
Basile

LP: RCA Victor LM 2262
LP: RCA RB 16148
LP: RCA AGL1-1282
LP: RCA VICS 1752
LP: RCA (Germany) 26.41004

Macbeth

New York February 1959	Role of Lady Macbeth Warren, Hines, Bergonzi Metropolitan Opera Chorus & Orchestra Leinsdorf	LP: RCA LD 6147/LDS 6147 LP: RCA RE 25005-7/SER 4505-7 LP: RCA VICS 6121 LP: RCA VL 43543 CD: RCA GD 84516 Excerpts 45: RCA ERA 9793
New York February 1959	Role of Lady Macbeth Warren, Hines, Bergonzi Metropolitan Opera Chorus & Orchestra Leinsdorf	LP: Movimento Musica 03.029 Excerpt LP: Melodram MEL 085

Macbeth: Excerpts (1. Regna il sonno su tutti; 2. La luce langue; 3. Si colmi il calice...to end Act 2; 4. Una macchia è qui tuttora)

Munich 1953	Role of Lady Macbeth Peter Bavarian State Orchestra Eichhorn Sung in German	LP: Melodram MEL 042 LP: Rodolphe RP 12433-4 (1,2 and 4)

Nabucco

New York December 1960	Role of Abigaille Elias, Fernandi, MacNeil, Siepi Metropolitan Opera Chorus & Orchestra Schippers	LP: Melodram MEL 042 Excerpts LP: Rodolphe RP 12433-4

Otello

Rome 1960	Role of Desdemona Vickers, Gobbi Rome Opera Chorus & Orchestra Serafin	LP: RCA LD 6155/LDS 6155 LP: RCA SER 5646-8 LP: RCA (Germany) 26.35051 LP: RCA AGL3-1969 LP: RCA VL 43546 CD: RCA GD 81969 Excerpts LP: RCA LM 2741/LSC 2741 LP: RCA RB 6577/SB 6577 LP: RCA GL 42167

Otello: Excerpts (Piangea cantando; Ave Maria)

Rome June-July 1958	Role of Desdemona Rome Orchestra Basile	LP: RCA Victor LM 2262 LP: RCA RB 16148 LP: RCA AGL1-1282 LP: RCA VICS 1752 LP: RCA (Germany) 26.41004
New York February 1964	Role of Desdemona Metropolitan Opera Orchestra Santi	LP: Melodram MEL 238

Otello: Excerpt (Già nella notte densa)

Munich 1953	Role of Desdemona Aldenhoff Bavarian State Orchestra Jochum Sung in German	LP: Melodram MEL 085 LP: Rodolphe RP 12433-4

Requiem

Chicago 1958	Soprano soloist Resnik, Lloyd, Tozzi Chicago Symphony Chorus & Orchestra Reiner	LP: Melodram MEL 238

Sonntag, 15. April 1984 *Staatsoper*
21. Aufführung in dieser Inszenierung

Parsifal

Ein Bühnenweihfestspiel von Richard Wagner

Dirigent	Horst Stein
Inszenierung	August Everding
Ausstattung	Jürgen Rose
Choreographie	Ray Barra
Amfortas	Bernd Weikl
Titurel	Reid Bunger
Gurnemanz	Kurt Rydl
Parsifal	Siegfried Jerusalem
Klingsor	Gottfried Hornik
Kundry	Leonie Rysanek-Gausmann
Erster Knappe	Waltraud Winsauer
Zweiter Knappe	Heidrun Götz *
Dritter Knappe	Franz Kasemann
Vierter Knappe	Robert Riener
Erster Gralsritter	Ewald Aichberger
Zweiter Gralsritter	Hans Christian
Blumenmädchen: 1. Gruppe	Renate Holm
	Joanna Borowska
	Margareta Hintermeier
2. Gruppe	Ulrike Steinsky
	Graciela de Gyldenfeldt
	Anna Gonda
Stimme von oben	Czeslawa Slania
Kinderchor	Wiener Sängerknaben

Die Brüderschaft der Gralsritter,
Jünglinge und Knaben

* Mitglied des Opernstudios

Ort der Handlung   Auf dem Gebiete und in
der Burg der Gralshüter
„Montsalvat",
Gegend im Charakter der
nördlichen Gebirge
des gotischen Spaniens
Sodann   Klingsors Zauberschloß am
Südabhange derselben Gebirge.
dem arabischen Spanien
zugewandt anzunehmen

DEUTSCHE OPER BERLIN

Sonntag, den 2. Dezember 1979

Beginn: 17.30 Uhr · Ende: gegen 22.30 Uhr

18. Aufführung

PARSIFAL

Ein Bühnenweihfestspiel in 3 Aufzügen von Richard Wagner

Musikalische Leitung: Horst Stein
Inszenierung, Bühnenbild und Kostüm: Filippo Sanjust
Chöre: Walter Hagen-Groll

Amfortas	Jef Vermeersch
Titurel	Ivan Sardi
Gurnemanz	Martti Talvela
Parsifal	Siegfried Jerusalem
Klingsor	Hans Günter Nöcker
Kundry	Leonie Rysanek
Erster Gralsritter	Otto Heuer
Zweiter Gralsritter	Miomir Nikolić
Alt-Solo	Kaja Borris

Vier Knappen:
Maria Teresa Reinoso, Maria José Brill, Peter Maus, Klaus Lang

Blumenmädchen:
Erste Gruppe: Beverly Bergen, Gerti Zeumer, Barbara Scherler
Zweite Gruppe: Barbara Vogel, Marga Schiml, Ruthild Engert

Das Orchester der Deutschen Oper Berlin
Der Chor der Deutschen Oper Berlin
Abendspielleitung: Roberto Goldschlager
Leitung der Statisterie: Erie Hardtke
Inspizienz: Gerd Heruth / Karlheinz Masuhr
Souffleur: Dieter Bahr
Technische Direktion: Rudolf Kück · Beleuchtung: Hans-Albrecht Neelsen
Bühnentechnik: Horst Hannemann
Tontechnik: Rolf Riethausen / Klaus Wendt
Kostümdirektion: Dietlinde Calsow · Maske: Eva Weber/Herbert Brehmer

Für Zuspätkommende Einlaß auf Klingelzeichen

Das Fotografieren sowie Film- und Tonaufnahmen während der Vorstellung sind nicht gestattet.
Photographing, video recording and sound recording during the performance is prohibited.

Wagner

Der fliegende Holländer

Bayreuth July 1959	Role of Senta Fischer, London, Uhl, Greindl Bayreuth Festival Chorus & Orchestra Sawallisch	LP: Melodram MEL 590 CD: Melodram MEL 26101 Excerpts LP: Rodolphe RP 12433-4 LP: Melodram MEL 650 CD: Myto MCD 89002
London August 1961	Role of Senta Elias, London, Liebl, Tozzi Covent Garden Chorus & Orchestra Dorati	LP: RCA RE 25035-7/SER 4535-7 LP: Decca 2BB 109-111 CD: Decca 417 3192 Senta's Ballad LP: Decca 414 1771
Milan February 1966	Role of Senta Bessel, Crass, Heater, Ridderbusch La Scala Chorus and Orchestra Sawallisch	CD: Memories HR 4281-2

Der fliegende Holländer: Excerpt (Senta's Ballad)

Saarbrücken 1950	Role of Senta Saarland RO Michl	LP: Melodram MEL 085 LP: Rodolphe RP 12433-4 CD: Melodram MEL 37073
London April 1952	Role of Senta Philharmonia Schüchter	78: Columbia LX 1573 LP: Columbia 33C 1035 LP: Electrola 1C 147 29150-1M

Der fliegende Holländer: Excerpt (Wie aus der Ferne)

London April 1952	Role of Senta S.Björling Philharmonia Schüchter	LP: Columbia 33C 1035 LP: Electrola 1C 147 29150-1M

Der fliegende Holländer: Excerpts (Bleib', Senta!; Was muss ich hören?)

New York January 1963	Role of Senta Konya Metropolitan Opera Orchestra Böhm	LP: Melodram MEL 658

Götterdämmerung

Munich September 1955	Role of Gutrune Nilsson, Malaniuk, Aldenhoff, Uhde, Frick Bavarian State Chorus & Orchestra Knappertsbusch	LP: Melodram MEL 425

Lohengrin

Bayreuth July 1958	Role of Elsa Varnay, Konya, Wächter, Blanc, Engen Bayreuth Festival Chorus & Orchestra Cluytens	LP: Replica RPL 2489-92 CD: Myto MCD 89062 Excerpts LP: Melodram MEL 085 LP: Melodram MEL 590 LP: Rodolphe RP 12433-4 CD: Melodram MEL 37073

Parsifal: Abridged

Paris October 1982	Role of Kundry Jerusalem, Weikl, Moll, Becht, Rydl RTF Chorus Orchestre National Janowski	LP: HRE Records HRE 412 Contains all of Kundry's music

Tannhäuser

Naples March 1956	Role of Elisabeth Nilsson, Lustig, Terkal, Frick, Cordes San Carlo Chorus & Orchestra Böhm	CD: Melodram MEL 37073

Tannhäuser: Excerpt (Dich teure Halle)

Munich April 1955	Role of Elisabeth Munich PO Leitner	45: DG NL 32102 LP: DG LPEM 19069 LP: DG 2721 115
New York December 1960	Role of Elisabeth Metropolitan Opera Orchestra Solti	LP: Melodram MEL 085
San Francisco 1973	Role of Elisabeth San Francisco Opera Orchestra Suitner	LP: Rodolphe RP 12433-4
Munich 1979	Role of Elisabeth Bavarian State Orchestra Suitner	LP: Legendary LR 101

Tannhäuser: Excerpt (Allmächtige Jungfrau)

Munich April 1955	Role of Elisabeth Munich PO Leitner	45: DG NL 32102 LP: DG LPEM 19069

Tannhäuser: Excerpt (Zurück von ihm! Nicht ihr seid seine Richter)

New York December 1960	Role of Elisabeth Metropolitan Opera Orchestra Solti	LP: Melodram MEL 085

Die Walküre

Bayreuth August 1951	Role of Sieglinde Varnay, H.Ludwig, Treptow, Van Mill, S.Björling Bayreuth Festival Orchestra Karajan	Acts 1 and 2 Columbia unpublished Act 3 78: Columbia LX 1447-1454/LX 8835-8842 LP: Columbia 33CX 1005-6 LP: Electrola 1C 181 03035-6M LP: Toshiba EAC 60215-6
Bayreuth August 1951	Role of Sieglinde Varnay, Malaniuk, Treptow, Van Mill, S.Björling Bayreuth Festival Orchestra Knappertsbusch	Decca unpublished
Vienna September and October 1954	Role of Sieglinde Mödl, Klose, Suthaus, Frantz, Frick VPO Furtwängler	LP: HMV ALP 1257-61 LP: EMI HQM 1019-23 LP: Electrola 1C 149 00675-9M CD: EMI CHS 763 0452 Excerpts LP: Electrola 1C 063 00830 LP: Electrola 1C 147 29150-1M
Bayreuth July 1958	Role of Sieglinde Varnay, Gorr, Vickers, Hotter, Greindl Bayreuth Festival Orchestra Knappertsbusch	LP: Melodram MEL 587 CD: Hunt CDLSMH 34042 Excerpts LP: Melodram MEL 085/MEL 590 LP: Rodolphe RP 12433-4 CD: Melodram MEL 37073 CD: Myto MCD 89002
Bayreuth July and August 1967	Role of Sieglinde Nilsson, Burmeiseter, King, Adam, Nienstedt Bayreuth Festival Orchestra Böhm	LP: Philips 6747 037/6747 047 CD: Philips 412 4782/420 3252 Excerpts LP: Philips 6833 083

Die Walküre: Excerpts (Sieglinde's scenes from Acts 2 and 3)

Bayreuth August 1965	Role of Sieglinde Nilsson, King, Adam, Talvela Bayreuth Festival Orchestra Böhm	CD: Legato SRO 833

Die Walküre: Excerpt (Der Männer Sippe....to end Act 1)

Vienna June 1984	Role of Sieglinde King Austrian RO Zagrosek	LP: Amadeo 415 3111

BAYREUTHER FESTSPIELE
SAMSTAG, 15. AUGUST 1964
RICHARD WAGNER
TANNHÄUSER

DER BEGINN JEDES AKTES WIRD 15 MINU-
TEN VORHER MIT EINER FANFARE, 10 MINU-
TEN VORHER MIT ZWEI UND 5 MINUTEN
VORHER MIT DREI FANFAREN ANGEKÜNDIGT.
1. AKT 16.00 UHR · 2. AKT 18.00 UHR · 3. AKT
20.15 UHR · ENDE GEGEN 21.10 UHR / NACH
BEGINN DER AKTE KEIN EINLASS

MUSIKALISCHE LEITUNG · OTMAR SUITNER
REGIE UND INSZENIERUNG · WIELAND WAGNER
CHOREINSTUDIERUNG · WILHELM PITZ
CHOREOGRAPHIE DES BACCHANALS
GERTRUD WAGNER
TANNHÄUSER · WOLFGANG WINDGASSEN
ELISABETH · LEONIE RYSANEK
VENUS · ANJA SILJA
LANDGRAF HERMANN · MARTTI TALVELA
WOLFRAM VON ESCHENBACH · BARRY McDANIEL
WALTHER VON DER VOGELWEIDE · ARTURO SERGI
BITEROLF · HUBERT HOFMANN
HEINRICH DER SCHREIBER · HERMANN WINKLER
REINMAR VON ZWETER · GERD NIENSTEDT
EIN JUNGER HIRT · ELSE MARGRETE GARDELLI

MASKE · WILLI KLOSE — BELEUCHTUNG · PAUL EBERHARDT / ERICH HAGER — BÜHNENTECHNIK · REINHARD KRUMM — WERKSTÄTTEN HANS-WOLFGANG DAHM — REGIEASSISTENZ PETER LEHMANN — MUSIKALISCHE ASSISTENZ · CLAUS ROESSNER / HERBERT VOCKS GIOVANNI BRIA / HERMANN EMMERLING — CHOREOGRAPHISCHE ASSISTENZ · SVEA KÖLLER-ZWEIG

Weber

Oberon: Excerpt (Ozean du Ungeheuer)

London April 1952	<u>Role of Rezia</u> Philharmonia Schüchter	Columbia unpublished
Cologne 1953	<u>Role of Rezia</u> WDR Orchestra Keilberth	LP: Melodram MEL 085 LP: Rodolphe RP 12433-4

Oberon: Excerpts (1.Eil', edler Held!; 2.Traure, mein Herz)

Cologne 1953	<u>Role of Rezia</u> Litz (2) WDR Orchestra Keilberth	LP: Melodram MEL 085 LP: Rodolphe RP 12433-4 (2)

Rysanek:
roles performed with the Vienna State Opera

Includes performances with the Vienna company on tour
Figure against each role indicates number of times the part was performed

8	Agathe (Der Freischütz)
19	Aida (Aida)
24	Amelia (Un ballo in maschera)
30	Ariadne/Prima donna (Ariadne auf Naxos)
48	Chrysothemis (Elektra)
16	Desdemona (Otello)
3	Donna Anna (Don Giovanni)
14	Elisabeth (Tannhäuser)
9	Elisabetta (Don Carlo)
13	Elsa (Lohengrin)
*	Herodias (Salome)
*	Kabanicha (Katya Kabanova)
34	Kaiserin (Die Frau ohne Schatten)
2	Klytemnestra (Elektra)
6	Kostelnicka (Jenufa)
11	Kundry (Parsifal)
1	1st Lady (Die Zauberflöte)
2	Leonora (La forza del destino)
35	Leonore (Fidelio)
58	Marschallin (Der Rosenkavalier)
10	Medea (Medea)
5	Mlada (Dalibor)
3	Ortrud (Lohengrin)

1	Myrtocle (Die toten Augen)
38	Salome (Salome)
4	Santuzza (Cavalleria Rusticana)
16	Senta (Der fliegende Holländer)
43	Sieglinde (Die Walküre)
3	Tatiana (Eugene Onegin)
52	Tosca (Tosca)
3	Turandot (Turandot)

*   still performing these roles in 1991-92 season

Eberhard Wächter
Discography

compiled by John Hunt

Introduction

Although he had already appeared at Covent Garden in 3 important roles, I first became aware of this striking light baritone when Walter Legge brought Eberhard Wächter (1929-1992) back to London in 1959 for the concert performances of Mozart operas which followed Columbia's recording sessions under Carlo Maria Giulini. Here, for example, was a Count Almaviva of considerable suavity and assertiveness who resorted to a little self-defensive hectoring when intimidated by the dazzling presence of Elisabeth Schwarzkopf's Countess.

After the Columbia recording of "Don Giovanni", that role became Wächter's visiting card on the international circuit, whilst at home in Vienna he also remained a distinguished Verdian in the mould of Schöffler and Metternich. And it was to his home base that Wächter quite soon began to restrict his activities, being a firm believer in the ensemble spirit. It was in the administrative sphere, advocating a return to the Vienna Opera ensemble of old, that he achieved some notoriety in the 18 months before his unexpected death. As Director of the Staatsoper he upset many a sensibility by calling for a return to ensemble values. Certainly, if Wächter's rejection of the star system was also going to eradicate the excesses of modern "producers", then many would have gone along with the reform.

Eberhard Wächter's early recordings for DG and Amadeo are indeed rare collector's items, but his prime is well documented and accessible: the Mozart operas already mentioned, the role of Donner in the Solti "Das Rheingold", Kurwenal in Böhm's "Tristan", Jochanaan in "Salome" and Wolfram in "Tannhäuser". Pride of place would go, in my view, to the Schumann Lieder recital on Decca (accompanied by Brendel and already reissued on CD), where an artist not closely associated with such repertoire reveals some fine interpretative insights and a honeyed tone of rare distinction. Just as delectable, if you can locate a copy of the DG LP, is a selection from Wolf's "Italian Songbook" with Irmgard Seefried.

SALZBURGER FESTSPIELE 1960

40 JAHRE SALZBURGER FESTSPIELE

ACHTES ORCHESTER-KONZERT

WOLFGANG AMADEUS MOZART
REQUIEM
für Soli, Chor, Orchester und Orgel

ANTON BRUCKNER
TE DEUM
für Soli, Chor, Orchester und Orgel

Solisten
LEONTYNE PRICE
HILDE RÖSSEL-MAJDAN
FRITZ WUNDERLICH
WALTER BERRY
EBERHARD WÄCHTER

DIRIGENT
HERBERT VON KARAJAN

DIE WIENER PHILHARMONIKER
DER SINGVEREIN DER GESELLSCHAFT DER MUSIKFREUNDE WIEN

D'Albert

Tiefland

Vienna 1956	Role of Moruccio Brouwenstijn, Hopf, Kmennt, Schöffler, Czerwenka Vienna Opera Chorus VSO Moralt	LP: Epic 4SC 6025 LP: Philips 6768 026 Excerpts LP: Philips GL 5672

Beethoven

Fidelio

Vienna May 1962	Role of Fernando C.Ludwig, Janowitz, Vickers, Kmennt, Kreppel, Berry Vienna Opera Chorus VPO Karajan	LP: Movimento Musica 03.014

An die ferne Geliebte, song cycle

1957	H. Schmidt, piano	LP: DG LPE 17 112

6 Gellert-Lieder

1957	H. Schmidt, piano	LP: DG LPE 17 112

Berg

Wozzeck

Vienna October and November 1980	Role of Wozzeck Silja, Winkler, Zednik, Malta, Laubenthal Vienna Opera Chorus VPO Dohnanyi	LP: Decca D321 D2 CD: Decca 417 3482

Bizet

Carmen: Selection

Cologne Date uncertain	Role of Escamillo Malaniuk, Fahberg, Konya WDR Orchestra Marszalek Sung in German	LP: Polydor SLPHM 237 041

Brahms

Ein deutsches Requiem

Vienna May 1964	Baritone soloist Janowitz Singverein BPO Karajan	LP: DG KL33-39/SKL 133-139 LP: DG 2707 018 LP: DG 2726 078 CD: DG 427 2522

Liebeslieder-Walzer; Neue Liebeslieder-Walzer

Vienna February 1962	Seefried, Kostia Kmennt Werba, piano Weissenborn, piano	LP: DG LPM 18 792/SLPM 138 792

Dallapiccola

Il Prigioniero

Vienna
March 1956

Role of Prisoner
Pilarczyk, Krebs,
Kreppel
Bavarian Radio
Chorus & Orchestra
Scherchen
Sung in German

CD: Stradivarius STR 10034

Vienna
June 1971

Role of Prisoner
Poli, English,
Bösch
Austrian Radio
Chorus & Orchestra
Melles

LP: CBS (Italy) 61344

Cornelius

Der Barbier von Bagdad

London
May 1956

Role of 1st Muezzin
Schwarzkopf,
G. Hoffman, Gedda,
Unger, Prey
Chorus
Philharmonia
Leinsdorf

LP: Columbia 33CX 1400-1
LP: Electrola 1C 147 01448-9M

Donizetti

L'Elisir d'amore

Vienna
May 1973

Role of Dulcamara
Grist, Gedda,
Kerns
Vienna Opera Chorus
VSO
Varviso

LP: Melodiya M10 47035 004

La Favorita: Excerpt (Vien, Leonora, a piedi tuoi)

Berlin
November 1957

Role of Alphonso
Berlin RO
König
Sung in German

45: DG EPL 30328
LP: Preiser PR 135 015

Einem

Der Besuch der alten Dame

Vienna May 1971	Role of Ill C.Ludwig, Loose, Hotter, Beirer VPO Stein	LP: Amadeo 419 5521

Gluck

Iphigenie auf Tauris: Excerpts (Ihr, die ihr mich verfolgt, ihr, meiner Frevel Schöpfer !; Ihr, die das Land des wilden Volkes schützt...die Ruhe kehret mir zurück)

Berlin November 1957	Role of Orest Berlin RO König	LP: Preiser PR 135 015

Gounod

Faust: Excerpts (1. Avant de quitter ces lieux; 2. Par ici, par ici, mes amis !)

Munich February 1957	Role of Valentine Stader, Naaf Bavarian Radio Chorus Munich PO Leitner	45: DG EPL 30339 (1) LP: Preiser PR 135 015 Version in German LP: DG LPEM 19 095/89651 45: DG EPL 30338 (1) 45: DG EPL 30328 (2)

Humperdinck

Königskinder: Excerpt (Verdorben! Gestorben!)

Berlin November 1957	Role of Spielmann Berlin RO König	45: DG EPL 30309 LP: Preiser PR 135015

Kreutzer

Das Nachtlager in Granada: Excerpt (Ein Schütz' bin ich in des Regenten Sold)

Berlin November 1957	Role of Huntsman Berlin RO König	45: DG EPL 30309 LP: Preiser PR 135 015

Lehar

Die lustige Witwe

London July 1962	Role of Danilo Schwarzkopf, Steffek, Gedda Philharmonia Chorus & Orchestra Matacic	LP: EMI AN 101-2/SAN 101-2 LP: EMI SLS 823 CD: EMI CDS 747 1788 Excerpts LP: EMI ALP 2252/ASD 2252

Der Graf von Luxemburg: Selection

Munich Date uncertain	Role of René Sukis, Kunz Graunke Orchestra Goldschmidt	LP: Philips 6449 084 CD: Philips 420 6632

Leoncavallo

I Pagliacci: Selection

Cologne 1960	Role of Tonio Hollweg, Konya WDR Orchestra Marszalek Sung in German	LP: Polydor SLPHM 237 150

I Pagliacci: Excerpt (Nedda ! Silvio ! A quest' ora che imprudenza)

Berlin November 1957	Role of Silvio Schlemm Berlin RO König Sung in German	LP: Preiser PR 135 015

Liszt

Aus dem Nebel der Täler erschalle hervor (Die heilige Elisabeth); Die drei Zigeuner; Es muss ein Wunderbares sein

Berlin November 1957	Berlin RO König	45: DG EPL 30303

Loewe

Der Mönch zu Pisa; Die Glocken zu Speyer; Graf Eberhards Weissdorn; Der Edelfalk; Der gefangene Admiral; Gregor auf dem Stein

Vienna   Dokoupil, piano   LP: Preiser SPR 3211
Date uncertain

Erlkönig; Odins Meeresritt

Vienna   H.Schmidt, piano   LP: Amadeo AVRS 6257
Date uncertain

Lortzing

Zar und Zimmermann: Selection

Vienna   Role of Tsar Peter   LP: Eurodisc 201.587.250
1961   Holm, Kmennt,   Sonst spielt' ich mit Zepter
                 Welter   LP: Eurodisc 200.417.241
                 Volksoper   LP: Eurodisc 300.645.370
                 Chorus & Orchestra
                 Bauer-Theussl

Vienna   Role of Tsar Peter   LP: Decca LXT 6039/SXL 6039
1963   Güden, Kmennt,
                 Czerwenka
                 Vienna Opera Chorus
                 Volksoper Orchestra
                 Ronnefeld

Mascagni

Cavalleria Rusticana

Berlin 1960	Role of Alfio Hillebrecht, Schock Deutsche Oper Chorus & Orchestra Hollreiser Sung in German	LP: Eurodisc 27272 XDR/72245 XR Excerpts LP: Eurodisc 72614 KR/72615 KR LP: Eurodisc 200.417.241

Millöcker

Der Bettelstudent

Vienna 1956	Role of Janicki Lipp, Rethy, Christ, Preger, Dönch Vienna Opera Chorus VPO Paulik	LP: Vanguard PVL 7056-7

Monteverdi

L'Orfeo: Excerpts

Munich April 1954	Role of Orfeo Lindermeier, L.Fischer, Böhme Bavarian Radio Chorus & Orchestra Jochum	LP: Giolielli della lirica GML 79

SALZBURGER FESTSPIELE 1960

40 JAHRE SALZBURGER FESTSPIELE

DON GIOVANNI

DRAMMA GIOCOSO IN ZWEI AKTEN
VON LORENZO DA PONTE

MUSIK VON
WOLFGANG AMADEUS MOZART

DIRIGENT
HERBERT VON KARAJAN

INSZENIERUNG
OSCAR FRITZ SCHUH

BÜHNENBILD
TEO OTTO

KOSTÜME
GEORGE WAKHEWITCH

ORCHESTER
DIE WIENER PHILHARMONIKER
CHOR DER WIENER STAATSOPER

DON GIOVANNI

(in italienischer Sprache)

Dramma giocoso in zwei Akten von Lorenzo da Ponte
MUSIK VON WOLFGANG AMADEUS MOZART

Don Giovanni	Eberhard Wächter
Donna Elvira	Elisabeth Schwarzkopf
Il Commendatore	Nicola Zaccaria
Donna Anna	Leontyne Price
Don Ottavio	Cesare Valletti
Leporello	Walter Berry
Zerline	Graziella Sciutti
Masetto	Rolando Panerai

Technische Einrichtung und Beleuchtung: Sepp Nordegg

Nach dem ersten Aufzug eine größere Pause

Der offizielle Almanach «Salzburg — Festspiele 1960» ist auch für Sie der unentbehrliche Ratgeber
The official almanac "Salzburg Festivals 1960" is an indispensable guide for all Festival visitors
L'almanach officiel «Salzbourg Festival 1960» est indispensable à tous ceux qui s'intéressent au Festival

Mozart

Don Giovanni

London October 1959	Role of Giovanni Schwarzkopf, Sutherland, Sciutti, Alva, Taddei, Frick, Cappuccilli Philharmonia Chorus & Orchestra Klemperer	Columbia unpublished (recording incomplete)
London October and November 1959	Role of Giovanni Schwarzkopf, Sutherland, Sciutti, Alva, Taddei, Frick, Cappuccilli Philharmonia Chorus & Orchestra Giulini	LP: Columbia 33CX 1717-20/SAX 2369-72 LP: EMI SLS 5083 CD: EMI CDS 747 2608 Excerpts LP: Columbia 33CX 1918/SAX 2559 LP: EMI SXLP 30300 CD: EMI CDM 763 0782
Salzburg August 1960	Role of Giovanni Schwarzkopf, L.Price, Sciutti, Valletti, Berry, Panerai, Zaccaria Vienna Opera Chorus VPO Karajan	LP: HRE Records HRE 247 LP: Movimento Musica 03.001 CD: Movimento Musica 013.6012 CD: Curcio OP 6
Lisbon 1960	Role of Giovanni Caballé, Otto, Stich-Randall, Kmennt, Kunz, Peter, H.Hoffmann San Carlos Chorus & Orchestra Gielen	CD: Legato SRO 813
Vienna June 1963	Role of Giovanni Güden, Sciutti, L.Price, Berry, Wunderlich, Kreppel, Panerai Vienna Opera Chorus VPO Karajan	CD: Verona 27065-7
Vienna 1955	Role of Masetto Jurinac, Sciutti, Zadek, Simoneau, London, Weber, Ernster Chamber Choir VSO Moralt	LP: Philips ABL 3069-71 LP: Philips GL 5753-5 LP: Philips 6768 033

Idomeneo

Salzburg July 1956	Role of Arbace Hillebrecht, Goltz, Schock, Kmennt, Böhme Vienna Opera Chorus VPO Böhm	LP: Movimento Musica 03.017
Salzburg July 1961	Role of High Priest Lorengar, Grümmer, Kmennt, Haefliger, Capecchi Vienna Opera Chorus Fricsay	LP: Melodram MEL 701

Le Nozze di Figaro

London September and November 1959	Role of Count Schwarzkopf, Moffo, Cossotto, Taddei, Philharmonia Chorus & Orchestra Giulini	LP: Columbia 33CX 1732-5/SAX 2381-4 LP: EMI SLS 5152 CD: EMI CMS 763 2662 Excerpts LP: Columbia 33CX 1934/SAX 2573 LP: EMI SXLP 30303 CD: EMI CDM 763 4092

Die Zauberflöte

Vienna May 1962	Role of Speaker Lipp, Hallstein, Sciutti, Gedda, Kunz, Frick Vienna Opera Chorus VPO Karajan	LP: Movimento Musica 03.015 CD: Movimento Musica 051.028

Die Zauberflöte: Excerpt (Wo willst du, kühner Fremdling, hin?)

Vienna 1970	Role of Speaker Dermota VPO Krips	CD: Melodram CDM 26522

ROYAL FESTIVAL HALL
General Manager: T. E. BEAN, C.B.E.

PHILHARMONIA CONCERT SOCIETY LTD

ARTISTIC DIRECTOR:
WALTER LEGGE

MOZART
DON GIOVANNI
(Concert Performance)

PHILHARMONIA ORCHESTRA
LEADER: HUGH BEAN

Members of the PHILHARMONIA CHORUS

CONTINUO AND MUSICAL ASSISTANT: HEINRICH SCHMIDT

Harpsichord by Thomas Goff

CARLO MARIA GIULINI

Monday, February 20, 1961, at 7.30 p.m.

Programme Two Shillings

DON GIOVANNI

Cast in order of appearance

Leporello, *servant to Don Giovanni*	Giuseppe Taddei
Donna Anna, *betrothed to Don Ottavio*	Elisabeth Grümmer
Don Giovanni, *an extremely licentious young nobleman*	Eberhard Waechter
Il Commendatore, *father of Donna Anna*	Gottlob Frick
Don Ottavio	Ernst Haefliger
Donna Elvira, *a lady of Burgos, deserted by Don Giovanni*	Elisabeth Schwarzkopf
Zerlina, *a peasant girl, betrothed to Masetto*	Mirella Freni
Masetto, *a peasant*	Piero Cappuccilli

ONE INTERVAL OF TWENTY MINUTES AFTER THE FIRST ACT

Nicolai

Die lustigen Weiber von Windsor: Excerpt (In einem Waschkorb ?)

Munich April 1955	Role of Reich Borg Munich PO Leitner	LP: DG LPEM 19049 45: DG EPL 30277 LP: DG 89 648 LP: Preiser PR 135 015

Offenbach

La Vie Parisienne

Berlin February 1968	Role of Gondremarck Della Casa, Hallstein, Schramm, Schock, Gruber, Unger, Böhme, Deutsche Staatsoper Chorus Berlin SO Allers Sung in German	LP: Eurodisc XE 77485 Excerpts LP: Eurodisc IE 89889 CD: RCA GD 69028

Puccini

Tosca: Excerpt (Già, mi dicon venal)

Vienna 1961	Role of Scarpia Volksoper Orchestra Bauer-Theussl Sung in German	LP: Eurodisc 72614KR/72615KR LP: Eurodisc 200.417.241 LP: Eurodisc 25965 XBR

Rossini

Il Barbiere di Siviglia

Vienna April 1966	Role of Figaro Grist, Konetzni, Wunderlich, Kunz, Czerwenka Vienna Opera Chorus VPO Böhm Sung in German	LP: Teatro Dischi TD 502-3 CD: Myto MCD 91752 Teatro Dischi incorrectly dated 1965

Il Barbiere di Siviglia: Excerpts

Munich 1964	Role of Figaro Hallstein, Kmennt, Kusche, Frick Bavarian State Orchestra Löwlein Sung in German	LP: Eurodisc 72614 KR/72615 KR LP: Eurodisc 86802 KR LP: Eurodisc 200.417.241

Schumann

Dichterliebe

Vienna September 1961	Brendel, piano	LP: Decca LXT 5675/SXL 2310 CD: Decca 425 9492

Aus meinen Tränen spriessen (Dichterliebe)

Vienna Date uncertain	H.Schmidt, piano	LP: Amadeo AVRS 6257

In der Fremde; Wehmut (Liederkreis op 39)

Vienna Date uncertain	H.Schmidt, piano	LP: Amadeo AVRS 6257

Schöne Wiege meiner Leiden; Mit Myrthen und Rosen (Liederkreis op 24)

Vienna Date uncertain	H.Schmidt, piano	LP: Amadeo AVRS 6257
Vienna September 1961	Brendel, piano	LP: Decca LXT 5675/SXL 2310 CD: Decca 425 9492

Mein Wagen rollet langsam; Lehn' deine Wang' an meine Wang'

Vienna Date uncertain	H.Schmidt, piano	LP: Amadeo AVRS 6257
Vienna September 1961	Brendel, piano	LP: Decca LXT 5675/SXL 2310 CD: Decca 425 9492

Stolz

Die Rosen der Madonna

Vienna Date uncertain	Role of Pater Clemens Janowitz, Kmennt ORF Orchestra Stolz	LP: BASF 20.212610

Johann Strauss

Die Fledermaus

London June and July 1959	Role of Falke Lipp, Scheyrer, C.Ludwig, Terkal, Berry, Kunz Philharmonia Chorus & Orchestra Ackermann	LP: Columbia 33CX 1688-9/SAX 2336-7 LP: Electrola 1C 147 01652-3 LP: EMI CFPD 4702 CD: EMI CDCFPD 4702 Excerpts LP: EMI XLP 20091/SXLP 20091
Vienna July 1960	Role of Frank Güden, Köth, Resnik, Kmennt, Zampieri, Berry, Kunz Vienna Opera Chorus VPO Karajan	LP: Decca MET 201-3/SET 201-3 LP: Decca LXT 6015-6/SXL 6015-6 LP: Decca D247 D3 CD: Decca 421 0462 Excerpts LP: Decca LXT 6155/SXL 6155
Vienna December 1960	Role of Eisenstein Güden, Streich, Stolze, Zampieri, Kunz, Berry Vienna Opera Chorus VPO Karajan	LP: Foyer FO 1031 CD: Foyer 3CF-2021 CD: Hunt CDKAR 215 Excerpts LP: Gioielli della lirica GML 25
Vienna 1964	Role of Eisenstein Leigh, Rothenberger, Stevens, Konya, Kunz, London Vienna Opera Chorus VPO Danon	LP: RCA LSC 7029/SER 5514-5 LP: RCA (Germany) 26.35058
Vienna 1972	Role of Eisenstein Janowitz, Holm, Windgassen, Kunz, Kmennt, Holecek Vienna Opera Chorus VPO Böhm	LP: Decca SET 540-1
Munich December 1986	Role of Eisenstein Coburn, Perry, Fassbänder, Brendel, Hopferwieser, Kusche, Bavarian State Chorus & Orchestra C.Kleiber	VHS Video: DG 072 4003 Laserdisc: DG 072 4001

Cagliostro in Wien: Selection

Vienna 1961	Role of Cagliostro Scheyrer, Kmennt, C.Ludwig Vienna Opera Chorus VSO Salmhofer	LP: Philips A 02216 L

Der lustige Krieg: Selection

Vienna 1961	Roles of Groot and Franchetti Siebert, C.Ludwig, Kmennt Vienna Opera Chorus VSO E.Strauss	LP: Philips A 02216 L

Ritter Pasman

Vienna 1975	Role of Pasman Ghazarian, T.Schmidt, Hopferwieser, Korn Austrian Radio Chorus & Orchestra Wallberg	LP: Ed Smith UORC 333 Ein schlechter Spass LP: ORF private issue

Der Zigeunerbaron

Vienna 1955	Role of Carnero Loose, Scheyrer, Kmennt, Kunz, Preger Vienna Opera Chorus VSO Paulik	LP: Philips GO4200-1L LP: Philips GL 5724-5 LP: Vanguard PVL 7033-4/VRS 486-7
Berlin Date uncertain	Role of Homonay Hazy, Schädle, Konetzni, Schock, Schmitt-Walter, Kusche Deutsche Oper Chorus & Orchestra Stolz	LP: Eurodisc XF 71455 E Excerpts LP: Eurodisc I 89897 E LP: Eurodisc 200.417.241

Richard Strauss

Arabella

Vienna May and June 1957	Role of Dominik Della Casa, Güden, Malaniuk, Dermota, London, Edelmann Vienna Opera Chorus VPO Solti	LP: Decca LXT 5403-6/SXL 2050-3 LP: Decca GOS 571-3 CD: Decca 430 3872

Capriccio

London September 1957	Role of Count Schwarzkopf, Moffo, C.Ludwig, Gedda, Hotter, Fischer-Dieskau, Schmitt-Walter Philharmonia Sawallisch	LP: Columbia 33CX 1600-2 LP: World Records OC 230-2 LP: Electrola 143 5243 CD: EMI CDS 749 0148 Excerpts LP: World Records OH 233

Elektra

Salzburg August 1964	Role of Orest Varnay, Mödl, Hillebrecht, King VPO Karajan	LP: Estro Armonico EA 044 LP: Melodram MEL 718 CD: Melodram CDM 27044 CD: Hunt CDKAR
Vienna December 1965	Role of Orest Nilsson, Resnik, Rysanek, Windgassen VPO Böhm	LP: HRE Records HRE 314 CD: Legato SRO 833

Die Frau ohne Schatten

Vienna November and December 1955	Role of Watchman Rysanek, Goltz, Höngen, Hopf, Schöffler, Böhme Vienna Opera Chorus VPO Böhm	LP: Decca LXT 5180-4 LP: Decca GOM 554-7/GOS 554-7 CD: Decca 425 9812

SALZBURGER FESTSPIELE 1961

DON GIOVANNI

DRAMMA GIOCOSO IN ZWEI AKTEN
VON LORENZO DA PONTE

MUSIK VON
WOLFGANG AMADEUS MOZART

DIRIGENT
HERBERT VON KARAJAN

INSZENIERUNG
OSCAR FRITZ SCHUH

BÜHNENBILD
TEO OTTO

KOSTÜME
GEORGE WAKHEWITCH

ORCHESTER
DIE WIENER PHILHARMONIKER
CHOR DER WIENER STAATSOPER

DON GIOVANNI

(in italienischer Sprache)

Dramma giocoso in zwei Akten von Lorenzo da Ponte

MUSIK VON WOLFGANG AMADEUS MOZART

Don Giovanni	Eberhard Wächter
Donna Elvira	Wilma Lipp
Il Commendatore	Nicola Zaccaria
Donna Anna	Leontyne Price
Don Ottavio	Nicolai Gedda
Leporello	Walter Berry
Zerline	Graziella Sciutti
Masetto	Rolando Panerai

Technische Einrichtung und Beleuchtung: Sepp Nordegg

Nach dem ersten Aufzug eine größere Pause

Der offizielle Almanach „Salzburg — Festspiele 1961" ist auch für Sie der unentbehrliche Ratgeber
The official almanac "Salzburg Festivals 1961" is an indispensable guide for all Festival visitors
L'almanach officiel «Salzbourg Festival 1961» est indispensable à tous ceux qui s'intéressent au Festival

Der Rosenkavalier

London December 1956	Roles of Faninal, Footman and Waiter Schwarzkopf, C.Ludwig, Gedda, Stich-Randall, Edelmann Chorus Philharmonia Karajan	LP: Columbia 33CX 1492-5/SAX 2269-72 LP: EMI SLS 810 LP: EMI EX 29 00453 CD: EMI CDS 749 3548 Excerpts LP: Columbia 33CX 1777/SAX 2423 CD: EMI CDM 763 4522

Salome

Vienna October 1961	Role of Jochanaan Nilsson, G.Hoffman, Stolze, Kmennt VPO Solti	LP: Decca MET 228-9/SET 228-9 CD: Decca 414 4142

Heimliche Aufforderung; Morgen; Die Nacht; Traum durch die Dämmerung; Zueignung

Vienna Date uncertain	H.Schmidt, piano	LP: Amadeo AVRS 6257

Stravinsky

Les Noces

Vienna 1953	Baritone soloist Steingruber, Kenny, Wagner Kammerchor Instrumentalists Rossi Sung in Russian	LP: Vanguard PVL 7009

Verdi

Un Ballo in Maschera: Selection

Berlin 1965	Role of Renato Hillebrecht, Otto, Töpper, Schock Deutsche Oper Orchestra Hollreiser Sung in German	LP: Eurodisc 86812 KR Eri tu LP: Eurodisc 72614 KR/72615 KR LP: Eurodisc 200.417.241

Don Carlos

Vienna October 1970	Role of Posa Janowitz, Verrett, Corelli, Ghiaurov, Talvela Vienna Opera Chorus VPO Stein	LP: Morgan MOR 7003 CD: Legato SRO 514 Also issued on Rodolphe label

Rigoletto: Excerpts

Cologne 1963	Role of Rigoletto Hollweg, Konya Cologne RO Marszalek Sung in German	LP: Polydor SLPHM 237 152

Simone Boccanegra: Excerpt (Suona ogni labbro il mio nome)

Vienna March 1969	Role of Simone Ghiaurov VPO Krips	CD: Legato SRO 514

Il Trovatore: Excerpts

Cologne 1963	Role of Luna Hillebrecht, Malaniuk, Konya Cologne RO Marszalek Sung in German	LP: Polydor SLPHM 237 152

Il Trovatore: Excerpt (Il balen)

Berlin 1965	Role of Luna Deutsche Oper Orchestra Hollreiser Sung in German	LP: Eurodisc 72614 KR/72615 KR LP: Eurodisc 200.417.241

Wagner

Lohengrin

Bayreuth July 1958	Role of Heerrufer Rysanek, Varnay, Konya, Blanc, Engen Bayreuth Festival Chorus & Orchestra Cluytens	LP: Replica RPL 2489-92 CD: Myto MCD 89062
Bayreuth August 1960	Role of Heerrufer Nordmo-Lövberg, Varnay, Adam, Windgassen, Neidlinger Bayreuth Festival Chorus & Orchestra Maazel	LP: Melodram MEL 601

Parsifal

Bayreuth July 1958	Role of Amfortas Crespin, Beirer, Hines, Greindl, Blankenheim Bayreuth Festival Chorus & Orchestra Knappertsbusch	LP: Melodram MEL 583
Vienna April 1961	Role of Amfortas C.Ludwig, Höngen, Uhl, Hotter, Franc, Berry Vienna Opera Chorus VPO Karajan	CD: Hunt CDKAR 219 Opening of performance, up to and including first scene with Amfortas, inadvertently taken from Bayreuth 1959 performance with Wächter but with Hines as Gurnemanz and Mödl as Kundry

Parsifal: Opening, up to and including first scene of Amfortas (Recht so! Habt Dank!)

Bayreuth August 1959	Role of Amfortas Mödl, Hines, Bayreuth Festival Orchestra Knappertsbusch	CD: Hunt CDKAR 219 Incorrectly labelled Vienna 1961 (see above)

Die Meistersinger von Nürnberg

Bayreuth July 1958	Role of Kothner Grümmer, Schärtel, Traxel, Stolze, Wiener, Hotter, Blankenheim Bayreuth Festival Chorus & Orchestra Cluytens	LP: Melodram MEL 582
Bayreuth July 1959	Role of Kothner Grümmer, Schärtel, Schock, Stolze, Wiener, Greindl, Blankenheim Bayreuth Festival Chorus & Orchestra Leinsdorf	LP: Melodram MEL 592

Das Rheingold

Vienna September and October 1958	Role of Donner Flagstad, Watson, Madeira, Kuen, Kmennt, Svanholm, Neidlinger, London, Kreppel, Böhme VPO Solti	LP: Decca LXT 5495-7/SXL 2101-3 LP: Decca SET 382-4 LP: Decca 414 1011/414 1001 CD: Decca 414 1012/414 1002 Excerpts LP: Decca LXT 5586/SXL 2230 45: Decca CEP 632/SEC 5042

Tannhäuser

Rome November 1957	Role of Wolfram Brouwenstijn, Liebl, Ernster, Pernerstorfer RAI Rome Chorus & Orchestra Rodzinski	LP: Melodram MEL 472
Bayreuth July 1962	Role of Wolfram Silja, Bumbry, Windgassen, Greindl Bayreuth Festival Chorus & Orchestra Sawallisch	LP: Philips AL 3445-7/SAL 3445-7 LP: Philips 6747 249/6747 242 LP: Philips 6770 026 CD: Philips 420 1222 Excerpts LP: Philips 6527 108 LP: Philips 412 0231
Vienna January 1963	Role of Wolfram Brouwenstijn, C.Ludwig, Beirer, Frick, Franc Vienna Opera Chorus VPO Karajan	LP: Melodram MEL 427 CD: Nuova Era 6307-9 Also issued on Hunt label

Tannhäuser; Excerpts (Blick' ich umher; O du mein holder Abendstern)

Bamberg February 1956	Role of Wolfram Bamberg SO Leitner	LP: DG LPEM 19069 45: DG EPL 30234 LP: Preiser PR 135 015

Tristan und Isolde

Bayreuth July 1962	Role of Kurwenal Nilsson, Meyer, Windgassen, Greindl, Bayreuth Festival Chorus & Orchestra Böhm	LP: Melodram MEL 625
Bayreuth July and August 1966	Role of Kurwenal Nilsson, C.Ludwig, Windgassen, Talvela Bayreuth Festival Chorus & Orchestra Böhm	LP: DG SLPM 139 221-5 LP: DG 2713 001 LP: DG 2740 144 LP: Philips 6747 243 LP: DG 415 3951 CD: DG 419 8892 Excerpts LP: DG SLPEM 136 433 LP: DG 2537 001 Rehearsal extracts (Act 3) LP: DG SLPM 139 221-5 LP: DG 2713 001 LP: DG 2740 144
Bayreuth August 1966	Role of Kurwenal Nilsson, C.Ludwig, Windgassen, Talvela Bayreuth Festival Chorus & Orchestra	CD: Frequenz CML 3 Excerpts CD: Curcio-Hunt OPV 16

Weber

Der Freischütz

Munich December 1959	Role of Ottokar Seefried, Streich, Holm, Böhme, Kreppel Bavarian Radio Chorus & Orchestra Jochum	LP: DG LPM 18 639-40/SLPM 138 639-40 LP: DG 2707 009 LP: DG 2726 061 Excerpts LP: DG LPEM 19 221/SLPEM 136 221 CD: DG 423 8692
Vienna May 1972	Role of Ottokar Janowitz, Holm, King, Jungwirth, Ridderbusch Vienna Opera Chorus VPO Böhm	CD: Hunt CDMP 457

Wolf

Italienisches Liederbuch: Sterb' ich, so hüllt in Blumen; Und willst du deinen Liebsten sterben sehen; Wenn du mich mit den Augen

Vienna Date uncertain	H.Schmidt, piano	LP: Amadeo AVRS 6257

Mörike-Lieder: Gebet; Peregrina; Gesang Weylas

Vienna Date uncertain	H.Schmidt, piano	LP: Amadeo AVRS 6257

Spanisches Liederbuch: Die du Gott gebarst, du Reine; Ach, wie lang die Seele schlummert; Nun bin ich dein; Komm', o Tod; Alle gingen, Herz, zur Ruh'; Wer sein holdes Lieb verloren; Treibe nur mit Lieben Spott; Wunden trägst du (duet); Herr, was trägt der Boden (duet); other titles sung by Seefried

Vienna April and May 1959	Seefried Werba, piano	LP: DG LPM 18 591/SLPM 138 059

Zeller

Der Vogelhändler: Selection

Vienna 1956	Role of Würmchen Zadek, Lipp Patzak, Preger Vienna Opera Chorus VSO Moralt	LP: Philips S 04031 L LP: Philips SBL 5215

Wächter:
roles performed with the Vienna State Opera

Includes performances with the Vienna company on tour
Figure against each role indicates number of times the part was performed

2	Achilles (Penelope)*
8	Adam (Der Bettelstudent)
20	Amfortas (Parsifal)
6	Caesar (Giulio Cesare)
17	Coppelius (Les contes d'Hoffmann)
143	Count Almaviva (Le nozze di Figaro)
16	Danton (Dantons Tod)
17	Dappertuto (Les contes d'Hoffmann)
21	Don Alfonso (Così fan tutte)
10	Don Fernando (Fidelio)
83	Don Giovanni (Don Giovanni)
17	Donner (Das Rheingold)
60	Eisenstein (Die Fledermaus)
2	Escamillo (Carmen)
18	Falke (Die Fledermaus)
12	Figaro (Il Barbiere di Siviglia)
13	Ford (Falstaff)
2	Gérard (Andrea Chenier)
36	Germont (La Traviata)
10	Golaud (Pelléas et Melisande)
14	Heerrufer (Lohengrin)
1	Herald (Alceste)
5	Homonay (Der Zigeunerbaron)

5	Igor (Prince Igor)
9	Ill (Der Besuch der alten Dame)**
32	Jochanaan (Salome)
13	King (Der Kuhreigen)***
17	Lindorf (Les contes d'Hoffmann)
12	Lord Cookburn (Fra Diavolo)
13	Kothner (Die Meistersinger von Nürnberg)
2	Kurt (Das Werbekleid)****
12	Lerma (Don Carlo)
7	Lescaut (Manon Lescaut)
19	Liebenau (Der Waffenschmied)
3	Luna (Il Trovatore)
25	Mandryka (Arabella)
54	Marcello (La Bohème)
3	Melchior (Amahl and the Night Visitors)
5	Melot (Tristan und Isolde)
17	Mirakel (Les contes d'Hoffmann)
1	Morales (Carmen)
10	Morone (Palestrina)
9	Music Master (Ariadne auf Naxos)
3	Nachtigall (Die Meistersinger v.Nürnberg)
4	Nick Shadow (The Rake's Progress)
5	Officer (Notre Dame)
9	Orest (Elektra)
12	Ottokar (Der Freischütz)
16	Ping (Turandot)
55	Posa (Don Carlo)
7	Prospero (The Tempest)*****
8	Renato (Un ballo in maschera)
13	Rigoletto (Rigoletto)

15	St. Brioche (The Merry Widow)
48	Scarpia (Tosca)
6	Schlemihl (Les contes d'Hoffmann)
61	Sharpless (Madama Butterfly)
13	Silvio (I Pagliacci)
15	Simone Boccanegra (Simone Boccanegra)
84	Speaker (Die Zauberflöte)
7	Tomsky (The Queen of Spades)
12	Valentine (Faust)
6	Vladislav (Dalibor)
30	Wolfram (Tannhäuser)
1	Wotan (Das Rheingold)

*	Liebermann
**	Von Einem
***	Kienzl
****	Salmhofer
*****	Frank Martin

Maria Reining
Discography

compiled by John Hunt

MARIA REINING

TO SUCCEED Lotte Lehmann as *the* Marschallin of the Vienna State Opera was no easy task, but this is what the charming Viennese soprano, Maria Reining, has been able to do. For she has the typical Viennese graciousness and breeding to her finger-tips.

Maria Reining's career has been mostly spent in two of Europe's most important opera houses, the Munich Opera and the Vienna State Opera. From 1931 to 1933 she sang in Vienna, from 1933 to 1937 in Munich, and from 1937 to the present time again in Vienna.

Maria Reining's roles in Vienna have included Pamina, the Countess, Agathe, Euryanthe, Majenka, Eva, Elsa, Elisabeth, Sieglinde, Ariadne, Arabella, Leonora in *Il Trovatore*, Elizabeth de Valois, Desdemona, Butterfly, Mimì, Marguerite, and Manon.

In 1937 she sang Eva under Toscanini at Salzburg, and since then has been a constant visitor there, her 1947 Arabella and 1949 Marschallin being especially remembered. In 1938 she sang in Chicago, in the same year as Elsa at Covent Garden, and in 1949 at the New York City Centre.

In recent seasons she has confined herself mostly to the Strauss and Wagner repertory, with occasional appearances as the Countess in *Figaro*.

From the Decca Book of Opera

SALZBURG
AUSTRIA

FESTIVAL 1953
JULY 26TH – AUGUST 31TH

CONDUCTORS:
KARL BÖHM · GUIDO CANTELLI · EDWIN FISCHER
WILHELM FURTWÄNGLER · CLEMENS KRAUSS
IGOR MARKEVITCH · BERNH. PAUMGARTNER
VICTOR de SABATA · BRUNO WALTER

PRODUCERS:
JOSEF GIELEN · HERBERT GRAF · ERNST LOTHAR
OSCAR FRITZ SCHUH

OFFICIAL PROSPECTUS
EDITED BY THE
MANAGEMENT OF THE SALZBURG FESTIVALS
SALZBURG · FESTSPIELHAUS

D'Albert

Die toten Augen: Excerpt (Psyche wandelt durch Säulenhallen)

Vienna 1942	Role of Myrtocle VPO Moralt	LP: Preiser LV 1315

Bizet

Carmen: Excerpt (Parle-moi de ma mère...Ma mère, je la vois!)

Stuttgart 1936	Role of Micaëla F.Krauss Stuttgart Opera Orchestra Görlich Sung in German	LP: BASF 22.221229

Giordano

Andrea Chenier: Excerpt (La mamma morta)

Vienna 1942	Role of Maddalena VPO Moralt Sung in German	78: Electrola DB 7648 LP: Electrola E 60632 LP: Preiser LV 1315

Lehar

Eva: Excerpt (Im heimlichen Dämmer)

Vienna	VPO	78: Electrola DB 5694
January 1942	Lehar	LP: EMI EX 769 7411
		CD: EMI CMS 769 7412

Friederike: Excerpt (Warum hast du mich wachgeküsst?)

Vienna	VPO	78: Electrola DB 5694
January 1943	Lehar	LP: Electrola 1C 147 30639-40
		LP: EMI EX 29 01313

Paganini: Excerpt (Liebe, du Himmel auf Erden)

Berlin	Deutsches	78: Telefunken E 3074
1939	Opernhaus Orchestra	LP: Preiser PR 9829
	Lutze	CD: Preiser 90083

Der Zarewitsch: Excerpt (Einer wird kommen)

Berlin	Deutsches	78: Telefunken E 3074
1939	Opernhaus Orchestra	LP: Preiser PR 9829
	Lutze	CD: Preiser 90083

Mozart

Le Nozze di Figaro: Excerpt (Porgi amor)

Berlin 1942	Role of Countess Staatskapelle Müller Sung in German	78: Electrola DB 7665 LP: Preiser LV 1315
Vienna June 1950	Role of Countess VPO Krips Sung in German	LP: Decca LXT 2685 CD: Preiser 90083

Le Nozze di Figaro: Excerpt (Dove sono)

Berlin 1942	Role of Countess Staatskapelle Müller Sung in German	78: Electrola DA 4508 LP: Preiser LV 1315
Vienna June 1950	Role of Countess VPO Krips Sung in German	LP: Decca LXT 2685 CD: Preiser 90083

Le Nozze di Figaro: Excerpt (Deh vieni non tardar)

Berlin 1942	Role of Susanna Staatskapelle Müller Sung in German	78: Electrola DB 7665 LP: Preiser LV 1315

Die Zauberflöte: Excerpt (Bald prangt, den Morgen zu verkünden)

Berlin 1943	Role of Pamina Berlin RO Steinkopf	LP: BASF 22.221229

Puccini

La Bohème: Excerpt (Mi chiamano Mimì)

Vienna   Role of Mimì   LP: Preiser LV 1315
1942   VPO
                Moralt
                Sung in German

Madama Butterfly: Excerpt (Che tua madre)

Vienna   Role of Butterfly   LP: Preiser LV 1315
1942   VPO
                Moralt
                Sung in German

Manon Lescaut: Excerpt (In quelle trine morbide)

Vienna   Role of Manon   LP: Preiser LV 1315
1942   VPO
                Moralt
                Sung in German

Tosca: Excerpts (Perchè chiuso...Quale occhio al mondo può star di paro all' ardente occhio tuo nero?; Vissi d'arte)

Berlin   Role of Tosca   LP: BASF 22.221229
1941   Rosvaenge
                Berlin RO
                Steinkopf
                Sung in German

The Puccini arias on LV 1315 are previously unpublished Electrola 78s

Smetana

The Bartered Bride: Excerpt (Gern will ich dir vernehmen)

Berlin 1942	Role of Marenka Berlin RO Steinkopf Sung in German	LP: BASF 22.221229

Johann Strauss

Die Fledermaus: Klänge der Heimat

Berlin 1939	Role of Rosalinde Deutsches Opernhaus Orchestra Lutze	78: Telefunken E 3055 LP: Preiser PR 9829 CD: Preiser 90083

DER ROSENKAVALIER

Octavian **Jurinac**   Feldmarschallin **Reining**
Sophie **Gueden**   Ochs **Weber**

and supporting cast
with **The Vienna State Opera Chorus**
and **The Vienna Philharmonic Orchestra**
conducted by **Erich Kleiber**

Ⓜ LXT 2954-7   Highlights   Ⓜ LXT 5623

THE GREATEST OPERA CATALOGUE IN THE WORLD

The Decca Record Company Ltd   Decca House   Albert Embankment   London   S E 1

Opertheater

Donnerstag den 25. November 1937
Anfang 6 ½ Uhr
Erhöhte Preise

Die Meistersinger von Nürnberg

Oper in drei Aufzügen von Richard Wagner

Spielleitung: Dr. Lothar Wallerstein   Dirigent: . * .

Hans Sachs, Schuster		. * .
Veit Pogner, Goldschmied		Herbert Alsen
Kunz Vogelgesang, Kürschner		Georg Maikl
Konrad Nachtigall, Spengler		Georg Monthy
Sixtus Beckmesser, Stadtschreiber		Hermann Wiedemann
Fritz Kothner, Bäcker		Fritz Krenn
Balthasar Zorn, Zinngießer	Meistersinger	Anton Arnold
Ulrich Eißlinger, Würzkrämer		Eduard Fritsch
Augustin Moser, Schneider		Richard Tomek
Hermann Ortel, Seifensieder		Walter Hellmich
Hans Schwarz, Strumpfwirker		Hermann Reich
Hans Foltz, Kupferschmied		Karl Ettl
Walther von Stolzing, ein junger Ritter aus Franken		. * .
David, Sachsens Lehrbube		. * .
Eva, Pogners Tochter		Maria Reining
Magdalena, Evas Amme		Enid Szantho
Ein Nachtwächter		Karl Ettl

Bürger und Frauen aller Zünfte, Gesellen, Lehrbuben, Mädchen, Volk

Schauplatz der Handlung: Nürnberg. Um die Mitte des 16. Jahrhunderts

Erster Aufzug: Im Innern der Katharinenkirche — Zweiter Aufzug: In den Straßen vor den Häusern Pogners und Sachsens — Dritter Aufzug: a) Sachsens Werkstatt, b) ein freier Wiesenplan an der Pegnitz
In Szene gesetzt von Dr. Lothar Wallerstein

Tanz auf der Festwiese einstudiert von Margarete Wallmann

Entwürfe der Bühnenbilder und Kostüme von Ludwig Sievert

Elektrische Musikwiedergabe-Einrichtung durchgeführt von Ing. Hermann May, mit Lautsprecher und Verstärker der Firma Czeija, Nißl & Co., Wien

. * . „Hans Sachs" **Karl Hammes**, Opernhaus Chemnitz, a. G.

. * . „Stolzing" Kammersänger **Max Lorenz**

. * . „David" Kammersänger **Erich Zimmermann**
Staatsoper Berlin, als Gäste

. * . Dirigent: **Dr. Wilhelm Furtwängler** a. G.

Nach dem ersten Aufzug eine größere Pause

Das offizielle Programm nur bei den Billetteuren erhältlich. Preis 50 Groschen — Garderobe frei

Kassen-Eröffnung vor 6 Uhr   Anfang 6 ½ Uhr   Ende 11 ½ Uhr

Während der Vorspiele und der Akte bleiben die Saaltüren zum Parkett, Parterre und den Galerien geschlossen. Zuspätkommende können daher nur während der Pausen Einlaß finden

Telephonische Bestellungen von Sitzen, R-20-320 (ausgenommen Säulensitze) zum Preise von S 4.— aufwärts werden für folgende Vorstellungen entgegengenommen.

Der Kartenverkauf findet heute statt für obige Vorstellung und für
Freitag   den 26. Wallenstein, im Abonnement II. Gruppe (Anfang 7 Uhr)
Samstag   den 27. Der Bettelstudent, im Abonnement II. Gruppe (Anfang 7 Uhr)

Richard Strauss

Arabella

Salzburg
August 1947

Role of Arabella
Della Casa, Anday,
Patzak, Hotter,
Hann
VPO
Böhm

LP: Melodram MEL 101

Ariadne auf Naxos

Vienna
June 1944

Role of Ariadne
Seefried, Noni,
Lorenz, Kunz,
Schöffler
VPO
Böhm

LP: DG LPM 18 850-2
LP: Acanta DE 23.309-10
Excerpts
LP: DG 88017
LP: BASF 22.221229
LP: Acanta DE 23.280-1

Der Rosenkavalier

Salzburg
August 1949

Role of Marschallin
Güden, Novotna,
Rosvaenge, Hann,
J.Prohaska
Vienna Opera Chorus
VPO
Szell

LP: Cetra LO 69

Vienna
May and June
1954

Role of Marschallin
Güden, Jurinac,
Dermota, Weber,
Poell
Vienna Opera Chorus
VPO
Kleiber

LP: Decca LXT 2954-7
LP: Decca 4BB 115-8
CD: Decca 425 9502

Vienna
November 1955

Role of Marschallin
Güden, Jurinac,
Terkal, Böhme,
Poell
Vienna Opera Chorus
VPO
Knappertsbusch

LP: Hans-Knappertsbusch-Gesellschaft
(Japan) HK 1012-5

Der Rosenkavalier: Excerpt (Da geht er hin)

Berlin
1944

Role of Marschallin
Staatskapelle
Heger

LP: BASF 22.221229

Zürich
1949

Role of Marschallin
Tonhalle Orchestra
Knappertsbusch

LP: Decca LX 3021
LP: Preiser PR 9829
CD: Preiser 90083
This version commences at Kann mich auch
an ein Mädel erinnern

Cäcilie

Vienna 1942	VPO Moralt	LP: Preiser LV 1315
Vienna 1942	Strauss, piano	LP: Rococo 5350 LP: Preiser PR 3262 CD: Preiser 93262

Freundliche Vision

Vienna 1942	Strauss, piano	LP: Rococo 5350 LP: Preiser PR 3262 CD: Preiser 93262

Meinem Kinde

Vienna 1942	VPO Moralt	LP: Preiser LV 1315
Vienna 1942	Strauss, piano	LP: Rococo 5350 LP: Preiser PR 3262 CD: Preiser 93262

Morgen

Vienna 1942	VPO Moralt	LP: Preiser LV 1315

Traum durch die Dämmerung

Vienna 1942	Strauss, piano	LP: Rococo 5350 LP: Preiser PR 3262 CD: Preiser 93262

Wiegenlied

Vienna 1942	VPO Moralt	LP: Preiser LV 1315
Vienna 1942	Strauss, piano	LP: Preiser PR 3262 CD: Preiser 90083/93262

Zueignung

Vienna 1942	Strauss, piano	LP: Rococo 5350 LP: Preiser PR 3262 CD: Preiser 93262

The 4 orchestral songs on LV 1315 are previously unpublished Electrola 78s

Suppé

Boccaccio: Excerpt (Hab' ich nur deine Liebe)

Berlin	Deutsches	78: Telefunken E 3055
1939	Opernhaus Orchestra	LP: Preiser PR 9829
	Lutze	CD: Preiser 90083

Verdi

Don Carlos: Excerpts (Io vengo a domandar (Act 2); Fragment from Act 5 duet)

Vienna	Role of Elisabetta	LP: Teletheater 76.23596-7
November 1937	Masaroff	
	VPO	
	Walter	
	Reining sings in German, Masaroff in Swedish	

Otello: Excerpts (Già nella notte densa; Ave Maria)

Berlin	Role of Desdemona	LP: BASF 22.221229/10.21360
1943	Rosvaenge	LP: Acanta BB 21360
	Staatskapelle	
	Elmendorff	
	Sung in German	

Il Trovatore: Excerpt (Tacea la notte placida)

Stuttgart	Role of Leonora	LP: BASF 22.221229
1936	Stuttgart RO	
	Leonhardt	
	Sung in German	

Wagner

Lohengrin: Excerpt (Einsam in trüben Tagen)

Berlin 1939	Role of Elsa Deutsches Opernhaus Orchestra Lutze	78: Telefunken E 3052 LP: Preiser PR 9829 CD: Preiser 90083
Berlin 1944	Role of Elsa Berlin RO Rother	LP: BASF 22.221229 LP: Acanta 40.23502

Lohengrin: Excerpt (Euch Lüften, die mein Klagen)

Berlin 1939	Role of Elsa Deutsches Opernhaus Orchestra Lutze	78: Telefunken E 3052 LP: Preiser PR 9829 CD: Preiser 90083

Die Meistersinger von Nürnberg

Salzburg August 1937	Role of Eva Thorborg, Noort, Sallaba, Nissen, Alsen, Wiedemann Vienna Opera Chorus VPO Toscanini	LP: Toscanini Society ATS 1062-6 np LP: Morgan MR 2006 LP: MRF Records MRF 16 LP: Accent ACC 150040 LP: Melodram MEL 012 CD: Melodram MEL 47041

Die Meistersinger von Nürnberg: Excerpt (Guten Abend, Meister)

Zürich 1949	Role of Eva Schöffler Tonhalle Orchestra Knappertsbusch	78: Decca X 312 LP: Decca LX 3021 LP: Preiser PR 9829 CD: Preiser 90083

Die Meistersinger von Nürnberg: Excerpt (O Sachs, mein Freund)

Zürich 1949	Role of Eva Schöffler Tonhalle Orchestra Knappertsbusch	Decca unpublished

Tannhäuser: Excerpts (Dich teure Halle; Allmächtige Jungfrau)

Berlin 1942-3	Role of Elisabeth Berlin RO Rother	LP: BASF 22.221229
Zürich 1949	Role of Elisabeth Tonhalle Orchestra Knappertsbusch	LP: Decca LX 3021 LP: Preiser PR 9829 CD: Preiser 90083

Tannhäuser: Excerpt (O Fürstin)

Vienna 1942	Role of Elisabeth Lorenz VPO Moralt	78: Electrola DB 7624 LP: Electrola E 60571 LP: Electrola 1C 147 29154-5M LP: Preiser LV 1315/1333 LP: EMI EX 29 02133

Tannhäuser: Excerpt (Sängerkrieg, Act 2)

Berlin 1942-3	Role of Elisabeth Lorenz, W.Ludwig, Grossmann, L.Hoffmann, Schmitt-Walter Deutsches Opernhaus Chorus Berlin RO Rother	LP: BASF 22.221199 LP: Acanta 40.23502 Auch ich darf mich so glücklich nennen; Zum Heil den Sündigen zu führen: LP: BASF 22.221202

Die Walküre, Act 1 Scene 3

Berlin 1942	Role of Sieglinde Lorenz Berlin RO Rother	LP: DG LPM 19 259 LP: DG 88029 LP: Acanta DE 23.221-2 Dich selige Frau...to end LP: BASF 22.221202 Du bist der Lenz...to end LP: BASF 22.221229

Die Walküre: Excerpt (Schläfst du, Gast...Der Männer Sippe)

Stuttgart 1938	Role of Sieglinde F.Krauss Stuttgart Reichssender Orchestra Leonhardt	LP: BASF 22.221229

Die Walküre: Excerpt (Todesverkündigung to end Act 2)

Stuttgart 1938	Role of Sieglinde Schlüter, F.Krauss, Manowarda, Bockelmann Stuttgart Reichssender Orchestra Leonhardt	LP: Acanta 40.23502

Weber

Euryanthe	Role of Euryanthe	LP: Melodram MEL 424
	Rössl-Majdan, Radko,	
Vienna	Kamann	
1949	Austrian Radio	
	Chorus & Orchestra	
	Zallinger	

Reining: a postscript

In Volume 4 of EMI's "Record of Singing" (LP and CD) is to be found the track which encapsulates the art of Maria Reining (1903-1991), a lyric soprano whose career fell somewhat under the shadows of both Lotte Lehmann and the dark years of the Third Reich. For even in this song from Lehar's operetta "Eva" can be heard the extremely feminine warmth which must have commended her other Eva, in Wagner's "Meistersinger", to both Furtwängler and Toscanini, combined as it is in the Lehar recording with the subtle lilt of Reining's Viennese background.

By the time that Reining came to be taken seriously as a Decca recording artist after the war, the bloom of youth had passed from her instrument, leaving her elegance less vivid than before. Like her colleague Viorica Ursuleac, also a specialist in the Richard Strauss repertoire, Reining created her operatic portrayals in what I would describe as pastel shades as opposed to the full oil colours of a Lehmann or a Jeritza.

Reining:
roles performed with the Vienna State Opera

Includes performances with the Vienna company on tour
Figure against each role indicates number of times the part was performed
Some roles performed only before 1945 may be missing

17	Agathe (Der Freischütz)
4	Annina (Eine Nacht in Venedig)
13	Arabella (Arabella)
12	Ariadne/Prima donna (Ariadne auf Naxos)
15	Butterfly (Madama Butterfly)
82	Countess Almaviva (Le nozze di Figaro)
8	Daphne (Daphne)
36	Desdemona (Otello)
39	Elisabeth (Tannhäuser)
16	Elisabetta (Don Carlo)
31	Elsa (Lohengrin)
4	Eva (Die Meistersinger von Nürnberg)
5	Frau Fluth (The Merry Wives of Windsor)
4	Gretchen (Der Wildschütz)
4	Kathrin (Die Kathrin)*
9	Leonore (Fidelio)
4	Manon (Manon)
9	Marenka (The Bartered Bride)
43	Marschallin (Der Rosenkavalier)
13	Mimi (La Bohème)
7	Myrtocle (Die toten Augen)
8	Pamina (Die Zauberflöte)
13	Rosalinde (Die Fledermaus)
3	Sieglinde (Die Walküre)
10	Tatiana (Eugene Onegin)
8	Tosca (Tosca)

* Korngold

Erich Kunz
Discography

compiled by John Hunt

ERICH KUNZ

ONE OF THE MOST popular members of the Vienna State Opera, Erich Kunz was born in Vienna. His father was an engineer, and young Kunz began his musical studies with Professor Lierhammer, the teacher of Ljuba Welitsch, and later with Hans Duhan, a famous baritone of the Vienna Opera. His first engagement was in the small town of Troppau, where he made his début as Osmin in Die Entführung aus dem Serail during the 1935-6 season; then followed seasons at Plauen and Breslau until 1939, and he joined the Vienna State Opera in 1940. It is not generally known that Kunz came to Glyndebourne in 1935 as an understudy and was a member of the chorus.

Kunz appeared at Salzburg for the first time in 1942 as Figaro, and then he was heard at Bayreuth in 1943 and 1944 as Beckmesser. He has sung at nearly every post-war Salzburg Festival, where his roles have included, besides Figaro, Guglielmo in Cosi fan tutte, Leporello, and Papageno. London first heard him in 1947 when he came with the Vienna State Opera to Covent Garden in the September of that year and was heard as Figaro, Leporello, and Guglielmo, roles he repeated when the company again visited London in 1954. He has also sung at Edinburgh and the post-war Glyndebourne Festivals, at Florence, Munich, Buenos Aires, and elsewhere in Europe and America.

His début at the Metropolitan Opera, New York, took place during the 1952-3 season. Besides the roles already mentioned, Kunz's repertory includes Malatesta in Don Pasquale, Gianni Schicchi, Spalanzani in Hoffmann, Faninal, and numerous roles in the operettas of Johann Strauss, Lehár, and Millöcker. He is married to Friede Kurzbauer, a former dancer.

From the Decca Book of Opera

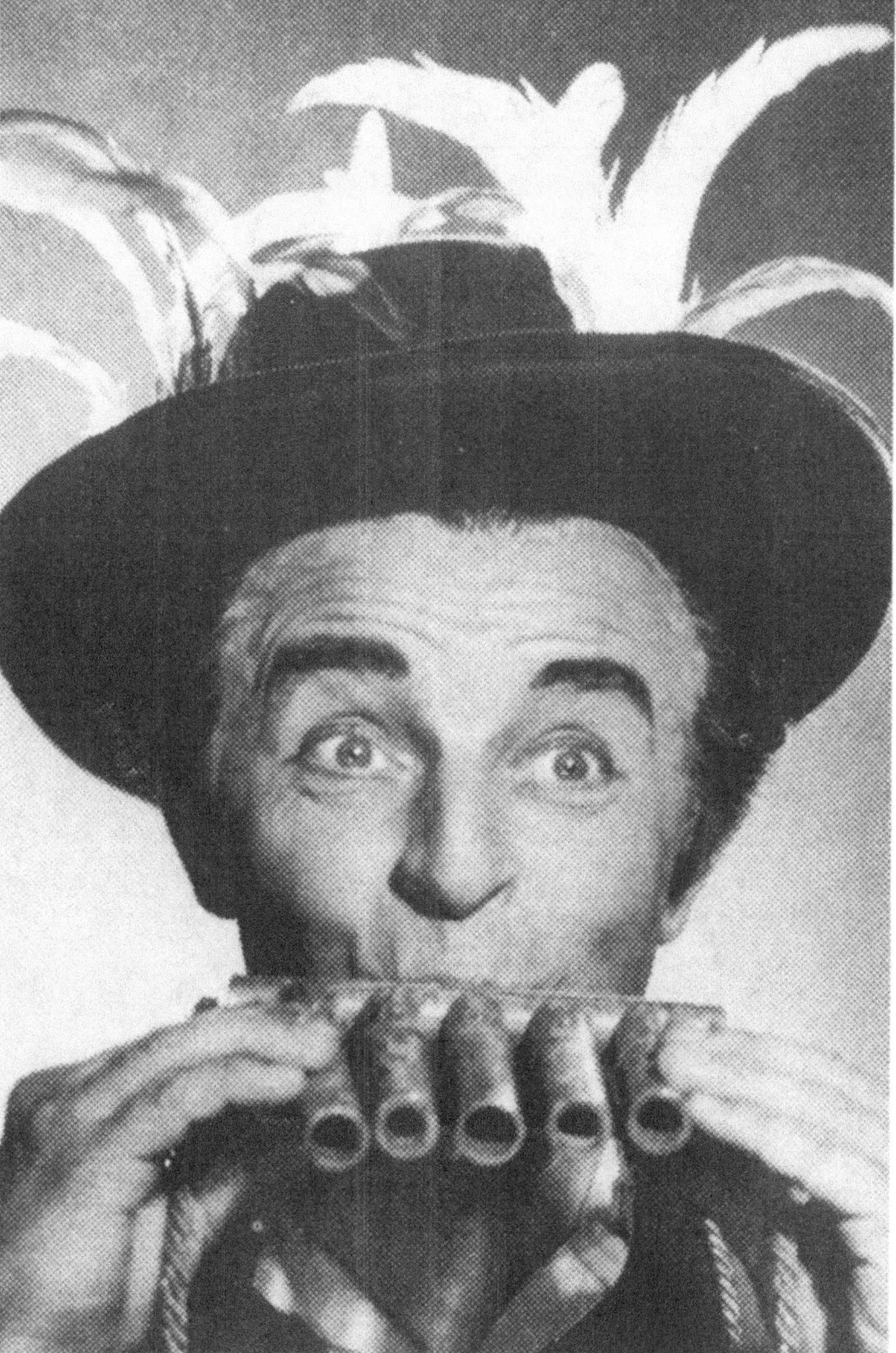

STAATSOPER

WIEDERERÖFFNUNG

Mittwoch, den 1. September 1965
Bei aufgehobenem Abonnement – Beschränkter Kartenverkauf
Preise IV

In italienischer Sprache

Die Hochzeit des Figaro

Komische Oper in vier Akten von Wolfgang Amadeus Mozart
Text nach Beaumarchais von Lorenzo da Ponte

Dirigent: Josef Krips
Inszenierung: Günther Rennert
Spielleitung: Josef Witt
Bühnenbild und Kostüme: Ita Maximowna

Graf Almaviva	Eberhard Wächter
Gräfin Almaviva	Hilde Güden
Susanne, deren Kammermädchen	Graziella Sciutti
Figaro, Kammerdiener des Grafen	Erich Kunz
Cherubino, Page des Grafen	Olivera Miljakovic
Marcelline, Haushälterin im Schlosse des Grafen	Hilde Rössel-Majdan
Basilio, Musikmeister im Dienste des Grafen	Murray Dickie
Don Curzio, Richter	Erich Majkut
Bartolo, Arzt aus Sevilla	Alois Pernerstorfer
Antonio, Gärtner des Grafen und Onkel der Susanne	Ljubo Pantscheff
Barbarina, seine Tochter	Lucia Popp
Erstes Bauernmädchen	Anna Vajda
Zweites Bauernmädchen	Edith Hintermeyer

Ort der Handlung ist das Schloß des Grafen Almaviva

Choreographie: Erika Hanka
Ausführende: Die Damen Fiala, Macholan, Philipp;
die Herren Jandosch, Hiess, Zajetz

Technische Einrichtung: Hans Felkel – Beleuchtung: Albin Rotter

Nach dem zweiten Akt eine größere Pause

Anfang 19 Uhr   Ende nach 22 Uhr

Preis des Programms S 6,–

Lehar

Der Graf von Luxemburg: Selection

Munich	Role of Basil	LP: Philips 6449 084
Date uncertain	Sukis, Wächter	CD: Philips 420 6632
	Graunke Orchestra	
	Goldschmidt	

Das Land des Lächelns

London	Role of Gustl	LP: Columbia 33CX 1114-5
April and	Schwarzkopf,	LP: EMI SXDW 3044
June 1953	Loose, Gedda	CD: EMI CHS 769 5232
	BBC Chorus	Excerpts
	Philharmonia	LP: Columbia 33CX 1712
	Ackermann	LP: EMI RLS 763

Die lustige Witwe

London	Role of Danilo	LP: Columbia 33CX 1051-2
April 1953	Schwarzkopf,	LP: EMI SXDW 3045
	Loose, Gedda	CD: EMI CDH 769 5202
	BBC Chorus	Excerpts
	Philharmonia	78: Columbia LX 1597
	Ackermann	LP: Columbia 33CX 1712
		45: Columbia SEL 1559
		LP: EMI RLS 763

Lortzing

Der Waffenschmied: Excerpt (Auch ich war ein Jüngling mit lockigem Haar)

London April 1953	Role of Stadinger Philharmonia Ackermann	45: Columbia SEL 1608 LP: Columbia (Germany) C 70407 LP: Electrola 1C 147 03580-1M

Der Wildschütz: Excerpt (Fünftausend Thaler)

London April 1953	Role of Baculus Philharmonia Ackermann	78: Columbia LB 143 LP: Columbia (Germany) C 70407 LP: Electrola 1C 147 03580-1M

Zar und Zimmermann: Excerpt (O sancta justitia)

London April 1953	Role of Van Bett Philharmonia Ackermann	45: Columbia SEL 1608 LP: Columbia (Germany) C 70407 LP: Electrola 1C 147 03580-1M

Millöcker

Der Bettelstudent: Excerpt (Ach, ich hab' sie ja nur)

Vienna January 1951	Role of Ollendorf VPO Moralt	Columbia unpublished

Gasparone: Excerpt (Dunkelrote Rosen)

Vienna January 1951	Role of Stranger VPO Moralt	Columbia unpublished

Mozart

Così fan tutte

Vienna May 1955	Role of Guglielmo Della Casa, Loose, C.Ludwig, Dermota, Schöffler Vienna Opera Chorus VPO Böhm	LP: Decca LXT 5107-9 LP: Decca GOM 543-5/GOS 543-5 Excerpts LP: Decca LXT 5511/SXL 2058 LP: Decca BR 3085 45: Decca CEP 572

Così fan tutte: Excerpts (La mia Dorabella capace non è; Una bella serenata; Sento, o Dio !; Di scrivermi ogni giorno; Il core vi dono; other excerpts without Kunz)

Glyndebourne July 1950	Role of Guglielmo Jurinac, Thebom, Lewis, Borriello Glyndebourne Orchestra Busch	78: HMV DB 21116-20 LP: World Records SH 397 Il core vi dono LP: Electrola 1C 147 03580-1M

THE ROYAL OPERA HOUSE, COVENT GARDEN

Sole Lessees: BOOSEY & HAWKES, LTD.

House Manager: PETER WALLER

Box Office Manager: A. M. WOLSTENHOLME

THE COVENT GARDEN OPERA TRUST

(General Administrator: DAVID L. WEBSTER)

present

THE VIENNA STATE OPERA

with

THE VIENNA STATE OPERA ORCHESTRA

Conductors: JOSEF KRIPS and CLEMENS KRAUSS

The Covent Garden Opera Trust works in full association with the Arts Council of Great Britain

Thursday, September 18th, 1947

COSI FAN TUTTE

A Comic Opera in Two Acts

Libretto by Lorenzo da Ponte

German Version following the tradition and the original
by George Schumann

Music by Mozart

Conductor: Josef Krips

Producer: Oscar Fritz Schuh

Decor: Robert Kautsky

Costumes: Caspar Neher

Fiordiligi } Two sisters { IRMGARD SEEFRIED

Dorabella } Ladies of Ferrara { ELISABETH HOENGEN

Guglielmo, an Officer, in love with Fiordiligi . ERICH KUNZ

Ferrando, an Officer, in love with Dorabella ANTON DERMOTA

Despina, Maid to the sisters . . EMMY LOOSE

Don Alfonso, an old Philosopher . PAUL SCHOEFFLER

Choreography by Willy Franzl

Don Giovanni

Salzburg July and August 1950	Role of Leporello Schwarzkopf, Welitsch, Seefried, Dermota, Gobbi, Greindl, Poell Vienna Opera Chorus VPO Furtwängler	LP: Ed Smith EJS 419 LP: Olympic 9109 LP: Discocorp RR 407 LP: Turnabout THS 65154-6 LP: Melodram MEL 713 CD: RCA (Japan) R30C 1014-6 CD: Priceless D 16581 CD: Laudis LCD 34001
Hamburg 1951	Role of Leporello Martinis, Danco, L.Hoffmann, Dermota, Schöffler, Neidlinger NDR Chorus and Orchestra L.Ludwig	LP: Melodram MEL 015
Lisbon 1960	Role of Leporello Caballé, Otto, Stich-Randall, Kmennt, Wächter, Peter, H.Hoffmann San Carlo Chorus & Orchestra Gielen	CD: Legato SRO 813
Chicago November 1964	Role of Leporello Stich-Randall, Curtin, Panni, Kraus, Ghiaurov, Marangoni, Uppman Chicago Lyric Opera Chorus & Orchestra Krips	LP: Melodram MEL 464

Don Giovanni: Excerpt (Madamina)

Vienna February 1949	Role of Leporello VPO Ackermann	78: Columbia LB 81 45: Columbia SEL 1574 LP: Electrola 1C 147 03580-1M LP: EMI RLS 764

Don Giovanni: Excerpt (Là ci darem la mano)

Vienna December 1947	Role of Giovanni Seefried VPO Karajan	LP: EMI RLS 764

Le Nozze di Figaro

Vienna June and October 1950	Role of Figaro Schwarzkopf, Seefried, Jurinac, London Vienna Opera Chorus VPO Karajan	78: Columbia (Austria) LWX 410-425 LP: Columbia 33CX 1007-9 LP: Electrola 1C 197 54200-8M CD: EMI CMS 769 6392 Excerpts LP: Columbia 33CX 1558
Salzburg August 1953	Role of Figaro Schwarzkopf, Seefried, Güden, Schöffler Vienna Opera Chorus VPO Furtwängler Sung in German	LP: Ed Smith GMR 999 LP: Discocorp IGI 343 LP: Fonit Cetra LO 8 LP: Fonit Cetra FE 27 CD: Rodolphe RPC 32527-30
Milan February 1954	Role of Figaro Schwarzkopf, Seefried, Jurinac, Petri La Scala Chorus & Orchestra Karajan	LP: Fonit Cetra LO 70 CD: Hunt CDKAR 225 CD: Melodram CDM 37075 Excerpts LP: Gioielli della lirica GML 30
Salzburg July 1957	Role of Figaro Schwarzkopf, Seefried, C.Ludwig, Fischer-Dieskau Vienna Opera Chorus VPO Böhm	LP: Melodram MEL 709 CD: Di Stefano Records GDS 31019 Excerpts CD: Verona 27092-4

Le Nozze di Figaro: Excerpt (Non più andrai)

Vienna December 1947	Role of Figaro VPO Karajan	78: Columbia LX 1123 LP: Columbia (Germany) C 70407 LP: Electrola 1C 147 03580-1M 45: Columbia SEL 1574 LP: EMI RLS 764

Le Nozze di Figaro: Excerpt (Se vuol ballare)

Vienna November 1948	Role of Figaro VPO Karajan	Columbia unpublished

Die Zauberflöte

Vienna November 1950	Role of Papageno Seefried, Lipp, Loose, Dermota, Weber, London Singverein VPO Karajan	78: Columbia (Austria) LWX 426-444 LP: Columbia 33CX 1013-5 LP: EMI SLS 5052 LP: Electrola 1C 197 54200-8M CD: EMI CMS 769 6312 Excerpts LP: Columbia 33CX 1572 LP: EMI RLS 764 LP: Electrola 1C 187 29225-6M
Salzburg August 1951	Role of Papageno Seefried, Lipp, Oravez, Dermota, Greindl, Schöffler Vienna Opera Chorus VPO Furtwängler	LP: Fonit Cetra LO 9 LP: Foyer FO 1028 LP: Fonit Cetra FE 19 CD: Foyer 3CF-2008 CD: Priceless D 16603 CD: Rodolphe RPC 32527-30 CD: Hunt CDWFE 361 Excerpts LP: Gioielli della lirica GML 14
Vienna May 1962	Role of Papageno Lipp, Hallstein, Sciutti, Gedda, Frick, Wächter Vienna Opera Chorus VPO Karajan	LP: Movimento Musica 03.015 CD: Movimento Musica 051.028

Die Zauberflöte: Excerpt (Der Vogelfänger bin ich ja)

Vienna November 1947	Role of Papageno VPO Moralt	LP: EMI EX 769 7411 CD: EMI CHS 769 7412
Munich Date uncertain	Role of Papageno Bavarian RO Hollreiser	LP: Eurodisc 73739 KR LP: Eurodisc 300.645.370

Die Zauberflöte: Excerpt (Ein Mädchen oder Weibchen)

Vienna November 1947	Role of Papageno VPO Moralt	78: Columbia LX 1123 45: Columbia SEL 1574 LP: Columbia (Germany) C 70407 LP: Electrola 1C 147 03580-1M LP: EMI RLS 764 LP: EMI EX 29 05983 CD: EMI CMS 763 7502
Munich Date uncertain	Role of Papageno Bavarian RO Hollreiser	LP: Eurodisc 73739 KR LP: Eurodisc 300.645.370

Die Zauberflöte: Excerpt (Bei Männern, welche Liebe fühlen)

Vienna December 1947	Role of Papageno Schwarzkopf VPO Karajan	Columbia unpublished

Rossini

Il Barbiere di Siviglia

Vienna April 1966	<u>Role of Bartolo</u> Grist, Koneztni, Wunderlich, Wächter, Czerwenka Vienna Opera Chorus VPO Böhm <u>Sung in German</u>	LP: Teatro Dischi TD 502-3 CD: Myto MCD 91752 <u>Teatro Dischi incorrectly dated 1965</u>

Schubert, arr. Berté

Das Dreimäderlhaus: Selection

Berlin Date uncertain	Köth, Schock, M.Schmidt Arndt-Chor FFB Orchestra Fox	LP: Electrola SME 73453 LP: EMI 5C 047 50563

Mittwoch, 14. April 1982 — *Staatsoper*
173. Aufführung in dieser Inszenierung

In italienischer Sprache

La Bohème

Szenen aus „Vie de Bohème" von Henry Murger
in vier Bildern von G. Giarosa und L. Illica

Musik	Giacomo Puccini
Dirigent	Ernst Märzendorfer
Inszenierung und Bühnenbild	Franco Zeffirelli
Regie	Peter Busse
Kostüme	Marcel Escoffier
Rudolf, Poet	Luis Lima
Schaunard, Musiker	Reid Bunger
Marcel, Maler	Robert Kerns
Collin, Philosoph	Tugomir Franc
Benois, der Hausherr	Erich Kunz
Mimi	Ilona Tokody
Musette	Renate Holm
Alcindor	Anton Wendler
Parpignol	Gregor Caban *
Sergeant bei der Zollwache	Nikolaus Simkowsky
Ein Zollwächter	Walter Zeh
Ein Obstverkäufer	Ingo Koblitz
Kinderchor	Wiener Sängerknaben

Studenten, Näherinnen, Hutmacherinnen, Bürger, Verkäufer in Läden und Hausierer, Soldaten Kellner, Buben und Mädchen usw.

Balletteleven der Ballettschule der Österreichischen Bundestheater

* Mitglied des Opernstudios

Ort der Handlung	Paris
1. Bild	In der Mansarde
2. Bild	Im Quartier Latin
3. Bild	Die Barriére d'Enfer
4. Bild	In der Mansarde

Sonntag, 3. April 1977   *Staatsoper*
36. Aufführung

Salome

Musikdrama in einem Aufzug nach
der gleichnamigen Dichtung von   Oscar Wilde
Deutsche Übersetzung von   Hedwig Lachmann

Musik	Richard Strauss
Dirigent	Gerd Albrecht
Inszenierung	Boleslaw Barlog
Bühnenbild und Kostüme	Jürgen Rose
Herodes	Ragnar Ulfung a. G.
Herodias	Ruth Hesse
Salome	Gwyneth Jones
Jochanaan	Rudolf Holtenau
Narraboth	Waldemar Kmentt
Ein Page der Herodias	Rohangiz Yachmi
Erster Jude	Heinz Zednik
Zweiter Jude	Ewald Aichberger
Dritter Jude	Dimiter Usunow
Vierter Jude	Karl Terkal
Fünfter Jude	Erich Kunz
Erster Nazarener	Tugomir Franc
Zweiter Nazarener	Georg Tichy
Erster Soldat	**Alfred Sramek**
Zweiter Soldat	Frederick Guthrie
Ein Cappadocier	Hans Christian
Ein Sklave	Horst Nitsche
Ein Henker	Werner Hammer
Abendspielleiter	Anton Wendler
Musikalische Studienleitung	Norbert Scherlich
Technische Einrichtung	Hans Langer
Beleuchtung	Robert Stangl
Leitung der Kostümwerkstätten	Alice Maria Schlesinger
Leitung der Dekorationswerkstätten	Pantelis Dessyllas
Maske	Konrad Keilich
Dekorations- und Kostümherstellung	Werkstätten der Bundestheater
Beginn	19.30 Uhr
Ende	nach 21 Uhr

Preis des Programms   S 12,—

Beachten Sie bitte unsere Informationsschrift „SZENE"

Johann Strauss

Die Fledermaus

London April 1955	Role of Falke Schwarzkopf, Streich, Christ, Krebs, Dönch Chorus Philharmonia Karajan	LP: Columbia 33CX 1309-10 LP: EMI RLS 728 CD: EMI CHS 769 5312 Excerpts LP: Columbia 33CX 1516 LP: Electrola 1C 047 01953
London June and July 1959	Role of Frosch Lipp, Scheyrer, C.Ludwig, Terkal, Berry, Wächter Philharmonia Chorus & Orchestra Ackermann	LP: Columbia 33CX 1688-9/SAX 2336-7 LP: Electrola 1C 147 01652-3 LP: EMI CFPD 4702 CD: EMI CDCFPD 4702 Excerpts LP: EMI XLP 20091/SXLP 20091
Vienna July 1960	Role of Frosch Güden, Köth, Resnik, Kmennt, Zampieri, Berry, Wächter Vienna Opera Chorus VPO Karajan	LP: Decca MET 201-3/SET 201-3 LP: Decca LXT 6015-6/SXL 6015-6 LP: Decca D247 D3 CD: Decca 421 0462 Excerpts LP: Decca LXT 6155/SXL 6155
Vienna December 1960	Role of Frank Güden, Streich, Stolze, Zampieri, Berry, Wächter, Vienna Opera Chorus VPO Karajan	LP: Foyer FO 1031 CD: Foyer 3CF-2021 CD: Hunt CDKAR 215 Excerpts LP: Gioielli della lirica GML 25
Vienna 1964	Role of Frank Leigh, Rothenberger, Stevens, Konya, Wächter, London Vienna Opera Chorus VPO Danon	LP: RCA LSC 7029/SER 5514-5 LP: RCA (Germany) 26.35058
Vienna November 1971	Role of Frank Janowitz, Holm, Windgassen, Kmennt, Holecek, Wächter, Schenk Vienna Opera Chorus VPO Böhm	LP: Decca SET 540-1

Der lustige Krieg: Excerpt (Nur für Natur)

Vienna January 1951	Role of Umberto VPO Moralt	78: Columbia LX 1544 45: Columbia SEB 3507 LP: Electrola 1C 147 03580-1M LP: World Records SH 284

Eine Nacht in Venedig

London May and September 1954	Role of Caramello Schwarzkopf, Loose, Gedda, Dönch Chorus Philharmonia Ackermann	LP: Columbia 33CX 1224-5 LP: EMI SXDW 3043 CD: EMI CDH 769 5302 Excerpts LP: EMI RLS 763

Eine Nacht in Venedig: Selection

Munich 1974	Role of Dell' Acqua Geszty, Migenes, De Ridder Munich RO Eichhorn	LP: Philips 6305 265

Eine Nacht in Venedig: Excerpt (Komm' in die Gondel)

Vienna November 1949	Role of Caramello Volksoper Orchestra Paulik	78: Columbia LX 1544 45: Columbia SEB 3507 LP: Electrola 1C 147 03580-1M LP: World Records SH 284

Eine Nacht in Venedig: Excerpt (Ach, wie so herrlich)

Vienna November 1949	Role of Caramello Volksoper Orchestra Paulik	78: Columbia LB 86 45: Columbia SEB 3507 LP: Electrola 1C 147 03580-1M LP: Electrola 1C 147 30226-7M LP: World Records SH 284

Eine Nacht in Venedig: Excerpt (Treu sein, das liegt mir nicht)

Vienna January 1951	Role of Caramello VPO Moralt	78: Columbia LB 117 LP: World Records SH 284

SALZBURGER FESTSPIELE 1960

40 JAHRE SALZBURGER FESTSPIELE

DER ROSENKAVALIER

KOMÖDIE FÜR MUSIK IN DREI AUFZÜGEN
VON HUGO VON HOFMANNSTHAL

MUSIK VON
RICHARD STRAUSS

DIRIGENT
HERBERT VON KARAJAN

INSZENIERUNG
RUDOLF HARTMANN

BÜHNENBILD
TEO OTTO

KOSTÜME
ERNI KNIEPERT

ORCHESTER
DIE WIENER PHILHARMONIKER
CHOR DER WIENER STAATSOPER

DER ROSENKAVALIER
Komödie für Musik in drei Aufzügen von Hugo von Hofmannsthal
MUSIK VON RICHARD STRAUSS

Die Feldmarschallin Fürstin Werdenberg . . .	Lisa Della Casa
Der Baron Ochs von Lerchenau	Otto Edelmann
Oktavian, genannt Quinquin, ein junger Herr aus großem Haus	Sena Jurinac
Herr von Faninal, ein reicher Neugeadelter . .	Erich Kunz
Sophie, seine Tochter	Anneliese Rothenberger
Jungfer Marianne Leitmetzerin, die Duenna . .	Judith Hellwig
Valzacchi, ein Intrigant	Renato Ercolani
Annina, seine Begleiterin	Hilde Rössel-Majdan
Ein Polizeikommissär	Alois Pernerstorfer
Der Haushofmeister bei der Feldmarschallin . .	Erich Majkut
Der Haushofmeister bei Faninal	Siegfried Rudolf Frese
Ein Notar	Josef Knapp
Ein Wirt	Fritz Sperlbauer
Ein Sänger	Giuseppe Zampieri
Ein Friseur	Hans Kres
Eine adelige Witwe	Betty Kodidek
Drei adelige Waisen	Liselotte Maikl / Ute Frey / Evelyn Labruce
Eine Modistin	Mary Richards
Ein Tierhändler	Kurt Equiluz
Vier Lakaien der Marschallin	Fritz Mayer / Rudolf Stumper / Otto Vajda / Alois Buchbauer
Kellner	Karl Kolowratnik / Ludwig Fleck / Kurt Bernhard / Norbert Balatsch
Leopold	Hermann Tichavsky
Ein Arzt	Georg Pichler
Ein Mohr	Wolfgang Kres

Ein Gelehrter, ein Flötist, Lauffer, Heiducken, Küchenpersonal, Gäste,
Musikanten, Wächter, Kinder, verschiedene verdächtige Gestalten

Bühnenmusik: Das Mozarteum-Orchester
Technische Einrichtung und Beleuchtung: Sepp Nordegg
In Wien, in den ersten Jahren der Regierung Maria Theresias
Nach dem ersten und zweiten Aufzug eine größere Pause

Der offizielle Almanach „Salzburg — Festspiele 1960" ist auch für Sie der unentbehrliche Ratgeber
The official almanac "Salzburg Festivals 1960" is an indispensable guide for all Festival visitors
L'almanach officiel «Salzbourg Festival 1960» est indispensable à tous ceux qui s'intéressent au Festival

Wiener Blut

London May 1954	Role of Josef Schwarzkopf, Gedda, Köth, Loose, Dönch Chorus Philharmonia Ackermann	LP: Columbia 33CX 1186-7 LP: EMI SXDW 3042 CD: EMI CDH 769 5292 Excerpt LP: Electrola 1C 147 03580-1M
Vienna June 1965	Role of Kagler Güden, Lipp, Schramm, Schock, Gruber, Kusche Chorus VSO Stolz	LP: Eurodisc XE 72750-1 Excerpts LP: Eurodisc IE 89896

Der Zigeunerbaron

Vienna 1955	Role of Homonay Loose, Scheyrer, Kmennt, Wächter, Preger Vienna Opera Chorus VSO Paulik	LP: Vanguard VRS 486-7 LP: Philips G04200-1L LP: Philips GL 5724-5
London May and September 1954	Role of Zsupan Schwarzkopf, Köth, Sinclair, Gedda, Prey Chorus Philharmonia Ackermann	LP: Columbia 33CX 1329-30 LP: EMI SXDW 3046 CD: EMI CHS 769 5262
Vienna 1961	Role of Zsupan Güden, Terkal, Rothenberger, Rössl-Majdan, Berry Vienna Opera Chorus VPO Hollreiser	LP: HMV ALP 1812-3/ASD 394-5 Excerpts LP: HMV ALP 1875/ASD 444 LP: EMI CFP 40251

Der Zigeunerbaron: Excerpt (Ja, das Schreiben und das Lesen)

Vienna November 1949	Role of Zsupan Volksoper Orchestra Paulik	78: Columbia LB 86 45: Columbia SEB 3507 LP: Electrola 1C 147 03580-1M LP: Electrola 1C 147 30226-7M LP: World Records SH 284

Richard Strauss

Ariadne auf Naxos

Vienna June 1944	Role of Harlekin Reining, Seefried, Noni, Lorenz, Schöffler VPO Böhm	LP: DG LPM 18 850-2 LP: Acanta DE 23309-10
London 1978	Role of Major Domo L.Price, Troyanos, Gruberova, Kollo, Berry LPO Solti	LP: Decca D103 D3 CD: Decca 430 3842

Der Rosenkavalier

Salzburg July 1960	Role of Faninal Della Casa, Güden, Jurinac, Edelmann, Zampieri Vienna Opera Chorus VPO Karajan	CD: Hunt CDKAR 213
Salzburg August 1960	Role of Faninal Schwarzkopf, Rothenberger, Jurinac, Edelmann, Zampieri Vienna Opera Chorus VPO Karajan	VHS Video: Rank 7015 E
Moscow October 1971	Role of Faninal Rysanek, De Groote, C.Ludwig, Jungwirth, Blankenship Vienna Opera Chorus VPO Krips	LP: Melodiya C10 28033 007

Verdi

Falstaff

Vienna March 1966	Role of Pistol Ligabue, Resnik, Rössl-Majdan, Sciutti, Oncina, Fischer-Dieskau, Panerai Vienna Opera Chorus VPO Bernstein	LP: CBS BRG 72493-5/SBRG 72493-5 LP: CBS 77392 CD: CBS M2K 42535

Wagner

Die Meistersinger von Nürnberg

Bayreuth July 1951	Role of Beckmesser Schwarzkopf, Malaniuk, Hopf, Unger, Edelmann, Dalberg Bayreuth Festival Chorus & Orchestra Karajan	CD: Hunt CDKAR 224 This is a complete performance, whereas the Columbia recording was taken from the rehearsal on 27 July and 4 further performances during August
Bayreuth July and August 1951	Role of Beckmesser Schwarzkopf, Malaniuk, Hopf, Unger, Edelmann, Dalberg Bayreuth Festival Chorus & Orchestra Karajan	78: Columbia LX 1465-1498/auto 8851-8884 LP: Columbia 33CX 1021-5 LP: EMI RLS 778 LP: EMI RLS 143 3903 CD: EMI CMS 763 5002 Excerpt LP: Electrola 1C 147 03580-1M
Vienna November 1955	Role of Beckmesser Seefried, Anday, Beirer, Dickie,
Schöffler, Frick Vienna Opera Chorus VPO Reiner	CD: Melodram CDM 47083

Die Meistersinger von Nürnberg: Extract Act 2 (Herr Stadtschreiber - Jerum! Jerum! O Ihr boshafter Geselle! - Ach, Himmel! David!)

Berlin 1944	Role of Beckmesser T.Kempff, Schilp, Noort, Fügel, Hann, Schirp Deutsches Opernhaus Chorus & Orchestra Rother	LP: Acanta 40.23502

Zeller

Der Vogelhändler: Excerpt (Wie mein Ahn'l zwanzig Jahr')

Vienna January 1951	Role of Adam VPO Moralt	78: Columbia LB 117 LP: Electrola 1C 147 03580-1M LP: World Records SH 284

Collections

Schrammel Songs: Es steht ein alter Nussbaum; Denk' dir, die Welt wär' ein Blumenstrauss

Vienna	Kemmeter-Faltl	Columbia unpublished
November 1948	Schrammel	

Schrammel Songs: 1. S'Nussdorfer Sterndel; 2. Wenn der Herrgott ne will; 3. Mutterl-Lied

Vienna	Kemmeter-Faltl	78: Columbia LB 111 (1)
November 1948	Schrammel	78: Columbia LB 83 (2)
		78: Columbia LB 129 (3)
		LP: Columbia 33C 1032 (1 and 2)
		45: Columbia SEB 3505 (3)
		LP: Electrola 1C 147 03580-1M (2 and 3)
		LP: Seraphim 65034
		LP: World Records SH 284

Schrammel Songs: 1. Wiener Fiakerlied; 2. Es steht ein alter Nussbaum; 3. Denk' dir, die Welt wär' ein Blumenstrauss

Vienna	Kemmeter-Faltl	78: Columbia LB 83 (1)
January 1949	Schrammel	78: Columbia LB 129 (2)
		78: Columbia LB 111 (3)
		LP: Columbia 33C 1032 (1 and 2)
		45: Columbia SEB 3505 (3)
		LP: Electrola 1C 147 03580-1M (1)
		LP: Seraphim 65034 (1 and 2)
		LP: World Records SH 284

Schrammel Songs: 1. Das Glück is' a Vogerl; 2. Ewiges Wien; 3. Wenn der Frantzel; 4. Mei Mutterl war a Weanerin

Vienna	Kemmeter-Falth	78: Columbia LB 98 (1 and 3)
October 1949	Schrammel	78: Columbia LB 115 (2)
		78: Columbia LB 90 (4)
		LP: Columbia 33C 1032 (4)
		45: Columbia SEB 3505 (2 and 3)
		LP: Electrola 1C 147 03580-1M (4)
		LP: Seraphim 65034
		LP: World Records SH 284 (2, 3 and 4)

Schrammel Songs: 1. Da draussen in der Wachau; 2. Du guater Himmelvater; 3. In Grinzing gibt's a Himmel Strass'n; 4. Secht's Lent'ln...so war's anno dreissig

Vienna	Kemmeter-Faltl	78: Columbia LB 100 (1 and 3)
November 1949	Schrammel	78: Columbia LB 90 (2)
		78: Columbia LB 115 (4)
		LP: Columbia 33C 1032 (2, 3 and 4)
		LP: Electrola 1C 147 03580-1M (2 and 4)
		LP: Seraphim 65034 (2, 3 and 4)
		LP: World Records SH 284

Schrammel Songs: Fiakerlied; Es wird ein Wien sein; Es steht ein alter Nussbaum; Wenn ich den Schlüssel hätte; Mei Mutterl war a Weanerin; Wenn der Herrgott ne will; Erst wenn's aus wird sein; Secht's Lent'ln..so war's anno dreissig; I' riach an Wien; Ich hab' mir für Grinzing ein Dienstmann engagiert; In einem klein Café in Hernals; Stellt's mein Ross in den Stall; Da fahren ma' halt nach Nussdorf 'naus

Vienna	Orchestral	CD: Preiser 90012
Date uncertain	accompaniment	

Schrammel Songs: Geh' langsam die alten Gassen; Kellerpartie; Das klingt wie ein Märchen aus Wien; Du bist ein klein dünnes Tschappel; Hinter Grinzing am Berg liegt der Himmel; Ich verdank' es dem Wein; Um Wien zu erleben; Denk' dir, die Welt wär' ein Blumenstrauss; Was denn, was denn?; Nussdorfer Stern Sterndel; Trink's letzte Viertel aus

Vienna	Orchestral	LP: Philips 6464 505
Date uncertain	accompaniment	

Schrammel duets with Erich Kunz and Julius Patzak: Was Oest'reich is; 's Herz in der Brust; Aber Hausknecht mei Peitsch'n; Was glaub'n S' was g'scheg'n is; other items with Patzak alone

Vienna	Patzak	LP: Amadeo AVRS 9078
Date uncertain	Grinzinger	LP: Musical Heritage MHS 3111
	Schrammel	

Erich Kunz singt Weihnachtslieder (Christmas songs)

Vienna	Volksoper Orchestra	LP: Vanguard SRV 100
Date uncertain	Schwarzbauer	

German Lieder in Orchestral Arrangement: Die beiden Grenadiere; Der Nussbaum; Sandmännchen; Ständchen; Lachen und Weinen; An die Musik; An Sylvia; O lieb' so lang du lieben kannst; Die Lorelei (Liszt); Die Ehre Gottes aus der Natur; Ich liebe dich; Die Lorelei (Silcher); Das Veilchen; Epiphanias; Schlafendes Jesuskind

Vienna	Male Chorus	LP: Vanguard SRV 477
1961	Volksoper Orchestra	LP: Philips A 04304 L
	Paulik	LP: Philips 838 204 AY

Studenten-, Trink- und Volkslieder

Vienna	Male Chorus	LP: Vanguard PVL 7042/SRV 278
1961	Volksoper Orchestra	LP: Amadeo AVRS 14503
	Litschauer	

Three Telefunken LPs are mentioned in "Das musikalische Selbstporträt" (Nannen-Verlag, Hamburg 1963), on which Erich Kunz sings Viennese and other popular melodies accompanied by the Hans Faltl-Quintett and Grosses Unterhaltungsorchester conducted by Willy Mattes and Richard Müller-Lampertz. The catalogue numbers are given as DX 1924, UX 4797 and LA 6272

Kunz: a postscript

Erich Kunz (born 1909) has become during his long career probably the epitome of Viennese male singing, combining his warm and endearing baritone with the inflections of Viennese speech to produce a sound with its own very personal "face". He presented himself to London audiences during those post-war London visits of the Vienna State Opera, almost taking the lion's share with the roles of Guglielmo, Leporello and Figaro. When his impersonation of Papageno in "Die Zauberflöte" was later added to the list, Kunz seemed to hold a deserved monopoly of these parts. When they were later relinquished or shared with younger colleagues, Kunz continued to serve the Staatsoper in a host of character parts, retaining many of these in his repertory even into his seventies.

Together with his tenor colleague Julius Patzak, Erich Kunz was also the very embodiment of Viennese song or Schrammellieder, and his presence almost became de rigueur in every operetta recording which a major company might be considering.

As the role of Papageno was very much the joint creation of Mozart and his librettist Schikaneder, it was fitting that Kunz should be selected to play the part of that impresario in an Austrian film based on Mozart's life which was made around the time of the 1956 bi-centenary and entitled "Reich mir die Hand, mein Leben". Mozart was played by Oskar Werner, and the scenario was far removed from the type of "Amadeus" extravaganza which would be expected nowadays.

Kunz:
roles performed with the Vienna State Opera

Includes performances with the Vienna company on tour
Figure against each role indicates number of times the part was performed
Some roles performed only before 1945 may be missing

9	Adelhof (Der Waffenschmied)
4	Arlecchino (Die schalkhafte Witwe)*
11	Baculus (Der Wildschütz)
40	Bartolo (Il Barbiere di Siviglia)
26	Bartolo (Le nozze di Figaro)
50	Beckmesser (Die Meistersinger v.Nürnberg)
53	Benoit (La Bohème)
15	Bottom (A Midsummer Night's Dream)
68	Caramello (Eine Nacht in Venedig)
10	Carnero (Der Zigeunerbaron)
100	Dancairo (Carmen)
89	Faninal (Der Rosenkavalier)
340	Figaro (Le nozze di Figaro)
94	Frank (Die Fledermaus)
2	Frosch (Die Fledermaus)
18	Giacomo (Fra Diavolo)
8	Gianni Schicchi (Gianni Schicchi)
117	Guglielmo (Così fan Tutte)
84	Harlekin (Ariadne auf Naxos)
60	Haushofmeister (Ariadne auf Naxos)
23	Hermosa (Die Insel Tulipatan)**
31	5th Jew (Salome)
138	Josef (Wiener Blut)

7	Kammerdiener (Kabale und Liebe)***
29	Kardinal von Lothringen (Palestrina)
12	Kolja (Ivan Tarassenko)****
220	Leporello (Don Giovanni)
40	Malatesta (Don Pasquale)
2	Masetto (Don Giovanni)
9	7th Master (Palestrina)
3	Melot (Tristan und Isolde)
11	Menelaus (La belle Hélène)
4	Micha (The Bartered Bride)
4	Monk (Don Carlo)
4	Mourzouk (Girofle-Girofla)*****
6	Olivier (Capriccio)
249	Papageno (Die Zauberflöte)
12	Pietro (Les brigands)******
28	Pistol (Falstaff)
99	Sacristan (Tosca)
9	Schaunard (La Bohème)
18	Sindulpho (Gasparone)
140	Spalanzani (Les contes d'Hoffmann)
19	Spinelloccio (Gianni Schicchi)
18	Lord Tristan (Martha)
6	3rd Vagabond (Die Kluge)
87	Zirkusdirektor (The Bartered Bride)

```
     *    Wolf-Ferrari
    **    Offenbach
   ***    Von Einem
  ****    Salmhofer
 *****    Lecocq
******    Offenbach
```

Rita Streich

additions

The following are additional items to the Rita Streich discography which appeared in the earlier volume "Italian conductors/Viennese sopranos"; corrections to existing entries are not included here but will be incorporated in a later up-date.

Bruckner

Te Deum

Perugia Soprano soloist CD: Hunt CD 705
September 1952 D. Hermann,
 Häfliger, Braun,
 Singverein
 VSO
 Karajan

Gilbert/Jarno

Die Försterchristl: Selection

Berlin Role of Christl 45: Odeon 28 435
Date uncertain Orchestra
 Dobrindt
 Streich sings under
 the pseudonym of
 Gina Berger

Henze

Muriel ou le temps d'un retour

Place and Orchestra LP: Milan A 248
date uncertain Henze

Jessel

Das Schwarzwaldmädel: Selection

Hamburg 1949	Role of Bärtele Glawitsch NDR Orchestra Hermann	78: Polydor HM 5737 45: Polydor EPH 20053 LP: Polydor 736 012

Millöcker

Gasparone: Selection

Hamburg October 1951	Role of Sora NDR Orchestra Stephan	LP: RCA VL 30421/VL 30446

Mozart

Le Nozze di Figaro

Aix-en-Provence July 1955	Role of Susanna Stich-Randall, Lorengar, Panerai Paris Conservatoire Orchestra Rosbaud	LP: Pathé DTX 206-8/DTX 30391-3 LP: Pathé 2C 167 16312-4 CD: Stradivarius STR 10039-40 CD: Ca' d'Oro CAD 1001-7 Excerpts LP: Vox OPL 190 Review in "Gramophone" (May 1992) suggests that the performance on Ca' d'Oro label is different from the one previously available

Puccini

La Bohème: Selection

Cologne 1960	Role of Musetta Fahberg, Konya, Kusche WDR Orchestra Marszalek Sung in German	LP: Polydor LPHM 46 541 LP: Polydor 635 096/237 041

La Bohème: Excerpt (Quando m'en vo)

Berlin Date uncertain	Role of Musetta Berlin RO Märzendorfer	45: DG EPL 30 485 LP: DG LPEM 19 137

Smetana

The Bartered Bride

Berlin Date uncertain	Role of Esmeralda T.Richter, Blatter, Hauser, Böhme, Koffmane Städtische Oper Chorus & Orchestra Lenzer Sung in German	LP: Urania URLP 210 LP: Vox OPBX 148 LP: Turnabout THS 65164-5

Johann Strauss

Die Fledermaus: Selection

Place and date uncertain	Role of Adele Konya Orchestra	LP: Polydor 46 541/237 041

Die Fledermaus: Excerpt (Spiel' ich die Unschuld vom Lande)

Hamburg December 1950	Role of Adele NDR Orchestra Schüchter	LP: Koch F.121 246

Draussen in Sievering (Die Tänzerin Fanny Elssler)

Hamburg February 1952	NDR Orchestra Müller-Lampertz	LP: RCA VL 30875

Richard Strauss

Ariadne auf Naxos: Excerpt (Circe! Circe!)

Cologne 1954	Role of Naiad Zadek, Ilosvay, Sommerschuh, Hopf, Müller-Sipermann WDR Orchestra Keilberth	LP: Melodram MEL 651

Suppé

Boccaccio: Selection

Place and date uncertain	Role of Fiametta Konya Orchestra	LP: Polydor 46 562/237 062

Verdi

La Traviata: Selection

Place and date uncertain	Role of Violetta Kozub, Günter, Grosses Opernorchester R.Wagner Sung in German	LP: Philips G 03142 L/837 020 LP: Pergola 659.3007

Wagner

Siegfried

Bayreuth July 1952	Role of Woodbird Varnay, Bugarinovic, Aldenhoff, Kuen, Hotter, Neidlinger, Bayreuth Festival Orchestra Keilberth	LP: Melodram MEL 528 CD: Paragon PCD 84021-4
Bayreuth August 1953	Role of Woodbird Mödl, Ilosvay, Windgassen, Kuen, Hotter, Neidlinger Bayreuth Festival Orchestra Keilberth	LP: Allegro-Elite 3133-7 LP: Melodram MEL 538 <u>This is additional to the performance conducted at Bayreuth in 1953 by Krauss and already listed in the Rita Streich discography; the above catalogue numbers were incorrectly attributed to the Krauss performance</u>
Rome November 1953	Role of Woodbird Mödl, Klose, Suthaus, Patzak, Pernerstorfer, Frantz RAI Rome Orchestra Furtwängler	LP: MRF Records MRF 23 LP: EMI RLS 702 LP: EMI EX 29 06703 CD: EMI CZS 767 1232/767 1312

List of record labels

This list is intended as a guide to the origins of the many record labels mentioned in these discographies. There can now be few collectors of historical material who are not indebted to the enterprise of the many private or unofficial labels which have circulated at different times (and sometimes for only limited periods of time), even if the documentation supplied with many of those issues was often unreliable or even non-existent.

Acanta	Germany
Allegro-Elite	USA
Allegro-Royale	USA
Amadeo	Austria
Angel	USA
Arabesque	USA
AS-Disc	Italy
BASF	Germany
Bach Guild	USA
Bayer DaCapo	Germany
Bella Musica	Italy
BIS	Sweden
BJR	USA
Brunswick	USA
CBS	Various countries
CLS	Italy
Cambria	USA
Capitol	USA
Cetra	Italy
Chaconne	Italy
Classical Collection	Italy
Classical Disk	Holland
Columbia (EMI)	Various countries
Curcio-Hunt	Italy
DG	Various countries
Da Camera Magna	Germany
Danacord	Denmark
Decca	Various countries
Dial Discos	Spain
Discocorp	USA

Discophilia	Germany	Opera Italiana	Italy
Di Stefano	Italy	Orfeo	Germany
Documents	Italy	Orfeus	Sweden
EMI	Various countries	Palette	Japan
EMI Italiana	Italy	Parlophone	Various countries
Ed Smith	USA (includes the prefixes EJS, GMR, RHR, UORC, ANNA and others)	Past Masters	USA
		Pathé (EMI)	France
		Paragon	Italy
		Pearl	UK
Erato	France	Penzance	USA
Estro Armonico	Italy	Period	USA
Eurochord	France	Philips	Various countries
Eurodisc	Germany	Pickwick	UK
Everest	USA	Pilz	Germany
FWR	USA	Polydor	Various countries
Fonit Cetra	Italy	Preiser	Austria
Fonoteam	Germany	Priceless	USA
Foyer	Italy	Quadrofoglio	Italy
Frequenz	Italy	RCA	Various countries
Furtwängler Soc.	UK, France, Germany	Refrain	Japan
Gallus	Jugoslavia	Relief	Switzerland
Gemma	Italy	Remington	USA
Gioielli della lirica	Italy	Replica	USA
		Ricordi	Italy
HMV (EMI)	Various countries	Rococo	Canada
HRE	USA	Rodolphe	France
Haydn Society	USA	Saga	UK
Homochord	Germany	Seven Seas	Japan
Hope	USA	Stradivarius	Italy
Hunt	Italy	Supraphon	Czechoslovakia
Intercord	Germany	Symposium	UK
JVC	Japan	Teatro dischi	Italy
Joker	Italy	Telefunken (now Teldec)	Germany
Knappertsbusch Society	Japan	Teletheater	Austria
Koch	USA	Timpani	France
Laudis	Italy	Top Rank	UK
Legato	USA	Toscanini Society	USA
Legendary	USA	Toshiba	Japan
Longanesi	Italy	Turnabout	USA, UK
London	USA, Japan	Tuxedo	Switzerland
Lyrichord	USA	Ultraphon	Czechoslovakia
MCA	USA	Unicorn	UK
MRF	USA	Urania	USA
Marco Polo	UK	Vanguard	USA, UK
Melodiya	Russia	Varèse Sarabande	USA
Melodram	Italy	Verona	Holland
Memories	Italy	Victor (now RCA/BMG)	USA
Mercury	USA	Virtuoso	Italy
Morgan	USA	Vox	Various countries
Movimento Musica	Italy	Westminster	USA
Murray Hill	USA	World Records	UK
Music and Arts	USA		
Myto	Italy		
Nippon Columbia	Japan		
Nixa	USA		
Novello	UK		
Nuova Era	Italy		
Oceanic	USA		
Odeon	Germany		
Olympic	USA		
Opera Viva	Italy		

Japanese issues:
Many of these have appeared without any name being given to the label or series, sometimes not even country of origin is mentioned

Still available

The Furtwängler Sound, 2nd edition (1985 incorporating
Furtwängler and Great Britain
Survey of the conductor's British appearances, with extensive press comments and reviews.

Price £5 (£7 outside UK)
Cheque payable to Wilhelm Furtwängler Society UK

Philharmonia Orchestra: Complete discography and
The Recordings of Herbert von Karajan
2 separate discographies in 1 volume (537 pages)

Price £9 (£13 outside UK)
Cheque payable to John Hunt

Both available from:
John Hunt
Flat 6
37 Chester Way
London SE11 4UR

Still available

Italian conductors & Viennese sopranos
10 separate discographies in 1 volume
(480 pages)

Price £18 (£22 outside UK)

Available from:
John Hunt
Flat 6
37 Chester Way
London SE11 4UR

'I actually like reading old record catalogues'

John Hunt talks to Robert Hartford about discography, detective work and Mr and Mrs Furtwängler.

Photo by Hanya Chlala

Some of the best-informed and wickedly scurrilous musical gossip comes across the counters of record shops. Years ago, I was amazed to find the fellow who had not only sold me my LPs but had been to last night's performance but had better-informed views about it than the morning's papers. After seeing him regularly at Wigmore Hall recitals, Goodall *Ring* performances and even the Bayreuth Festival, I discovered his name to be John Hunt. Since then I have seen his activities as an amateur musical journalist come to outweigh those of many a professional. He runs the Wilhelm Furtwängler Society (WFS) in the UK, publishes discographies and lectures to music groups and record clubs.

John Hunt studied German at London University. It did not take him long to find out his metier lay not in school teaching, nor in personnel management. His abiding interest in music took him into record retailing which, during the 1970s, was booming due to the removal of price fixing. John went through the ups and downs of the discount trade for a decade or so but has now opted for the safer haven of bibliographical work in a government agency.

'I reckon it was seeing Callas in *La Traviata* in 1958 that really hooked me,' says Hunt, adding wryly, 'And when I was studying in Würzburg I rang the Bayreuth box office and bought a ticket for *Die Meistersinger* just a week or two before the performance. Then a group of us went to Salzburg and heard Mitropoulos, Böhm and Karajan conduct operas with legendary casts on four successive evenings. Can anybody do that now?'

To his regret, John did not hear Furtwängler (the conductor died in 1954). 'I had his records of Schubert's Ninth and Beethoven's *Choral* and thought they were something special. I became involved with the WFS shortly after it was founded – it is now the oldest such society anywhere – and have been chairman since 1977. We have more than 300 members now, but had even more before France, Japan and the US set up their own societies along similar lines to ours.' The aims of the WFS are to promote Furtwängler's art, to keep its members informed of developments by means of a newsletter, edited by Hunt, largely in the field of recordings and publications which appear with surprising regularity.

There is detective work too. Because the avid, worldwide interest in Furtwängler is not satisfied by his commercial records, a supplementary stream of releases has appeared, taken from broadcasts. Many are valuable and some, such as the EMI *Ring*, put out at the behest of the WFS. 'But a lot are spurious,' claims Hunt, 'either somebody else conducting or a known Furtwängler recording doctored with audience noise and applause to make it sound genuine. We used to find some really crude efforts and set about sorting the fakes out from the good ones.' Hunt and his associates checked the alleged dates of performances against true ones and, using their knowledge of the style and repertoire, exposed several recordings as not what they are claimed to be: Dvořák's *New World* and Haydn's *London* symphonies being withdrawn.

Hunt's work has brought him the friendship of Frau Elisabeth Furtwängler, the conductor's widow, and he visits her home in Switzerland. 'She is a very active 80-year-old,' he says. 'She has her family and grandchildren and still finds time to take an interest in all we do. When she went to Japan, where there is great enthusiasm for Furtwängler, even though he never conducted there, she found herself mobbed "like one of the Beatles".' With some diffidence, Hunt admits, 'She did tell me I had done more for Furtwängler's reputation than any of the record companies.'

A natural development of discography, the *Furtwängler Sound*, publishers being shy of a list of record numbers, he decided to publish it himself. It was a success, went into second and third editions (a fourth is in preparation) and grew into substantial proportions; neatly laid out, printed on good paper and solidly bound in laminated covers, the books are truly expert jobs. Now illustrated with playbills, autographs and concert programmes they also include a list of all Furtwängler's performances from 1906 to 1954. Astonishingly, these take in Wimbledon and Watford.

'I must be a bit of a freak,' Hunt confesses, 'I actually like reading old record catalogues!' The success of the Furtwängler discographies took Hunt on to another conductor whose career he has followed: Herbert von Karajan. By chance, he discovered somebody had done work similar to his on the Philharmonia Orchestra so, noting the connection, John published the two as a 530-page blockbuster in 1987. Like his others, it sells at a price leaving no margin for profit. This year Hunt extended his cover to a volume devoted to Italian maestros (Toscanini, Cantelli, Giulini) and sopranos (Schwarzkopf, Grümmer, Güden etc), in the same attractive format. He is now planning similar treatment of the likes of Sabata, Serafin and Knappertsbusch, coupled with singers such as Rysanek, Dermota and Kunz etc.

Not content with these labours of love Hunt also travels to give his talks up and down the country and across the seas to Ireland. His is a story of dedication to music and musicians for, in his seemingly narrow territory of discography, a purposeful pattern of research is being carried out and a history written.

CLASSICAL MUSIC 18 APRIL 1992

Discographies by Travis & Emery:
Discographies by John Hunt.

1987: 978-1-906857-14-1: From Adam to Webern: the Recordings of von Karajan.
1991: 978-0-951026-83-0: 3 Italian Conductors and 7 Viennese Sopranos: 10 Discographies: Arturo Toscanini, Guido Cantelli, Carlo Maria Giulini, Elisabeth Schwarzkopf, Irmgard Seefried, Elisabeth Gruemmer, Sena Jurinac, Hilde Gueden, Lisa Della Casa, Rita Streich.
1992: 978-0-951026-85-4: Mid-Century Conductors and More Viennese Singers: 10 Discographies: Karl Boehm, Victor De Sabata, Hans Knappertsbusch, Tullio Serafin, Clemens Krauss, Anton Dermota, Leonie Rysanek, Eberhard Waechter, Maria Reining, Erich Kunz.
1993: 978-0-951026-87-8: More 20th Century Conductors: 7 Discographies: Eugen Jochum, Ferenc Fricsay, Carl Schuricht, Felix Weingartner, Josef Krips, Otto Klemperer, Erich Kleiber.
1994: 978-0-951026-88-5: Giants of the Keyboard: 6 Discographies: Wilhelm Kempff, Walter Gieseking, Edwin Fischer, Clara Haskil, Wilhelm Backhaus, Artur Schnabel.
1994: 978-0-951026-89-2: Six Wagnerian Sopranos: 6 Discographies: Frieda Leider, Kirsten Flagstad, Astrid Varnay, Martha Moedl, Birgit Nilsson, Gwyneth Jones.
1995: 978-0-952582-70-0: Musical Knights: 6 Discographies: Henry Wood, Thomas Beecham, Adrian Boult, John Barbirolli, Reginald Goodall, Malcolm Sargent.
1995: 978-0-952582-71-7: A Notable Quartet: 4 Discographies: Gundula Janowitz, Christa Ludwig, Nicolai Gedda, Dietrich Fischer-Dieskau.
1996: 978-0-952582-72-4: The Post-War German Tradition: 5 Discographies: Rudolf Kempe, Joseph Keilberth, Wolfgang Sawallisch, Rafael Kubelik, Andre Cluytens.
1996: 978-0-952582-73-1: Teachers and Pupils: 7 Discographies: Elisabeth Schwarzkopf, Maria Ivoguen, Maria Cebotari, Meta Seinemeyer, Ljuba Welitsch, Rita Streich, Erna Berger.
1996: 978-0-952582-77-9: Tenors in a Lyric Tradition: 3 Discographies: Peter anders, Walther Ludwig, Fritz Wunderlich.
1997: 978-0-952582-78-6: The Lyric Baritone: 5 Discographies: Hans Reinmar, Gerhard Huesch, Josef Metternich, Hermann Uhde, Eberhard Waechter.
1997: 978-0-952582-79-3: Hungarians in Exile: 3 Discographies: Fritz Reiner, Antal Dorati, George Szell.
1997: 978-1-901395-00-6: The Art of the Diva: 3 Discographies: Claudia Muzio, Maria Callas, Magda Olivero.
1997: 978-1-901395-01-3: Metropolitan Sopranos: 4 Discographies: Rosa Ponselle, Eleanor Steber, Zinka Milanov, Leontyne Price.
1997: 978-1-901395-02-0: Back From The Shadows: 4 Discographies: Willem Mengelberg, Dimitri Mitropoulos, Hermann Abendroth, Eduard Van Beinum.
1997: 978-1-901395-03-7: More Musical Knights: 4 Discographies: Hamilton Harty, Charles Mackerras, Simon Rattle, John Pritchard.
1998: 978-1-901395-94-5: Conductors On The Yellow Label: 8 Discographies: Fritz Lehmann, Ferdinand Leitner, Ferenc Fricsay, Eugen Jochum, Leopold Ludwig, Artur Rother, Franz Konwitschny, Igor Markevitch.
1998: 978-1-901395-95-2: More Giants of the Keyboard: 5 Discographies: Claudio Arrau, Gyorgy Cziffra, Vladimir Horowitz, Dinu Lipatti, Artur Rubinstein.
1998: 978-1-901395-96-9: Mezzo and Contraltos: 5 Discographies: Janet Baker, Margarete Klose, Kathleen Ferrier, Giulietta Simionato, Elisabeth Hoengen.

1999: 978-1-901395-97-6: The Furtwaengler Sound Sixth Edition: Discography and Concert Listing.
1999: 978-1-901395-98-3: The Great Dictators: 3 Discographies: Evgeny Mravinsky, Artur Rodzinski, Sergiu Celibidache.
1999: 978-1-901395-99-0: Sviatoslav Richter: Pianist of the Century: Discography.
2000: 978-1-901395-04-4: Philharmonic Autocrat 1: Discography of: Herbert Von Karajan [Third Edition].
2000: 978-1-901395-05-1: Wiener Philharmoniker 1 - Vienna Philharmonic and Vienna State Opera Orchestras: Discography Part 1 1905-1954.
2000: 978-1-901395-06-8: Wiener Philharmoniker 2 - Vienna Philharmonic and Vienna State Opera Orchestras: Discography Part 2 1954-1989.
2001: 978-1-901395-07-5: Gramophone Stalwarts: 3 Separate Discographies: Bruno Walter, Erich Leinsdorf, Georg Solti.
2001: 978-1-901395-08-2: Singers of the Third Reich: 5 Discographies: Helge Roswaenge, Tiana Lemnitz, Franz Voelker, Maria Mueller, Max Lorenz.
2001: 978-1-901395-09-9: Philharmonic Autocrat 2: Concert Register of Herbert Von Karajan Second Edition.
2002: 978-1-901395-10-5: Sächsische Staatskapelle Dresden: Complete Discography.
2002: 978-1-901395-11-2: Carlo Maria Giulini: Discography and Concert Register.
2002: 978-1-901395-12-9: Pianists For The Connoisseur: 6 Discographies: Arturo Benedetti Michelangeli, Alfred Cortot, Alexis Weissenberg, Clifford Curzon, Solomon, Elly Ney.
2003: 978-1-901395-14-3: Singers on the Yellow Label: 7 Discographies: Maria Stader, Elfriede Troetschel, Annelies Kupper, Wolfgang Windgassen, Ernst Haefliger, Josef Greindl, Kim Borg.
2003: 978-1-901395-15-0: A Gallic Trio: 3 Discographies: Charles Muench, Paul Paray, Pierre Monteux.
2004: 978-1-901395-16-7: Antal Dorati 1906-1988: Discography and Concert Register.
2004: 978-1-901395-17-4: Columbia 33CX Label Discography.
2004: 978-1-901395-18-1: Great Violinists: 3 Discographies: David Oistrakh, Wolfgang Schneiderhan, Arthur Grumiaux.
2006: 978-1-901395-19-8: Leopold Stokowski: Second Edition of the Discography.
2006: 978-1-901395-20-4: Wagner Im Festspielhaus: Discography of the Bayreuth Festival.
2006: 978-1-901395-21-1: Her Master's Voice: Concert Register and Discography of Dame Elisabeth Schwarzkopf [Third Edition].
2007: 978-1-901395-22-8: Hans Knappertsbusch: Kna: Concert Register and Discography of Hans Knappertsbusch, 1888-1965. Second Edition.
2008: 978-1-901395-23-5: Philips Minigroove: Second Extended Version of the European Discography.
2009: 978-1-901395--24-2: American Classics: The Discographies of Leonard Bernstein and Eugene Ormandy.

Discography by Stephen J. Pettitt, edited by John Hunt:
1987: 978-1-906857-16-5: Philharmonia Orchestra: Complete Discography 1945-1987

Available from: Travis & Emery at 17 Cecil Court, London, UK. (+44) 20 7 240 2129. email on sales@travis-and-emery.com .

© Travis & Emery 2009

Music and Books published by Travis & Emery Music Bookshop:
Anon.: Hymnarium Sarisburiense, cum Rubricis et Notis Musicis.
Agricola, Johann Friedrich from Tosi: Anleitung zur Singkunst.
Bach, C.P.E.: edited W. Emery: Nekrolog or Obituary Notice of J.S. Bach.
Bateson, Naomi Judith: Alcock of Salisbury
Bathe, William: A Briefe Introduction to the Skill of Song
Bax, Arnold: Symphony #5, Arranged for Piano Four Hands by Walter Emery
Burney, Charles: The Present State of Music in France and Italy
Burney, Charles: The Present State of Music in Germany, The Netherlands …
Burney, Charles: An Account of the Musical Performances … Handel
Burney, Karl: Nachricht von Georg Friedrich Handel's Lebensumstanden.
Cobbett, W.W.: Cobbett's Cyclopedic Survey of Chamber Music. (2 vols.)
Corrette, Michel: Le Maitre de Clavecin
Crimp, Bryan: Dear Mr. Rosenthal … Dear Mr. Gaisberg …
Crimp, Bryan: Solo: The Biography of Solomon
d'Indy, Vincent: Beethoven: Biographie Critique
d'Indy, Vincent: Beethoven: A Critical Biography
d'Indy, Vincent: César Franck (in French)
Frescobaldi, Girolamo: D'Arie Musicali per Cantarsi. Primo & Secondo Libro.
Geminiani, Francesco: The Art of Playing the Violin.
Handel; Purcell; Boyce; Geene et al: Calliope or English Harmony: Volume First.
Häuser: Musikalisches Lexikon. 2 vols in one.
Hawkins, John: A General History of the Science and Practice of Music (5 vols.)
Herbert-Caesari, Edgar: The Science and Sensations of Vocal Tone
Herbert-Caesari, Edgar: Vocal Truth
Hopkins and Rimboult: The Organ. Its History and Construction.
Hunt, John: Adam to Webern: the recordings of von Karajan
Isaacs, Lewis: Hänsel and Gretel. A Guide to Humperdinck's Opera.
Isaacs, Lewis: Königskinder (Royal Children) A Guide to Humperdinck's Opera.
Kastner: Manuel Général de Musique Militaire
Lacassagne, M. l'Abbé Joseph : Traité Général des élémens du Chant.
Lascelles (née Catley), Anne: The Life of Miss Anne Catley.
Mainwaring, John: Memoirs of the Life of the Late George Frederic Handel
Malcolm, Alexander: A Treaty of Music: Speculative, Practical and Historical
Marx, Adolph Bernhard: Die Kunst des Gesanges, Theoretisch-Practisch
May, Florence: The Life of Brahms
May, Florence: The Girlhood Of Clara Schumann: Clara Wieck And Her Time.
Mellers, Wilfrid: Angels of the Night: Popular Female Singers of Our Time
Mellers, Wilfrid: Bach and the Dance of God
Mellers, Wilfrid: Beethoven and the Voice of God
Mellers, Wilfrid: Caliban Reborn - Renewal in Twentieth Century Music

Music and Books published by Travis & Emery Music Bookshop:

Mellers, Wilfrid: François Couperin and the French Classical Tradition
Mellers, Wilfrid: Harmonious Meeting
Mellers, Wilfrid: Le Jardin Retrouvé, The Music of Frederic Mompou
Mellers, Wilfrid: Music and Society, England and the European Tradition
Mellers, Wilfrid: Music in a New Found Land: ... ... American Music
Mellers, Wilfrid: Romanticism and the Twentieth Century (from 1800)
Mellers, Wilfrid: The Masks of Orpheus: ...... the Story of European Music.
Mellers, Wilfrid: The Sonata Principle (from c. 1750)
Mellers, Wilfrid: Vaughan Williams and the Vision of Albion
Panchianio, Cattuffio: Rutzvanscad Il Giovine
Pearce, Charles: Sims Reeves, Fifty Years of Music in England.
Playford, John: An Introduction to the Skill of Musick.
Purcell, Henry et al: Harmonia Sacra ... The First Book, (1726)
Purcell, Henry et al: Harmonia Sacra ... Book II (1726)
Quantz, Johann: Versuch einer Anweisung die Flöte traversiere zu spielen.
Rameau, Jean-Philippe: Code de Musique Pratique, ou Methodes.
Rastall, Richard: The Notation of Western Music.
Rimbault, Edward: The Pianoforte, Its Origins, Progress, and Construction.
Rousseau, Jean Jacques: Dictionnaire de Musique
Rubinstein, Anton : Guide to the proper use of the Pianoforte Pedals.
Sainsbury, John S.: Dictionary of Musicians. Vol. 1. (1825). 2 vols.
Serré de Rieux, Jean de : Les dons des Enfans de Latone
Simpson, Christopher: A Compendium of Practical Musick in Five Parts
Spohr, Louis: Autobiography
Spohr, Louis: Grand Violin School
Tans'ur, William: A New Musical Grammar; or The Harmonical Spectator
Terry, Charles Sanford: J.S. Bach's Original Hymn-Tunes for Congregational Use.
Terry, Charles Sanford: Four-Part Chorals of J.S. Bach. (German & English)
Terry, Charles Sanford: Joh. Seb. Bach, Cantata Texts, Sacred and Secular.
Terry, Charles Sanford: The Origins of the Family of Bach Musicians.
Tosi, Pierfrancesco: Opinioni de' Cantori Antichi, e Moderni
Van der Straeten, Edmund: History of the Violoncello, The Viol da Gamba ...
Van der Straeten, Edmund: History of the Violin, Its Ancestors... (2 vols.)
Waltern: Musikalisches Lexicon
Walther, J. G.: Musicalisches Lexikon ober Musicalische Bibliothec

Travis & Emery Music Bookshop
17 Cecil Court, London, WC2N 4EZ, United Kingdom.
Tel. (+44) 20 7240 2129

© Travis & Emery 2009

www.ingramcontent.com/pod-product-compliance
Lightning Source LLC
Chambersburg PA
CBHW070925230426
43666CB00011B/2319